# CENSORING GOD

*The History of the Lost Books (and other Excluded Scriptures)*

# ABOUT THE AUTHOR

Having earned his master's degree in theology from Andover Newton Theological School, Jim Willis has been an ordained minister for more than forty years. He has also taught college courses in comparative religion and cross-cultural studies. In addition, Willis has been a professional musician, high school orchestra and band teacher, arts council director, and even a drive-time radio show host. His background in theology and education led to his writings on religion, the apocalypse, cross-cultural spirituality, and the mysteries of the unknown. His books include Visible Ink Press' *Ancient Gods: Lost Histories, Hidden Truths, and the Conspiracy of Silence; The Religion Book: Places, Prophets, Saints, and Seers; Supernatural Gods: Spiritual Mysteries, Psychic Experiences, and Scientific Truths;* and *Armageddon Now: The End of the World A to Z.* He also published *Faith, Trust & Belief: A Trilogy of the Spirit.* Willis resides in the woods of South Carolina with his wife, Barbara, and their dog, Rocky.

# GOD

## The History
## of the Lost Books
### (and other Excluded Scriptures)

#### JIM WILLIS

# OTHER VISIBLE INK PRESS BOOKS BY JIM WILLIS

*Ancient Gods: Lost Histories, Hidden Truths, and the Conspiracy of Silence*
ISBN: 978-1-57859-614-0

*Armageddon Now: The End of the World A to Z*
With Barbara Willis
ISBN: 978-1-57859-168-8

*Hidden History: Ancient Aliens and the Suppressed Origins of Civilization*
ISBN: 978-1-57859-710-9

*Lost Civilizations: The Secret Histories and Suppressed Technologies of the Ancients*
ISBN: 978-1-57859-706-2

*The Religion Book: Places, Prophets, Saints, and Seers*
ISBN: 978-1-57859-151-0

*Supernatural Gods: Spiritual Mysteries, Psychic Experiences, and Scientific Truths*
ISBN: 978-1-57859-660-7

# ALSO FROM VISIBLE INK PRESS

*Alien Mysteries, Conspiracies, and Cover-Ups*
by Kevin D. Randle
ISBN: 978-1-57859-418-4

*Angels A to Z*, 2nd edition
by Evelyn Dorothy Oliver, Ph.D., and James R Lewis, Ph.D.
ISBN: 978-1-57859-212-8

*The Astrology Book: The Encyclopedia of Heavenly Influences*, 2nd edition
by James R. Lewis
ISBN: 978-1-57859-144-2

*The Bigfoot Book: The Encyclopedia of Sasquatch, Yeti, and Cryptid Primates*
by Nick Redfern
ISBN: 978-1-57859-561-7

*Conspiracies and Secret Societies: The Complete Dossier*, 2nd edition
by Brad Steiger and Sherry Hansen Steiger
ISBN: 978-1-57859-368-2

*The Dream Encyclopedia*, 2nd edition
by James R Lewis, Ph.D., and Evelyn Dorothy Oliver, Ph.D.
ISBN: 978-1-57859-216-6

*The Dream Interpretation Dictionary: Symbols, Signs, and Meanings*
By J. M. DeBord
ISBN: 978-1-57859-637-9

*The Encyclopedia of Religious Phenomena*
by J. Gordon Melton
ISBN: 978-1-57859-209-8

*The Fortune-Telling Book: The Encyclopedia of Divination and Soothsaying*
by Raymond Buckland
ISBN: 978-1-57859-147-3

*The Government UFO Files: The Conspiracy of Cover-Up*
By Kevin D. Randle
ISBN: 978-1-57859-477-1

*Hidden Realms, Lost Civilizations, and Beings from Other Worlds*
by Jerome Clark
ISBN: 978-1-57859-175-6

*The Horror Show Guide: The Ultimate Frightfest of Movies*
By Mike May
ISBN: 978-1-57859-420-7

*The Illuminati: The Secret Society That Hijacked the World*
By Jim Marrs
ISBN: 978-1-57859-619-5

*The Monster Book: Creatures, Beasts, and Fiends of Nature*
By Nick Redfern
ISBN: 978-1-57859-575-4

*Real Aliens, Space Beings, and Creatures from Other Worlds,*
by Brad Steiger and Sherry Hansen Steiger
ISBN: 978-1-57859-333-0

*Real Encounters, Different Dimensions, and Otherworldly Beings*
by Brad Steiger with Sherry Hansen Steiger
ISBN: 978-1-57859-455-9

*Real Ghosts, Restless Spirits, and Haunted Places,*
2nd edition
by Brad Steiger
ISBN: 978-1-57859-401-6

*Real Miracles, Divine Intervention, and Feats of Incredible Survival*
by Brad Steiger and Sherry Hansen Steiger
ISBN: 978-1-57859-214-2

*Real Monsters, Gruesome Critters, and Beasts from the Darkside*
by Brad Steiger and Sherry Hansen Steiger
ISBN: 978-1-57859-220-3

*Real Vampires, Night Stalkers, and Creatures from the Darkside*
by Brad Steiger
ISBN: 978-1-57859-255-5

*Real Visitors, Voices from Beyond, and Parallel Dimensions*
By Brad Steiger and Sherry Hansen Steiger
ISBN: 978-1-57859-541-9

*Real Zombies, the Living Dead, and Creatures of the Apocalypse*
by Brad Steiger
ISBN: 978-1-57859-296-8

*The Sci-Fi Movie Guide: The Universe of Film from Alien to Zardoz*
By Chris Barsanti
ISBN: 978-1-57859-503-7

*Secret History: Conspiracies from Ancient Aliens to the New World Order*
By Nick Redfern
ISBN: 978-1-57859-479-5

*Secret Societies: The Complete Guide to Histories, Rites, and Rituals*
By Nick Redfern
ISBN: 978-1-57859-483-2

*The Spirit Book: The Encyclopedia of Clairvoyance, Channeling, and Spirit Communication*
by Raymond Buckland
ISBN: 978-1-57859-172-5

*UFO Dossier: 100 Years of Government Secrets, Conspiracies, and Cover-Ups*
By Kevin D. Randle
ISBN: 978-1-57859-564-8

*Unexplained! Strange Sightings, Incredible Occurrences, and Puzzling Physical Phenomena*, 3rd edition
by Jerome Clark
ISBN: 978-1-57859-344-6

*The Vampire Book: The Encyclopedia of the Undead*, 3rd edition
by J. Gordon Melton
ISBN: 978-1-57859-281-4

*The Werewolf Book: The Encyclopedia of Shape-Shifting Beings*, 2nd edition
by Brad Steiger
ISBN: 978-1-57859-367-5

*The Witch Book: The Encyclopedia of Witchcraft, Wicca, and Neo-paganism*
by Raymond Buckland
ISBN: 978-1-57859-114-5

*The Zombie Book: The Encyclopedia of the Living Dead*
By Nick Redfern and Brad Steiger
ISBN: 978-1-57859-504-4

# "REAL NIGHTMARES"
# E-BOOKS BY BRAD STEIGER

Book 1: *True and Truly Scary Unexplained Phenomenon*

Book 2: *The Unexplained Phenomena and Tales of the Unknown*

Book 3: *Things That Go Bump in the Night*

Book 4: *Things That Prowl and Growl in the Night*

Book 5: *Fiends That Want Your Blood*

Book 6: *Unexpected Visitors and Unwanted Guests*

Book 7: *Dark and Deadly Demons*

Book 8: *Phantoms, Apparitions, and Ghosts*

Book 9: *Alien Strangers and Foreign Worlds*

Book 10: *Ghastly and Grisly Spooks*

Book 11: *Secret Schemes and Conspiring Cabals*

Book 12: *Freaks, Fiends, and Evil Spirits*

PLEASE VISIT US AT WWW.VISIBLEINKPRESS.COM.

## CENSORING GOD

Visible Ink Press®
43311 Joy Rd., #414
Canton, MI 48187-2075

Visible Ink Press is a registered trademark of Visible Ink Press LLC.

Most Visible Ink Press books are available at special quantity discounts when purchased in bulk by corporations, organizations, or groups. Customized printings, special imprints, messages, and excerpts can be produced to meet your needs. For more information, contact Special Markets Director, Visible Ink Press, www.visibleink.com, or 734-667-3211.

Managing Editor: Kevin S. Hile
Cover Design: Graphikitchen
Page Design: Allesandro Cinelli
Typesetting: Marco Divita
Proofreaders: Christa Gainor and Shoshana Hurwitz
Indexer: Larry Baker

Cover images: Shutterstock.

ISBN: 978-1-57859-732-1

Cataloging-in-Publication data is on file at the Library of Congress.

Printed in the United States of America.

# DEDICATION

*This book is dedicated to all those who have ever*

*sworn by,*

*sworn on,*

*or sworn at*

*the Bible.*

*It could have been quite a different book.*

# CONTENTS

# Photo Sources

Osama Shukir Muhammed Amin FRCP (Glasg): pp. 62, 140.

Armour, R. C. *North American Indian Fairy Tales Folklore and Legends*: p. 145.

Aukland Castle: p. 78.

Bibliotheca Philosophica Hermetica, Amsterdam: p. 275.

Bizzell Bible Collection, University of Oklahoma Libraries: p. 48.

Brigham Young University Museum of Art: p. 223.

British Museum: pp. 143, 155.

Cobija (Wikicommons): p. 162.

Corcoran Gallery of Art, Washington, D.C.: p. 43.

Dead Sea Scrolls Digital Project, Israel Museum: p. 87.

Eddo (Wikicommons): p. 248.

Edjoerv (Wikicommons): p. 265.

Bernard Gagnon: p. 164.

Gallica Digital Library: p. 184.

Gemäldegalerie Alte Meister: p. 210.

Government Press Office: p. 27.

Idont (Wikicommons): p. 212.

Morteza Jaberian: p. 183.

Kunsthistorisches Museum, Vienna: p. 292.

Lorax (Wikicommons): p. 252.

Mariner's Museum Collection: p. 125.

MesserWoland (Wikicommons): p. 276.

Museo del Palazzo del Buonconsiglio, Trento: p. 36.

Museum of Fine Arts, Budapest: pp. 108, 131.

Karl Musser: p. 95.

NASA: p. 150.

National Gallery, London: p. 13.

National Gallery of Art, Washington, D.C.: p. 168.

National Portrait Gallery, London: p. 137.

National Trust for Places of Historic Interest or Natural Beauty, England: p. 204.

Ohio State University: p. 242.

Thilo Parg: p. 126.

Pathfindermark (Wikicommons): p. 75.

Andreas Praefcke: p. 288.

Damien Halleux Radermecker: p. 57.

Rama (Wikicommons): p. 190.

D. Gordon E. Robertson: p. 146.

Sanna Saunaluoma: p. 264.

Sémhur (Wikicommons): p. 97.

Shakko (Wikicommons): p. 104.

Shutterstock: pp. 3, 6, 8, 9, 12, 16, 18, 19, 26, 28, 32, 40, 52, 53, 54, 56, 68, 79, 86, 90, 94, 99, 110, 111, 118, 120, 127, 134, 136, 152, 157, 160, 174, 188, 194, 198, 205, 214, 228, 229, 260, 302, 306, 307, 309, 310.

Sistine Chapel: p. 71.

U.S. Geological Survey: p. 114.

U.S. Government: p. 30.

U.S. National Archives and Records Administration: p. 148.

U.S. National Park Service: p. 254.

Victoria and Albert Museum: p. 130.

Michel Wal: p. 139.

Wellcome Images: p. 102.

Wiki Taro: p. 219.

William Blake Archive, University of North Carolina at Chapel Hill: p. 215.

Public domain: pp. 10, 22, 50, 66, 70, 81, 88, 122, 154, 161, 169, 170, 172, 176, 180, 182, 200, 206, 217, 220, 221, 231, 246, 247, 283, 285, 294, 300.

# PREFACE

History sings two siren songs.

The first is a simple and direct melody, sung in a major key that appeals to those who want their music straightforward and direct. It features tonic and dominant harmonies that revolve around the questions "when?," "who?," "where?," and "how?"

The second is much more complicated, often disturbing, and usually sung in a minor key. It dances around one question, "why?," and seems fiendishly designed to remain in the background, a *sotto voce* counterpoint motif to the clarion call of the composition called *Life*.

The first song has been dissected by academia, codified, neatly explained, and reproduced in history books and religious scriptures, accompanied by glorious illustrations in which the colors always remain within the lines.

The second is heard only by those who listen for the music of the spheres and remain open to its spell. It is the pianissimo response of a composition called *Meaning*.

The two songs always occur in counterpoint. Only when we listen to them both is reality made complete.

*Life* and *Meaning*. Most of us are comfortable with the first. But the second is what haunts our nights and quiet times.

Try this experiment. Retire to a quiet room where you know you will not be disturbed. Turn off your infernal smartphone, sit in a comfortable chair, center your mind, and contemplate the meaning of life. At first it will be easy. For a few seconds, maybe even a minute if you concentrate, you will be under the illusion that you are peaceful and calm.

Then your mind will start singing in loud, discordant tones. You will be reminded of your many obligations, all of which will demand immediate attention. You will recall the many times you have failed to do this or that and dredge up forgotten memories of past victories and defeats. Stick with it long enough and you will decide that this is not a good time to be quiet and peaceful. Tomorrow will be better. Maybe you can fit in another attempt as soon as things slow down at work. Once you get your life straightened out a little, perhaps next week, you will try again with greater success. But right now, you're too busy. Now, where did you leave that phone?

You rise from your chair and get back to singing the song of *Life*.

So much for hearing the soft melodies of *Meaning*.

This, in a nutshell, is the central problem of the human race in the souped-up, strident, boisterous, twenty-first century.

But you are left with a nagging feeling that something greater was at work during this experiment. Something subtle, something almost malicious, seems to have stepped in, taken over control of your mind, wrested it away from your grasp, and compelled you to obey its call for complexity and busy-ness.

What's going on, here? Aren't you in control of your own thoughts?

Maybe not.

If the mythology of the great religious systems, found in their ancient texts, is to be believed, something sinister is happening right here on planet Earth, and the human race is caught in the middle of a greater reality.

Here's the problem, though. The religious texts we hold in our hand today, from the Hebrew Talmud and Tanakh to both Testaments of the Christian Bible, from the Hindu Upanishads to the Mayan Popol Vuh—in short, all the ancient wisdom compiled to transport us from *Life* to *Meaning*—were put together by committee. Tradition tells us these books came directly from the hand of a god. History tells a different story. For every book that has stood the test of time and taken its revered place among the great religious texts of our day, there are dozens more that were rejected, destroyed, and thrown into the dustbins of history. Did those forgotten texts reveal wisdom that the old ones understood but we have forgotten? Did ancient writers who asked the illusive "why?" question know as much or even more than we do about meaning and purpose? Is that why their books were at best redacted or at worst consigned to the wastebasket?

During the last hundred years or so, portions, snippets, and fragments of some of those texts have found their way into the hands of scholars and wormed their way into the fabric of the academic tapestry. They reveal that there may be a deeper meaning behind the simple and obvious truth of materialistic dualism—a meaning that has been censored by committees with an already fully formed, in many cases, political, agenda that cared more for its own propagation than for spiritual integrity. Is the battle between good and evil more than just a metaphor? Is there something much bigger, much more complex, going on, carried out in a dimension beyond the reach of our sensory perception? And can these ancient, lost texts begin to show us the way?

Virtually every culture and civilization that ever existed told the story of the good and virtuous hero who either triumphed over evil or was destroyed by it. They all seemed to think it was important to remind us of our responsibility to resist the Devil so as not to be cast out of Eden. Wars have been fought and dictators brought low because the principle of fighting evil seemed to be more important at the time than merely defending a piece of turf. History is not a simple story of who did what and when they did it. It is also the story of why it happened at all.

*Meaning* is everything. Why?

Perhaps the answer lies in the fact that we *are* a part of something much bigger than our dawn-to-dusk daily existence. Maybe something more important *is* going on. Maybe our sometimes-comfortable home planet *is* part of a larger arena, the scene of an engagement destined to reach out into the vast reaches of the universe itself, and perhaps even universes beyond our own. And maybe, just maybe, the story of that engagement lies hidden in forgotten and previously unknown religious texts that are finally coming to the surface in our time.

As we progress, we might come to remember the song that sings to our inner hearts and souls. That's where we'll hear it best. For even in the midst of the clash and clamor of a noisy world, the music continues. It's not too late. We can still learn that beneath the song of *Life*, and even the song of *Meaning*, another song sings its eternal melody. It's a song called *Purpose,* and must be sung by each one of us individually.

To hear the song of *Purpose* might be our ultimate existential goal. It underlies everything we are and do, and its music forms the soundtrack of our life on Earth. We all want to know why we are here and what our function is in the great scheme of things. To paraphrase an early Hebrew writer in Proverbs 29:18, "Without *Purpose* the people perish." And the disclosure of *Purpose* was behind many of the censored texts of history that are now coming to light. These are texts that refused to remain buried away out of sight forever. They may have been censored, but they would not be silenced.

*Purpose* gives us a reason to get up in the morning and go to work. It sustains us through life's valleys of depression and discouragement. *Purpose* allows us to continue on in the midst of adversity and setback. It is more than a song. It is a symphony whose themes stitch together both the melodies and harmonies of our lives.

From the texts they left behind, there is evidence that the ancients knew something about this subject. Theirs is the voice we need to recover.

# INTRODUCTION

On April 4, 1969, a team of censors led by William S. Paley, president and CEO of the CBS television network, fired Dick and Tom Smothers, the stars of the immensely popular *Smothers Brothers Comedy Hour*. The official reason for the firing was that the brothers had refused to meet pre-airing delivery dates to various outlets around the country. These dates were specified by contract to give local censors enough time to vet the program's content, ensuring it was in line with community standards.

The show had originally been scheduled in what was, up to then, a time slot known as "the graveyard." On Sunday nights, American families watched *The Ed Sullivan Show* followed by *Bonanza*. A number of shows scheduled to go up against those two behemoths had withered on the Nielson rating's vine. No one really expected *The Smothers Brothers Comedy Hour* to fare any differently.

Much to the surprise of pundits and experts, who thought they had a good handle on what the public should see, the Smothers brothers began to grow a substantial audience. This was the era of Vietnam War protests and racial riots. America was divided, and, agree with the brothers or not, their show expressed those divisions. President Lyndon Johnson grew increasingly worried when young people began to move away from what the networks considered to be wholesome, family Sunday night fare to embrace a show that was becoming increasingly edgy in its treatment of social issues. When Richard Nixon took office in January 1969, the situation didn't improve. Both presidents took notice and, as the infamous Nixon tapes would later reveal, talked to CBS about it.

Although popular artists such as Peter, Paul, and Mary; The Who; George Harrison of the Beatles; Cass Elliot; Simon and Garfunkel; and Glen Campbell made their appearances, so did Pete Seeger, who had been banned from television ever since the McCarthy hearings had rocked the nation in the 1940s and '50s. His song "Waist Deep in the Big Muddy" was considered to be a personal attack on President Johnson. Young writers such as Steve Martin, Rob Reiner, Pat Paulson, and Mason Williams began to serve up controversial skits that criticized government policies. Paulson even staged mock runs for the presidency several times.

Censors tried hard to keep up, but the writers, encouraged by Tom Smothers, increasingly found ways to produce political commentary that was understood by their hip, ages 15 to 25, audience, but they angered the network executives who were almost all older, white males.

During the 1968 Democratic National Convention, a song sung by Harry Belafonte, "Lord, Don't Stop the Carnival," juxtaposed with pictures of the increasingly violent Chicago demonstrations outside the convention amphitheater, was too much for the conservative president of CBS.

In the course of a subsequent trial, which found in favor of the Smothers brothers and awarded them substantial monetary compensation, it was revealed that, under pressure from the White House, Paley had looked for an excuse to cancel his network's popular show. When the Smothers brothers missed their contractual censorship deadline by two days, witnesses revealed that he said, "I've got 'em!" That was the end of the *Smother Brothers Comedy Hour*.

At least, everyone thought so. Twenty years later, after the brothers had continued their successful career, CBS apologized and brought them back for a reunion special. The show was a huge hit, proving that you can't sustain censorship forever. Eventually, the truth will out.

I bring up this bit of TV trivia to illustrate an important point. Throughout history, much of the information that exposes the reality of who we are and what's going on in the world comes to us through filters. Almost always, a committee stands between actual events and our understanding of them.

These committees may act out of a genuine concern. They may feel they are preserving their version of reality for future generations, but what is often behind their agenda is an attitude towards the public that was best expressed by Jack Nicholson's character in the 1992 military court drama, *A Few Good Men*: "You can't handle the truth!" Ironically, that movie was directed by none other than Rob Reiner, who got his start writing for the Smothers brothers.

This whole process has a direct bearing on biblical studies. Most people who grow up in Jewish or Christian traditions learn early on that the Bible is "the Word of God." That's the official position of both church and synagogue. It's a clean description so easy to grasp that it is expressed on a popular bumper sticker: "God said it! I believe it! That settles it!" The Bible, or rather, one particular interpretation of it, becomes the filter through which they view the world.

But how did the Bible come to be? Did it really arrive on the world's stage as a fully formed product straight from the mouth of God? After all, that's where words come from, don't they—from somebody's mouth?

Take the Christian New Testament, for instance. It begins with what we call the four canonical Gospels that are traditionally attributed to Matthew,

Mark, Luke, and John. The word "Gospel" comes from two Old English words that mean "good news." It refers to the story of the birth, death, and resurrection of Jesus Christ. If we go only by what we find in our modern Bibles, these four accounts of the life of Jesus give us what we are told is the complete story.

But people are often surprised to discover that there are at least fifty more gospels—some of which exist only in fragments while others are complete and whole—that were considered and subsequently discarded by the committees who decided which books were determined to be inspired by God and which were not. This process didn't begin until late in the fourth century after Christ, and even today there is a difference of opinion between Roman Catholic, Eastern Orthodox, and Protestant believers.

Among the rejected gospels are those purportedly written by Thomas, Mary, Judas, and Philip. There are infancy gospels called Joseph the Carpenter and the Protoevangelium of James. We recently learned about a partially preserved work called The Gospel of Peter. Some are written in Greek, others in Coptic or other languages unknown to the original authors of the familiar books we recognize today. A few are lost, probably forever, but we know about them because texts that *have* been preserved quote them at length. All of them offer a slightly different, often contradictory, point of view. Some reveal glimpses into an unseen dimension of reality that goes far beyond our current materialistic world view.

Can you imagine what it would be like to go back to some of those fourth-century deliberations and peek into the wastebasket after their meetings ended?

This kind of study usually goes on in the rarified atmosphere of theological institutions, but it has implications far beyond the halls of academia. The Bible—and other sacred texts that have profoundly shaped our world view in ways we usually aren't even aware of—were put together by groups of men who had already formed and solidified their ideology. They had a fully developed point of view and an aggressive agenda. They really thought they knew best what should be released to the public and what should be destroyed. I sometimes call them "gatekeepers."

To be brutally honest, it appears as though we might have been patronized by a religious establishment that long ago lost any claim to relevancy. Religion as we know it, which comprises our search for meaning and purpose—the quest for what makes life important—was shaped by opinionated scholars who sincerely claimed they were doing the work of God while they secretly—maybe not fully understanding what they were doing—sought to use religion for their own purposes. It was seen as an instrument of power and control. Their decisions about which texts to accept and which to destroy, were, albeit perhaps not always knowingly, slanted in a particular direction.

In religious works far removed from the Bible, the story is the same. Hidden behind dogmas and doctrines that were already in place when the texts were finalized and assembled, what we now read and have access to are heavily edited treatises that express a religious ideology that was tied to a cultural time and geographical place. Once cast in stone, those documents were then often used for political purposes, as the persecution of Sir Isaac Newton or the case of the Salem witch trials more than adequately illustrate. When we read between the lines, we get the idea that perhaps the purpose behind the original writing was to reveal a timeless and eternal struggle against something a whole lot bigger than meets the eye.

Is history simply a record of what happened, or is there a behind-the-scenes story that a few gifted individuals intuited and sought to pass down for our edification?

Who was it that sought to use the human condition to fulfill their own ends for either good or evil? Who were the principal characters engaged in this subterfuge? Why did they hide behind the scenes and keep their faces hidden? Were cosmic forces engaged in an eternal battle for goodness and love, compassion and meaning? Does our very existence have a purpose and direction? Are we being watched from afar or even above?

To answer these questions we must turn to ancient texts written by those of our ancestors who first conceived of the whole magnificent affair, who first intuited its presence among us, and who began to compose vast theological and metaphysical structures of mythology around what seemed to them to be a very clear and present danger.

The Sumerians and Jews, for instance, believed the gods wanted to destroy the world with a great flood.

Why?

The Hopis believed their ancestors were forced to endure the destruction of three former worlds.

Why?

The Maya and Canaanites believed they needed to offer sacrifices to appease an angry god.

Why?

The Egyptians believed they needed to build great stone pyramids to send their leaders off to the stars.

Why?

The Christians believed Jesus needed to return to Earth in order to bring about Armageddon and the defeat of the Devil.

Why?

That's what the book you now hold in your hands is about. It attempts to help each of us answer the personal question "why?" by listening to the wisdom of those who have gone before. Perhaps, while traveling the fast lanes of busy hubris, we have forgotten how to hear the still, soft music of the spheres that was once available to our ancestors who lived in quieter times. Many of them devoted their whole lives to listening for its siren song. Their ideas may have been edited out of our immediate awareness, but now that we have discovered bits and pieces of their work, they might still have a lot to offer.

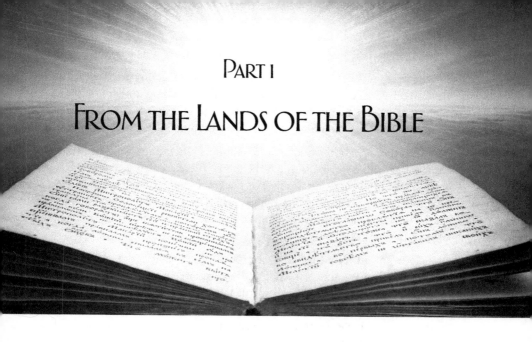

# Part I

# From the Lands of the Bible

## Books That Didn't Make the Final Cut

When Wolfgang Amadeus Mozart died at the age of 35, he was at the height of his creative powers, but the most well-known musician of his day was a man by the name of Carl Ditters von Dittersdorf. They both wrote music following the rules and theory of the classical period. They both wrote for the same ensembles and employed the same kinds of instruments. Von Dittersdorf was famous and gainfully employed. Mozart died a pauper. He never considered himself anything but brilliant, and he had great faith in his genius. But he mourned the fact that the general public didn't understand him, so he considered himself a commercial failure, which, in reality, he was.

Today, everyone calls Mozart one of the greatest composers who ever lived. Hardly anyone remembers the name Carl Ditters von Dittersdorf, let alone pays much attention to the music he left behind.

What causes some artists to achieve greatness and others to bequeath only mediocre work to future generations? Why do some paintings and musical compositions sparkle while others merely glimmer? What makes a piece of art immortal? It may employ the same material and follow the same rules as all the rest, but it alone is remembered long after its originator is gone.

When I was in music school, I was taught the music of Johann Sebastian Bach. He was the one who made the rules that guided Western classical music ever since the baroque period. Every pop artist you've ever heard, from the Beatles to the Rolling Stones, from Kenny G to Wynton Marsalis, from Merle Haggard to Dolly Parton, uses the same framework and music theory that Bach perfected. I learned all those rules and followed them explicitly. But my music never sounded like his—or like theirs, for that matter. Why not?

I asked my teachers and pondered the phenomenon myself, but I have never received a good answer. The only word I can come up with is "magic." Some works of art are touched by the gods. Others are merely craft. Some reach to the heavens and pull down the stars. The rest remain anchored to the earth.

Mythology, both secular and religious, including well-known and much-loved Bible stories, is much the same. There are passages that cause us to nod our heads and say, "Yes!" We understand something without being able to explain it. That's what art does. When we catch the hidden nugget of truth couched in a simple turn of phrase, we attempt to explain it with pages of text, but we fall short.

The ancient Hindus had a word for it. They called it *Brahman*. Brahman is the ultimate unexplained and unexplainable reality behind all that is. Brahman cannot be defined. All words fall short. If you think you've got it and try to explain what you've got, you don't have it at all. But when you hear and, probably even more important, feel a truth that cannot be defined in words, that's Brahman.

Brahman has a close companion called *Atman*. The nearest English equivalent is probably something like "soul." Brahman is transcendent. Atman is within. And the great realization of the Rishis 5,000 years ago was "Thou art that!" Brahman and Atman are one. When art is touched by the gods, it reaches out and kisses Brahman. When it is experienced within, it nurtures Atman, our inner, mysterious essence.

In that sense, when we ask why certain scriptural texts have become classics, we have to at least consider the fact that they are divinely inspired. But to even speak that phrase aloud is to polarize our audience. Some will accept the concept; others will not. Some will take it for granted that the Bible, for instance, is divinely inspired, while others will totally reject the idea.

No matter which camp you occupy, think for a minute what divine inspiration means. Those who reject the concept may not be rejecting divinity as much as they are rejecting a narrow definition of what the word "God" means. If that is the case, a simple broadening of the meaning of "divine" may be in order.

Why do some texts achieve immortality? Why are they still with us while others have been lost?

We might just as well ask why some entertainers become famous while others remain in obscurity. Maybe it's simply a matter of luck. But doesn't the word "luck" imply some kind of magic? What is luck? It is a process that exists outside the normal. When we experience luck, we thus experience a miraculous force. If we call that outside force God or Brahman or Spirit or anything else, we are implying a form of divine inspiration.

In short, if we open our-selves up to the idea that things happen outside our experience that are then manifested within our perception realm, what we are saying is that there is something bigger than us at work in the cos-mos. If you are uncomfortable cal-ling that "something" God, then use another word that works for you. The word "God," after all, is just a series of letters we invented to designate a reality beyond the ability of words to express.

Christians believe that the Bible is divinely inspired, but many people consider it simply a collection of man-made stories, myths, and some history.

Now, let's apply this to the work we are about to explore to-gether. Why did some religious texts make the final cut in the Bible while others fell by the wayside? Ultimately, it was because a group of men (there is very little ev-idence of women being allowed within the fraternity of early biblical redac-tors) decided that some books would make it and others would not.

If you believe God was somehow involved in their decision making, you can accept their work as divinely inspired. But if you wonder whether other, more mundane, earthly forces were at work, you've got to admit that the first redactors might be guilty of censoring the creative force at work in the universe or even God. I call original redactors like these the gatekeepers—those who decide for the rest of humanity which bits of knowledge, art, or philosophy we may access and which will be withheld.

Take the story of the Garden of Eden, for instance. In a few chapters, we're going to discover that there were many varied accounts that viewed the well-known story from different angles. We were given one of them. Did that version make the cut because it was inspired? Maybe, but we'll never know this side of heaven, assuming heaven exists.

Does the version we have received sparkle with the brilliance of a Mo-zart? Are the rest the equivalent of a von Dittersdorf symphony, popular at the time but destined to be forgotten?

That is what we're each going to have to decide for ourselves. But we can't make that decision without at least knowing what was rejected. That's the landscape we're going to explore in the coming pages. We'll listen for Mo-zartian motifs, but we'll hear von Dittersdorfian ditties as well. And who knows? Maybe we'll even experience some heretofore undiscovered, divinely inspired genius—genius that was censored by the gatekeepers but is now ready to burst forth into song.

# WHO WROTE THE BIBLE?

Before beginning any conversation about books that didn't make the final cut when the decision to form the Bible was made, we first have to come to grips with a basic question. Here it is in its simplest form: Who wrote the Bible in the first place?

If you ask that question to random people you meet on the street, many Jews, Christians, and Muslims will answer, "God!" Others will refer to un-named, unknown authors of the distant past. Quite a few will refer to mul-tiple authors such as Moses, Daniel, Isaiah, or Ezekiel. Most will probably shake their heads, admit they don't know, and continue with their business of the moment.

These will be rather diverse responses, considering the fact that the Bible is the best-selling book of all time and the single book that is apt to be in the houses of people who own more than one book. For the most popular book in the world, its contents and structure remain a mystery to a vast majority of those who swear by its supposed message.

Quite a few years ago, I was teaching a course in world religions at a small college in New England. At that time there was quite a conversation going on in the newspapers and on radio programs about whether or not a plaque containing the Ten Commandments should be allowed to be displayed on the walls of public school classrooms. The question was being debated in federal courts, and quite a few people were discussing the issue. I, of course, was always looking for ways to make sure my course content was relevant to current events, so I put the question to my students:

"Should the Ten Commandments be displayed on the walls of public school classrooms?"

One student in particular was very adamant. She answered with a firm "No!"

"Why not?" I asked.

"Because if there were some Jewish kids in the class, they might be of-fended!"

I had to gently explain that the Ten Commandments came from the Jewish scriptures, or what Christians call the "Old" Testament. She'd had no idea. She had assumed that the Ten Commandments were Christian dogma.

As the years went by, I discovered that she was by no means alone in her ignorance. Many of my students, including those who had been raised in

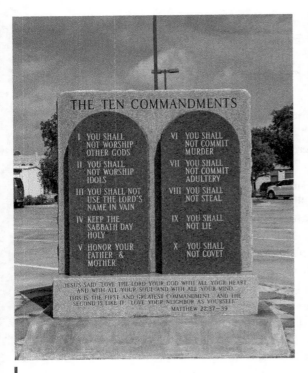

THE TEN COMMANDMENTS

| I   YOU SHALL NOT WORSHIP OTHER GODS | VI   YOU SHALL NOT COMMIT MURDER |
| II  YOU SHALL NOT WORSHIP IDOLS | VII  YOU SHALL NOT COMMIT ADULTERY |
| III YOU SHALL NOT USE THE LORD'S NAME IN VAIN | VIII YOU SHALL NOT STEAL |
| IV  KEEP THE SABBATH DAY HOLY | IX   YOU SHALL NOT LIE |
| V   HONOR YOUR FATHER & MOTHER | X    YOU SHALL NOT COVET |

JESUS SAID "LOVE THE LORD YOUR GOD WITH ALL YOUR HEART AND WITH ALL YOUR SOUL AND WITH ALL YOUR MIND, THIS IS THE FIRST AND GREATEST COMMANDMENT. AND THE SECOND IS LIKE IT: 'LOVE YOUR NEIGHBOR AS YOURSELF.'" MATTHEW 22:37-39

A display of the 10 Commandments was erected at a public parking lot in Cuero, Texas. Some people object to such displays—especially at schools and government buildings—because they can be offensive to those who practice other religions and also because they see such monuments and plaques as violating the principle of separation of church and state in America.

Bible-believing traditions—and some of whom could even rattle off the 66 books of the Protestant Bible in the correct order—had no idea how the book had come to be and what it was about. Perversely, for a while I even took great pleasure in quoting verses straight out of texts that most didn't know were there. While I read, I made sure that I was holding up the biggest, blackest, most holy-looking copy of the Bible that I owned:

And the LORD spake unto Moses, saying, "Avenge the children of Israel of the Midianites: afterward shalt thou be gathered unto thy people." And Moses said unto them, "Have ye saved all the women alive? Now therefore kill every male among the little ones, and kill every woman that hath known man by lying with him. But all the women children, that have not known a man by lying with him, keep alive for yourselves." (Numbers 31)

When a woman has a discharge, and the discharge in her body is blood, she shall be in her menstrual impurity for seven days, and whoever touches her shall be unclean until the evening. And everything on which she lies during her menstrual impurity shall be unclean. Everything also on which she sits shall be unclean. And whoever touches her bed shall wash his clothes and bathe himself in water and be unclean until the evening. And whoever touches anything on which she sits shall wash his clothes and bathe himself in water and be unclean until the evening. Whether it is the bed or anything on which she sits, when he touches it he shall be unclean until the evening. (Leviticus 15)

Slaves, obey your earthly masters with respect and fear, and with sincerity of heart. (Ephesians 6)

The response was always universal.

"Did God say *that*?"

I always asked whether any of them had ever heard a sermon or homily based on any of those texts or whether they had ever heard them discussed in a classroom. To this day I have yet to receive a positive response. In fact, I once received a phone call from an irate pastor who accused me of filling the heads of his impressionable young congregants with filth and blasphemy. When I pointed out that all I did was read from the Bible, he snorted and said, "Not *my* Bible."

> I ONCE RECEIVED A PHONE CALL FROM AN IRATE PASTOR WHO ACCUSED ME OF FILLING THE HEADS OF HIS IMPRESSIONABLE YOUNG CONGREGANTS WITH FILTH AND BLASPHEMY. WHEN I POINTED OUT THAT ALL I DID WAS READ FROM THE BIBLE, HE SNORTED AND SAID, "NOT MY BIBLE."

I then quoted chapter and verse to him. After a moment of silence, presumably while he checked out his Bible and, I assume, read for the first time verses that even he had never read before, he hung up. I never heard from him again. I secretly hoped it was because he was embarrassed, not angry.

Experiences such as these have made me wonder whether many people really reverence the Bible or just their idea of what the Bible should be.

All that being said, we return to our basic question. Who wrote the Bible?

A simple answer is that the Bible is not a single book as much as it is a collection of books. Indeed, the very word "bible" comes from the Latin word *biblia*, which means "holy books." That being the case, there were multiple authors, spread out over many years and geographical locations.

Tradition has it that during the time of King Hezekiah of Judah in the eighth century B.C.E., royal scribes began to gather together what by then had become a large body of texts that included history, legends, proclamations, songs, poems, and wise sayings that had accumulated over a span of time beginning as early as 1200 B.C.E. Some of them had been pressed into clay tablets. Others were inscribed on long parchment scrolls. Legend has it that some, such as the original Ten Commandments, were even carved into stone by the very finger of God.

Many scholarly books have been written about how all this took place. Rather than try to reproduce the voluminous information in all of them, let's look at only the first five books of the Bible. Jews call them the Torah or the

A man carries the sacred Torah during a holiday cele-bration by the Western Wall in Jerusalem, Israel. The Torah contains the first five books of the Bible.

Books of Moses. Sometimes, scholars refer to them as the Pentateuch—*penta* meaning five, or "five scrolls."

Traditionally, they are said to be the work of one author—Moses—who was thought to have lived somewhere between 1500 and 1300 B.C.E. They begin, quite literally, "in the beginning" and move rapidly, in only ten chapters, through creation, the Great Flood, the Tower of Babel and the birth of languages, the re-peopling of the earth, and the introduction of Abraham, who is said to be the patriarch of Judaism, Christianity, and Islam—the three great monotheistic religions, all of which revere the Bible.

Then the story slows down as it traces the foundation story of the Jewish people and nation through Isaac, the son of Abraham, Isaac's sons, Jacob and Esau, and finally the 12 sons of Jacob, whose name is changed to Israel. One of those sons, Joseph, is led by fate to Egypt. Thus, it is that at the end of the first book of the Bible, those who were to become the patriarchs of the 12 tribes of Israel are now living in Egypt.

At the beginning of the second book of the Bible, Exodus, the thread continues. The Jews are now enslaved. Exodus, Leviticus, Numbers, and Deuteronomy tell the story of the exodus out of Egypt, the giving of the law that bound the nation together, the beginning of the traditions concerning the building of the Ark of the Covenant and the first Tabernacle, or Tent of Meeting, the wilderness wanderings, and the final trek that brought them to the brink of the Promised Land. Joshua, the sixth book, begins the story of the final conquest of the land and the building of a nation. From there, the story continues.

All of these records up to the sixth book are traditionally attributed to one man—Moses. Indeed, any suggestions to the contrary are considered by some to be heresy of the first order. The five books that comprise the Pentateuch, or Torah, are called the Five Books of Moses, and they are identified as such in many modern Bibles.

But now let's narrow our study down a little. Can we say with certainty that the Torah was written by Moses?

The answer is no. Over the years, beginning as far back as the late seventeenth century, many scholars, both Jewish and Christian, have developed what is now called the documentary hypothesis, or the JEDP model. They suggest that at least four unknown authors wrote these books. The authors were not even aware of each other. Their work was later cobbled together by a committee to reproduce what appears to be the unified work of one author.

In other words, even the first books of the Bible, attrib-

Tradition says that Moses wrote the first books of the Bible, but scholars believe that they were actually penned by four different authors, none of whom knew of the others.

uted to one author, is, in one sense, a fraud perpetrated by a committee that may have, perhaps without even meaning to, redacted what was destined to become a holy text.

The JEDP model is based on the fact that various parts of the Torah use different names for God. These differences don't show up in translation, so English versions of the Bible don't always illustrate the nuances. But the basic idea is that there are parts of these texts that use the name *JHVH*, usually rendered *Jehovah*, for God. Hence, the letter "J" in the model's name. These documents were written, it is said, between 900 and 850 B.C.E.

Somewhere between 750 and 700 B.C.E., the name *Elohim* came into vogue. These are called the "E" documents.

During the time of King Josiah's reforms in 621 B.C.E., meant to bring the nation of Judah back into God's good graces, it is suggested that the book of Deuteronomy was written and attributed to Moses to give it heft, substance, and status. The books of 2 Kings and 2 Chronicles tell the story of a group of priests who were cleaning out the back rooms of Solomon's temple and "discovered" the forgotten book of Deuteronomy that Moses had written centuries before. It purports to be the final words of Moses before his death, and it warns the people away from following the very path of disobedience they seem to have followed—the path that led to the need for Josiah's reforms.

Many scholars question such a convenient coincidence and suggest the book was more about marketing and persuasion than historical accuracy. They claim it was written by at least one author, who is indicated with a "D" for Deuteronomy.

The final letter, "P," stands for Priest. This is a reference to the laws defined and codified by priests who forged the laws of Judaism to help the Jews maintain their separate and unique identity during the years of captivity in Babylon and Persia.

Thus was developed the JEDP documentary hypothesis. Its origin goes back at least as far as the late seventeenth century, but it was Dr. Julius Wellhausen who cemented the theory together in 1895. He believed that all four sources were written sometime after 900 B.C.E. In the words of the noted Old Testament scholar Gleason Archer,

German Orientalist and biblical scholar Dr. Julius Wellhausen specialized in the early history of Islam and the Torah/Pentateuch, including JEDP theory.

"Although Dr. Wellhausen contributed no innovations to speak of, he restated the documentary theory with great skill and persuasiveness, supporting the JEDP sequence upon an evolutionary basis."

Over the years the editors—those who combined the separate books into a whole work—began to be called "redactors," and the JEPD theory is now commonly taught at most seminaries and is widely believed, if not expressly taught, by liberal scholars the world over. Such luminaries as the twelfth century's Rabbi Ibn Ezra and the influential philosopher Baruch Spinoza were members of the long line of scholars who at least raised the possibility of multiple authorship.

Conservatives, of course, stick to the traditional "Books of Moses" explanation even to this day. In some Protestant circles, the very mention of multiple authorship of the Pentateuch, the book of Isaiah, and the book of Daniel, for instance, is enough to get you kicked out of church.

The Hebrew Scriptures, called the Tanach by Jews and the Old Testament by Christians, were written in Hebrew and Aramaic. The final book, attributed to Malachi and probably written in the early fifth century B.C.E., ushered in a period lasting 500 years in which no other books were added to the canon. The word "canon" indicates a set of texts, usually called books, that a particular religious community regards as authoritative scripture. It comes from the Greek word *kanon*, meaning either "ruler" or "measuring stick." During this time, Alexander the Great (356–323 B.C.E.) conquered much of his known world and superimposed the Greek language everywhere he went. Greek became the language of the realm. The Scriptures were translated into Greek to produce a work known as the Septuagint, or Work of the Seventy Scholars.

> DURING THIS TIME, ALEXANDER THE GREAT (356–323 B.C.E.) CONQUERED MUCH OF HIS KNOWN WORLD AND SUPERIMPOSED THE GREEK LANGUAGE EVERYWHERE HE WENT. GREEK BECAME THE LANGUAGE OF THE REALM.

Once again, a committee of gatekeepers enters the picture. Perhaps it might be a good idea to remember at this point the well-known joke that a camel is nothing but a horse designed by a committee. It might keep us grounded as we proceed.

What many Christians often overlook is the fact that the Old Testament, said to be the Bible of Jesus of Nazareth, didn't exist as such in his day. The texts were compiled and collected, of course, but their inclusion and arrangement were not finalized until, as the traditional story goes, the Council of Jamnia, which was held near the end of the first century, more than 60 years after Jesus died. The Jamnia theory has been disputed ever since the late 1960s, but for much of the twentieth century, it was believed that the Hebrew Bible wasn't fully formed until the Jewish authorities became alarmed at the number of Jews who were leaving their heritage behind to join the new Jesus cult that is now called Christianity.

If this was indeed the case, there is at least a possibility that Jesus himself may never have read from the Hebrew Scriptures as we know them. Instead, he and his contemporaries would have had access only to whatever scrolls their local religious authorities were able to compile. One assembly might have had access to one limited set and their neighbors to another. Perhaps they even exchanged collections from time to time.

All this raises a serious question. If we don't know for sure who wrote the Bible and can't even agree on when, where, and by whom it was compiled and codified, can we say with any authority that it is the infallible word of God? Or was it instead assembled by various and forgotten committees, each of whom

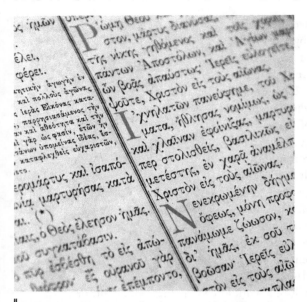

The New Testament books were originally written down in the language of Koine (common) Greek. Over the centuries, as these texts were copied, small errors were introduced and perpetuated, a problem exacerbated when the Greek was translated into other languages such as English.

had their own agenda, sometimes political, sometimes religious, and sometimes personal?

If all this isn't enough, we now need to throw in another layer of complexity. So far, we've been talking about the Hebrew Scriptures, or what Christians call the Old Testament. When we move to the New Testament, more problems arise. The New Testament was written in Koine Greek, or "common" Greek. But no original copies exist of the books written in this language, at least as far as anyone knows. What we have are copies of copies of copies, many of them produced hundreds of years or more after the originals had long since disappeared. When the committees that compiled the New Testament met, they dealt with texts that were very old but far short of being pristine editions. Copyists, even the best of them, make small mistakes from time to time. It's inevitable. So, if two copies of a manuscript exist and are placed side by side, small, often nonessential differences, are sure to be found.

Over the years, and in this case centuries, a general consensus arose as to which copies to use and which to discard. By the time a Dutch scholar named Erasmus (1469–1536), who lived in the sixteenth century, decided to compile a general-use, one-size-fits-all edition of the Bible, the Church had pretty much agreed to use what is now known as the Textus Receptus, or "received text." Erasmus worked for years, beginning in 1512, to produce a Latin translation that could be used by every Catholic church all over the world. He used the Textus Receptus as a base from which to start. He had to correct the Latin that some editions had already produced, saying famously, "It is only fair that Paul should address the Romans in somewhat better Latin." Although he never mentioned Greek, he undoubtedly used Greek translations in his work. After a long, involved process, he finally produced the Latin Vulgate, which was the standard text of the Bible used for many years, including as the basis for the venerable English translation called the King James Bible, or the King James Version, still used by many today. The name for that translation came from the fact that it was King James of England who ordered the translation to be made in 1611. Its official name was the Authorized Version, but the name King James Bible was the one that stuck.

In the nineteenth century, a new science called textual criticism arose. Scholars began to seek a more highly refined way to discover exactly what the original texts said. This produced a real problem. Suppose an academic had at his disposal 20 copies of a text of the Gospel according to Mark, for instance, that were all copied down during the twelfth century, and all were exactly the same. But he had one copy that was produced in the tenth century and featured a few words that were different from the received text. Does the fact that the one older copy was written closer in time to the original text mean that fewer chances of error had crept into the process, thus making it more reliable? Or does the fact that so many copies agree, even though written a few hundred years later, mean the preponderance of evidence lies on the side of the received text that so many had already agreed was the standard of excellence?

Desiderius Erasmus Roterodamus was a prominent Catholic priest and scholar who translated and prepared important editions of the Bible in Latin and Greek that were used as the basis for the later King James Version.

By the time the middle of the twentieth century rolled around, quite a few translations of the Bible had come out that claimed to have based their translation on the oldest versions of text rather than the Textus Receptus. The New American Standard Version of the Bible (NASV) and the New International Version (NIV) are just two examples. This created all sorts of problems in the Protestant Church. To this day, there are Southern Baptist churches who insist that the King James Bible, based on the Textus Receptus, is the only accurate English version of the Bible. On the other hand, a lot of people like the New International or Revised Standard Version because they read more easily, incorporate modern English, and feature nuances that make the language more accessible.

Take the well-known words of the Lord's Prayer, for instance. The King James Bible says, "Our Father, *which art* in heaven." A new rendition might

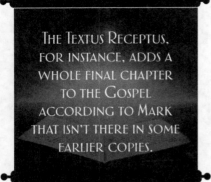

THE TEXTUS RECEPTUS,
FOR INSTANCE, ADDS A
WHOLE FINAL CHAPTER
TO THE GOSPEL
ACCORDING TO MARK
THAT ISN'T THERE IN SOME
EARLIER COPIES.

read, "Our Father, *who is* in heaven." Referring to God as a "which" rather than a "who" seems to move "his" character a bit closer to an "it."

The whole process gets more complicated than simply word choices, however. The Textus Receptus, for instance, adds a whole final chapter to the Gospel according to Mark that isn't there in some earlier copies. This is important because the chapter records the resurrection of Jesus. The earliest copies end with Jesus still in the tomb. Since Mark is considered to be the first Gospel written down, does that imply that the earliest copy of the earliest Gospel had nothing to say about Jesus being raised from the dead? It's an interesting thought.

All this is to say that the only way to claim with any kind of historical certainty that the Bible we read today came directly from God is to hold firmly to a faith statement. We must choose to believe God directed and safeguarded the whole process, from initial manuscripts through all the redactions and editing. This, of course, is a matter of opinion. That's why I call it a faith statement.

If you are a believer, maybe that's enough.

If not, you no doubt have questions.

It doesn't help that in many religious communities, those questions are deliberately covered over and never brought up, lest the faith of the congregation falter. One of the most frightening questions a religious leader faces is "Who wrote the Bible?" It can open a Pandora's box of problems.

# HOW DID THE
# OLD TESTAMENT BECOME "OLD"?

"Behold, the days come," saith the LORD, "that I will make a
new covenant with the house of Israel, and with the house of
Judah: Not according to the covenant that I made with their
fathers in the day that I took them by the hand to bring them
out of the land of Egypt; which my covenant they brake, although I was an husband unto them," saith the LORD: "But
this shall be the covenant that I will make with the house of
Israel; After those days," saith the LORD, "I will put my law
in their inward parts, and write it in their hearts; and will be
their God, and they shall be my people. And they shall teach
no more every man his neighbor, and every man his brother,
saying, Know the LORD: for they shall all know me, from the
least of them unto the greatest of them," saith the LORD: "for
I will forgive their iniquity, and I will remember their sin no
more." (Jeremiah 31:31–34)

The term "Old Testament" is a Christian term. The Christian Bible is divided into two sections, "Old" Testament and "New" Testament. The Old
Testament was written before Jesus was born—B.C.E.—or "before the Common Era." The era used to be called B.C., or "before Christ," but to measure
time in Israel or, indeed, among any non-Christians using the benchmark of
the birth of Jesus Christ was eventually recognized to be insensitive, to say
the least. So, the name of the era was changed. The New Testament was
written after the birth of Jesus Christ, or in the Common Era (C.E.). When
Christians read the passage from Jeremiah quoted above, they consider the
New Testament to tell the story of the new "covenant," or testament, of which
Jeremiah spoke.

A "testament" is a legal covenant, or agreement, between the "party of
the first part" and the "party of the second part," as contemporary legalese
would put it. In this case, the agreement is between God and humanity. Before Jesus, there was only one written contract or set of sacred writings within
the Jewish, and what was to become Christian, tradition. When Christians
began to assemble another set, describing quite a different contract, the first
set became known as the "old" set in order to distinguish it from what they
saw as God's "new" method of operation.

After the Great Flood, God made a covenant with Noah that he would never destroy the earth and humanity with water again.

In Christian terms, the Old Testament bound people to the law. They were judged on how well they kept it. That being said, the Hebrew Scriptures record not just one but a number of different covenants within the overall scope of the whole. Each separate covenant contains an admonition and a set of penalties for breaking the terms of agreement.

## 1. The Covenant God made with Adam and Eve

This was a simple agreement. There were two trees in the Garden of Eden that bore forbidden fruit. One was the Tree of the Knowledge of Good and Evil, sometimes called the tree of duality. The other was the Tree of Life. Every other tree was safe and at the disposal of our first parents. When they broke the terms of agreement and ate the forbidden fruit from the first tree— the original sin—the penalty went into effect. They were kicked out of the garden. Their penalty was passed on to their children. In the words of the old New England spelling primer, "In Adam's fall, we sinned all."

## 2. The Covenant with Noah

After the great biblical flood, the Bible records that God made another covenant, this time with Noah. If Noah and his family were to follow instructions to build an ark and fill it with representative animals of all species on the earth, there would be a new beginning for humanity. God would reward them by promising never again to destroy the earth and humanity with water. God even gave them an everlasting sign to remember the promise: the sign of the rainbow. Every time people saw a rainbow, they would find comfort in the fact that the rain was over and the earth was safe.

### 3. The Covenant with Abraham

This was another simple agreement. If Abraham would leave his home and go to a new place to live, the land that would later become known as Israel, God would bless the progeny of Abraham, hence the name Promised Land, or the land God promised to Abraham and his descendants. Jews believe this covenant is still in place today and represents the underpinnings of Israel's belief that they are the true inheritors of what was once called Canaan, later Israel, and even later Palestine. The sign of this covenant was not a rainbow but the tradition of circumcising all male children.

### 4. The Covenant with Moses

In this agreement God gave the people the law and promised to protect them if they would keep the commandments. They were to be, in the words of the Bible, "a peculiar (or special) people," set apart by the fact that they alone, of all the people on the earth, followed the laws of God. In this agreement God "chose" the Israelites and made them a unique people, hence the phrase "God's chosen ones."

When Moses received the Law from God, delivered to the Israelites after their escape from Egypt, he was told to build an ark upon which the glory of God would rest.

"Ark" comes from the Greek word for chest. "Covenant" means contract or agreement. Thus, the Ark of the Covenant became a constant reminder of God's contract with his chosen people.

It was a box about 2.5 feet high and wide and 4.5 feet long. It was made of wood, covered with gold leaf, transported by means of two long poles, and housed in the Holy of Holies, the inner sanctuary of the Tabernacle, or Tent of Meeting, during the 40 years the Israelites wandered in the wilderness. After the conquest of Canaan, it resided in the sanctuary at Shiloh, and it was later brought by King David to the site of the future temple in Jerusalem. This was the occasion that so inspired David that he "danced before the Lord," much to the disgust of his wife.

When the Babylonians destroyed Solomon's temple in 586 B.C.E., the Ark of the Covenant disappeared. Although many have tried to locate it (and it makes a pop culture appearance in the movie *Raiders of the Lost Ark*), its

A detail of the Gates of Paradise at the Baptistery of San Giovanni in Florence, Italy, depicts the Israelites carrying the Ark of the Covenant.

location has remained a mystery ever since. Some think it is hidden away in a temple in Ethiopia, brought there by the son of Solomon and the queen of Sheba. Others believe it is hidden in the caves of Qumran near the Dead Sea, buried under the Temple Mount in Jerusalem, or even hidden in a booby-trapped pit on Oak Island off the coast of Nova Scotia. Most scholars believe it was destroyed. A few doubt that it ever existed.

Three symbolic objects were placed within the Ark that, when taken together, represent the very essence of early Judaism and illustrate the covenant with Moses.

The first object was the stone tablet containing the Ten Commandments. These represented God's law. But the people had broken God's law. While Moses was on Mount Sinai receiving instructions that forbade the worship of idols, the people were down below dancing around a golden calf. The tablets would forever symbolize the people's rejection of God's law.

The second was a pot of manna. "Manna" literally means "what is it?" When the people needed food in the desert, God told Moses to have them go outside and gather a daily supply of a light bread that would form with the dew each morning. Only one day's supply could be gathered because it would spoil if hoarded. The bread gathered on Friday would keep for an extra day so that people would not have to break the Sabbath commandment forbidding work on the seventh day. When the people went outside on the first morning, they saw the manna and said, "What is it?" The idea was to teach the people to trust in God's provision. But after the novelty wore off, the people complained, longing for "the leeks and onions of Egypt." So, manna came to represent their rejection of God's provision.

The third item was "Aaron's rod that budded." Aaron, Moses's brother, had been selected by God to be the high priest. But the people wanted to elect their own leaders. They complained to Moses, who passed the word on to God. So, Moses was told to have each tribe select a candidate for high priest. Each candidate would place his "rod," or walking staff, in the ground to be in-

A replica of the Ark of the Covenant. The lost ark contained the 10 Commandments tablets, a pot of manna, and Aaron's rod.

spected during the next morning's convocation. The rod that "budded," or took root, would indicate God's choice. The implication was that God's leaders bear fruit.

Of course, Aaron's rod produced a bud, and he went on to become the first high priest of Israel. But the people would always be reminded that they had rejected God's leadership.

On the cover of the Ark stood the mercy seat. Two carved angels, one on each side with their arched wings meeting in the middle, looked down at the Ark's contents. There they saw rejection—rejection of God's law, God's provision, and God's leadership. That doesn't leave a lot more of God to be rejected.

But on one day a year—the Day of Atonement, or Yom Kippur—the high priest sprinkled the blood of a sacrificial lamb on the mercy seat. On that day the angels would see not rejection but the blood of the innocent substitute. Thus, the sins of the people would be pardoned. They would experience atonement, or "at-one-ment."

Much speculation has arisen over the true meaning of the Ark. Because the Bible makes a special point of saying Moses's face glowed when he came out from the visible presence of God, some have speculated it contained a source of light or even radiation. It was said that at the Ark, Moses would hear the voice of God. This has sparked tales of it being a transmitter through which Moses was in contact with aliens from outer space, having used details supplied from their blueprints to build the Ark to their specifications. Because of the Ark's supposed ability to inspire armies in war, and because at least one man is said to have died after he touched it without proper consecration, speculation arose as to its mystical or military powers.

The Ark of the Covenant is surrounded by mystery. Perhaps it still awaits discovery, resting in its 3,500-year-old hiding place. But its meaning to the Israelites was clear. The Ark reminded them of their contract, or covenant, between God and Moses.

### 5. The Covenant with David

In this covenant God promised to reward David's offspring if they were to build a unique temple of worship. This is how the covenant was framed, as recorded in 2 Samuel:

> When your days are fulfilled and you lie down with your fathers, I will raise up your offspring after you, who shall come from your body, and I will establish his kingdom. He shall build a house for my name, and I will establish the throne of his kingdom forever. I will be to him a father, and he shall be to me a son. When he commits iniquity, I will discipline him with the rod of men, with the stripes of the sons of men, but my steadfast love will not depart from him, as I took it from Saul, whom I put away from before you. And your house and your kingdom shall be made sure forever before me. Your throne shall be established forever. (2 Samuel 7:12–16)

## Conclusion

There are more covenants that Christians recognize in the New Testament, but these are the unique covenants that together make up the Old Testament. In essence they say that the party of the first part—God—lays the ground rules, the obeying of which will result in the promised blessing to the party of the second part—humanity. The history of the Old Testament is the history of people who broke those rules and reaped the penalty. It's important to remember, though, that this is a uniquely Christian perspective.

This is the point where the Hebrew Scriptures were given the name "Old Testament" by Christians. The theology of the Apostle Paul, himself a Jewish religious scholar before his conversion to Christianity, claimed that keeping the commands of God was an exercise in futility. Although his ideas were disputed, rebuffed, and later refined by Christians in the Roman era and beyond, the "new" covenant, or New Testament, can best be described using a simple courtroom metaphor:

Humans, under the influence of their original sin, need a savior. They are unable to be good enough to warrant God's grace. Forgiveness was provided in the form of Jesus the Christ (the "anointed one"), who came to earth to take upon himself the penalty for our sin, release us from a death sentence, and free us for eternity.

The basic idea behind Christian thought is this. Suppose you are arrested for speeding and brought before a judge.

"Are you guilty?" he asks.

"Yes," you reply. "I knowingly broke the law. I'm sorry. I wish I were different, but I did it."

> This doctrine is called substitutionary atonement. Our sins are "atoned for" by a substitute. In Jewish theology the substitute was an animal sacrifice, often a lamb. Christianity substituted the son of God—the "lamb" of God.

"Being sorry doesn't cut it," the judge declares. "You broke the law, and the penalty must be paid. That's the way the system works. The fine is $100."

"That may be," you say, "but I don't have $100. I am unable to pay the fine."

"That doesn't matter," declares the judge. "This is a nation of law, and you are guilty of breaking that law. If you cannot pay the fine, it's off to jail with you!"

But before the bailiff whisks you down to the dungeons, the judge does a strange thing. He takes off his black robe, the symbol of his power and authority, steps out from behind the high bench where he has been sitting, comes down to stand beside you, pulls $100 out of his pocket, and pays your fine himself.

The law has been satisfied. You were guilty of breaking it, but your penalty has been paid by the very judge who pointed out your fatal flaw. He has stepped from his world, the world of the high bench of superiority, into yours, the world of the fatal flaw. You are free to go ("and sin no more," hopefully!). This doctrine is called substitutionary atonement. Our sins are "atoned for" by a substitute. In Jewish theology the substitute was an animal sacrifice, often a lamb. Christianity substituted the son of God—the "lamb" of God. But the meaning is exactly the same.

At this point Christianity adds another step to the process—a step that has, from time to time, been censored out of the religion. In Christianity, God is not explained by just two manifestations—that of the "Father out there in heaven" and the "Son who came to earth to be our substitute." There

Johannes Tetzel, von Leipzig
S.S. Theol. Doctor und Professor ein Bruder
des Dominicaner Ordens, Ketzer Meister und
Päpstlicher Gnadenprediger, oder Ablas Cramer.

As the grand commissioner of indulgences in Germany, Holy Roman Empire Dominican friar and preacher Johann Tetzel made the practice of collecting money in exchange for guaranteeing the release of souls from purgatory.

are three "persons" who together form a Trinity, which is the complete expression of God. From heaven above to our earthly environment, they add a closer level of connection, that of the Holy Spirit, who moves "inside" us, so to speak. Michelangelo's "Father God" becomes Salvador Dali's "Substitute on the Cross" becomes the Quaker "Inner Witness." God moves from *heaven* to *earth* to *within* each person.

This third step, although probably the most important of all according to early Gnostic belief, which we will soon explore in detail, has often been censored by gatekeepers who want to control the process of individual connection with God. Rather than allowing immediate access to the Godhead, a priest, confessor, pastor, or even the Church itself becomes an intermediary to bolster the physical infrastructure between spirit and flesh.

This practice probably found its most meaningful expression in the late fifteenth century when the Dominican friar Johann Tetzel (1465–1519) began raising money for the Roman Church and its extensive building projects. The Church believed people went to purgatory when they died. That was an intermediate place of abode between earth and heaven. There they stayed until they were ransomed out by various acts of charity carried out by their living relatives on behalf of the deceased. Legend has it that Tetzel would ride into town on a fundraising mission singing a little ditty that went, "As soon as a coin in the coffer rings, another soul from purgatory springs."

In this way, the Christian Bible consists of the "New Testament" and "Old Testament." It's a way of justifying the tremendous difference that seems to separate the strict, vengeful God of the Old Testament from the "gentle Jesus, meek and mild" image of God in the New Testament.

Later, we'll examine how the New Testament was assembled by a committee that had its own unique political agenda. For now, however, while we look at the Hebrew Scriptures—the "Old" Testament—those who were raised in a Christian tradition and culture need to be careful not to judge Jewish tradition through non-Jewish eyes. Those who compiled the texts of the canon had their own unique agenda, ensconced as they were in their own culture.

But before we begin to seek out the texts that didn't make the final cut, the ones that were rejected for different reasons, is there any physical evidence that might indicate a higher power was at work that attempted to convey a hidden message in spite of the personal agendas, be they political or spiritual, followed by the redactors?

As it turns out, there just might be. That's where we'll go next.

# The Bible Code:
# Hidden Messages from Another Realm?

Human beings seem to have a natural tendency to look for order and patterns even in chaos. We find animals pictured in passing clouds, faces in sunbeams striking windowpanes, and human figures in natural rock formations. That being the case, it's only natural that we seek out codes buried in ancient texts.

But what if they're really there?

Michael Drosnin, the author of *The Bible Code* and *Bible Code II: The Countdown* who passed away in June 2020, claimed claims to have discovered a secret code hidden within the letters and phrases of the world's most popular book. If true, the implications are staggering. It would mean that a supernatural consciousness—or, at the very least, a highly evolved entity from an ancient civilization, either on earth or elsewhere in the galaxy—had the ability to foresee the future and sought to warn us about it in a way totally beyond our comprehension.

This code predicted the assassination of U.S. president John F. Kennedy in 1963. Of course, it was not discovered in time to prevent the murder, but that doesn't always have to be the case for a prediction to be accurate, said Drosnin. He sent a letter to Prime Minister Yitzhak Rabin of Israel warning him of an attempted assassination. The letter reached Rabin in plenty of time. It apparently was ignored, and in 1995 the assassination happened.

The Bible code, if we are to believe Drosnin, predicted World War II and Watergate. The Holocaust, the atomic bomb blast at Hiroshima, the moon walk, the Gulf War, and the Twin Towers attacks of September 11, 2001—all are predicted in a complicated code that is even now only in the first stages of being interpreted. It was there all along, but until the invention of computers it was impossible to decipher. Does this mean the code was meant to be discovered only after humankind had reached a sophisticated level of technology?

Drosnin did not appear to be a religious fanatic. He insists he does not believe in God. He is an investigative reporter who learned his trade working the night police beat for the *Washington Post* and covering corporate news for the *Wall Street Journal*. He didn't even discover the code himself. That honor goes to Dr. Eliyahu Rips, a Jewish mathematician who lived in Jerusalem, and his colleagues Doron Witztum and Yoav Rosenberg. But with the publication of *The Bible Code* in 1997, both Rips and Drosnin were thrown into

If Bible interpreters had read the code embedded in Scripture, and people believed its warnings, might the Twin Towers in New York City still be standing today?

the international spotlight, where they soon attracted a devout following of sincere believers while at the same time being attacked by those who did not think such a thing possible.

Drosnin said over and over again, especially at the beginning of his work, that he wished someone would debunk the code. Many attempts have been made and many claims published, but, according to his followers, the mathematics and statistical analysis of the Bible code have, so far at least, withstood the onslaught.

What exactly is the Bible code?

From ancient time, rabbis have passed on the tradition that the Torah, the first five books of the Bible, were given to Moses on Mount Sinai, written on stone tablets by the very finger of God. Tradition states that the books were written in Hebrew, with no breaks between words. The entire Torah contains 304,805 Hebrew letters. If the original text, or at least a close approximation, is reproduced in the form in which it might have been given to Moses and then arranged in columns of 40 rows, each row would contain 7,551 letters. (If you do the multiplication, this doesn't quite compute. Drosnin offers no explanation.) The letters would form a grid that could be read from right to left, as in Hebrew, or left to right, as in English. It could also be read up and down and corner to corner. In short, it would resemble a larger version of the find-the-words games that appear daily in many newspapers.

Of course, the code is more complicated than that. Sometimes, words and phrases appear to make sense only when a fixed number of letters are skipped. Drosnin gave the following sentence as an example:

> Rips explained that each code is a case of adding every fifth
> or tenth or fiftieth letter to form a word.

Now read that sentence again, this time emphasizing every fifth letter:

> Rips explained that each code is a case of adding every fifth
> or tenth or fiftieth letter to form a word.

Israeli prime minister Yitzhak Rabin (far right) is shown receiving the 1994 Nobel Peace Prize with PLO chairman Yasser Arafat (far left) and Israeli foreign minister Shimon Perez. Rabin was assassinated the next year, having not heeded Drosnin's warnings.

The message says: READ THE CODE.

The software that Drosnin used and made available to internet aficionados finds key words in context with other words or phrases in one direction or another. The combination of words that so startled Drosnin at the beginning of his search consisted of the name YITZHAK RABIN, crossed with the words ASSASSIN THAT WILL ASSASSINATE. When Rabin was shot and killed on November 4, 1995, a little more than a year after Drosnin wrote to warn him of this hidden message, Drosnin came to the astonishing belief that he was dealing with prophecies encoded 3,000 years ago. Many other such messages began to surface, including one supposedly predicting a terrifying event Drosnin later witnessed firsthand from his apartment in New York City. After the 1993 bomb attack at the World Trade Center, Drosnin had found the words TWIN and TOWERS in the Bible, encoded with the words THE WARNING, THE SLAUGHTER and crossed by the word TERROR. In his words, "It never occurred to me that lightning would strike twice—that there would be another terrorist attack on the same two monoliths eight years later, that it would succeed, and knock both towers down."

So, right after the 9/11 attack, Drosnin returned to his computer. There it was. Embedded in the same text were the words SIN, CRIME OF BIN LADEN, THE CITY AND THE TOWER, and the sentence THEY SAW SMOKE RISING ABOVE THE LAND LIKE THE SMOKE OF A FURNACE. Even the name of the alleged leader of the hijackers, Mohammed

Sir Isaac Newton believed that the Bible contained riddles and cryptograms that could be interpreted to predict the future.

Atta, appears, along with the words EGYPTIAN MAN. The word PENTAGON appears, crossed by the word DAMAGED and the phrase EMERGENCY FROM ARABIA.

At the same time Drosnin was making these discoveries, Eliyahu Rips, working from his home in Israel, discovered the same message and e-mailed it to Drosnin in New York. The words are in the Bible, and anyone who uses the proper software can find them, whether they read Hebrew or not. No one questions the method *per se*, only the significance of the results. How likely or unlikely is it that "messages" such as those Drosnin found will occur in a given text? That is the central question driving those who have attempted to discredit the code.

Drosnin himself professed to be mystified by the existence of the hidden word strings he discovered. Rips has no problem with believing the code exists because ancient Jewish tradition claims the Torah came first and then the creation. First the word, then the act. Doesn't the Torah itself claim God "spoke" the world into existence? "God said ... and it was so."

Even the Christian tradition makes that claim. The Gospel of John opens with: "In the beginning was the Word, and the Word was with God, and the Word was God." It only makes sense, according to these traditions, that all that exists and all that happens originates in God. For Rips, a devout Jew, the Bible code only affirms what the rabbis have been saying for 3,000 years.

English mathematician Isaac Newton (1642–1727) believed the Bible to be "a cryptogram set by the Almighty" and the "riddle of the Godhead, the riddle of past and future events divinely foreordained." According to Rips, the Bible code is now beginning to be understood because we have reached "the time of the end."

The prophet Daniel foretold this. When he was faced with visions beyond his comprehension, he asked the Almighty's angel: "My Lord, what will the outcome of all this be?" He was told: "Go your way Daniel, because the words are closed up and sealed until the time of the end" (Daniel 12:8, 9).

In 1998 Drosnin gave a sealed envelope to his lawyer, not to be opened until 2002. In the letter he predicted: "The world will face 'global economic collapse' starting in the Hebrew year 5762 (2002 in the modern calendar). This will lead to a period of unprecedented danger, as nations with nuclear weapons become unstable and terrorists can buy or steal the power to destroy whole cities. The danger will peak in the Hebrew year 5766 (2006 in the modern calendar), the year that is most clearly encoded with both 'world war' and 'atomic holocaust.'"

> OF COURSE, WHEN 2006 CAME AND WENT WITHOUT CONSEQUENCES OF THIS NATURE, THE WHOLE CONTROVERSY BEGAN TO FADE INTO THE MISTS OF CONSPIRACY THEORIES PAST AND PRESENT.

Of course, when 2006 came and went without consequences of this nature, the whole controversy began to fade into the mists of conspiracy theories past and present. But still, true believers continue to search the Scriptures for more information.

Drosnin was a master storyteller. *Bible Code II*, even though it is filled with charts and statistics, still reads like a good mystery novel. It may not be fair to jump right to the last page and reveal where Drosnin believed the Bible code originated, but at the risk of spoiling the surprise, he believed that the code came from aliens from another planet. He believed they "seeded" the earth with DNA to produce life, and because they were able to observe time from "outside," they could also warn us when our self-destruction approached. They did this with a code that came equipped with a time lock. We would not be able to destroy ourselves until we had perfected the technology to do so. That technology involves the invention of computers. Computers are also the key that unlocks the Bible code. It couldn't be easily deciphered without them.

Drosnin even claimed to know when and where the Bible code was delivered. He said that the code itself reveals this information. The event occurred at the time of the birth of civilization, the Agricultural Revolution of some 6,000 years ago. The place was what Drosnin called the Lisan Peninsula, a tongue of land extending into the Dead Sea from Jordan. The spacecraft landed there and perhaps even placed two obelisks that will one day be recovered. These contain the complete key to the Bible code.

The time frame he gives is significant. When Drosnin was in his prime and commanded his largest audience, most of academia agreed that civilization began just the way he presents it. But since the discovery of Göbekli Tepe, a Neolithic site in southeastern Turkey, the Agricultural Revolution and the rise of civilization has been relocated and redated. It is now believed that it happened further north, in Turkey, and much earlier in time, at least 11,800 years ago.

During their November 1985 meeting in Geneva, Switzerland, U.S. president Ronald Reagan and Soviet Union general secretary Mikhail Gorbachev reportedly discussed helping each other should one or the other nation be attacked by aliens from another world.

But the era of the discovery of writing is still in play. This was the time in which the very first stories of the Bible are placed. A literal reading of the Bible indicates that this was the time of creation, although Drosnin would argue against such an interpretation. The world was not created 6,000 years ago, he says. Our civilization was. If you define the word "our" to coincide with the monotheistic version of the birth of civilization, he may be in the ballpark. Cities and trade, modern science, and everything we associate with progressive life began much earlier. But our religious story began right there and right then, according to a conservative reading of the Bible and an acceptance of biblical chronology.

Why this sudden spurt of human progress some 6,000 years ago? According to Drosnin, it was because we had help.

Drosnin didn't necessarily believe that 2006 *had* to be the end. The Bible code doesn't predict as much as it warns, he reminds us. We can change our future, and perhaps, somehow, we did. The purpose of the predictions is to bring humanity to their collective senses. Many would argue that didn't seem to happen either, but at least it presents some wiggle room for his argument, which seems to be solid for many other objective reasons.

Quite a lot of people have wondered if there is other intelligent life in the universe. If evidence were discovered, they say, perhaps the world would change its ways. Maybe if we knew we were not alone, we might band together and work for the common good.

This is not simply idle thought. During a 2009 joint interview by television journalist Charlie Rose with George Shultz, President Ronald Reagan's secretary of state, and President Mikhail Gorbachev of the Soviet Union, it was revealed that something strange had happened during a summit meeting between Reagan and Gorbachev on November 19, 1985. The encounter took place in Geneva, Switzerland, as Schultz recalled, addressing Gorbachev.

> "All of a sudden you and President Reagan took a walk," Schultz explained. "You went down to some cabin on Lake Geneva where there was a fire in a fireplace and sat down there. I wasn't there, but I know when you came back, there were two friends, almost. Talking about what was going to happen. Then we went to the next—"

> "At the fireside house," Gorbachev cut in, through an interpreter. "President Reagan suddenly said to me, 'What would you do if the United States were attacked by someone from outer space? Would you help us?' I said, 'No doubt about it.' He said, 'We too.' So that's interesting."

Reagan was later quoted in a 1985 speech as saying:

> "I couldn't help but—one point in our discussions privately with General Secretary Gorbachev—when you stop to think that we're all God's children, wherever we may live in the world, I couldn't help but say to him, just think how easy his task and mine might be in these meetings that we held if suddenly there was a threat to this world from some other species, from another planet, outside in the universe. We'd forget all the little local differences that we have between our countries, and we would find out once and for all that we really are all human beings here on this Earth together. Well, I don't suppose we can wait for some alien race to come down and threaten us, but I think that between us we can bring about that realization."

Drosnin claimed that there is indeed evidence that we have been visited and are not alone. That evidence is the Bible code. It is irrefutable proof that other, more mature life forms are even now giving us a chance to grasp at the straw of a hopeful future rather than endure the gloomy tragedy of extinction.

Why the Bible? Why that particular book? Drosnin's answer was that the warfare occupying the world today is wrapped in religion. The power is technological. The forces are economic. But the people doing the acts are inspired by their religion. Muslim terrorists rage against America—the "Great

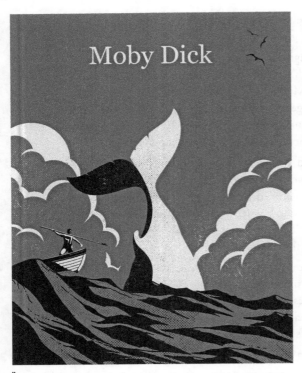

The same methods used to analyze hidden code in the Bible can be, and have been, used on other books such as the novel *Moby Dick*. This seems to indicate that Drosnin's methods are fallacious.

Satan." American leaders pray that God will "bless America." Israeli troops carry Torahs in their packs. Jew against Muslim. Christian against Jew. Muslim against Christian. And all these religions revere "the Book." That's why it is there, in the Bible, that we read about what might be our end but what must be our hope.

Drosnin's detractors were legion.

Foremost among them was Brendan McKay (1951–), a mathematician who taught in the Department of Computer Science at the Australian National University in Canberra. McKay insisted that the code merely illustrates mathematical probabilities inherent in any text of sufficient length. Using a Hebrew translation of Leo Tolstoy's *War and Peace*, McKay demonstrated that messages could be found supposedly encoded in texts other than the Bible. He also pointed out that the Hebrew of the Torah contains no vowels, making it easier to concoct meanings where none, in fact, exist.

McKay was so vocal in denouncing Drosnin's research that Drosnin issued what amounted to a challenge. He was quoted in the June 9, 1997, issue of *Newsweek* magazine as saying, "When my critics find a message about the assassination of a prime minister encrypted in *Moby Dick*, I'll believe them."

Such a challenge could not be ignored. Using the same software and techniques with which Drosnin supposedly deciphered the Bible code, McKay went to work on *Moby Dick*. There he found revealed the assassinations of, among others, Indira Gandhi, Martin Luther King Jr., John F. and Robert Kennedy, Abraham Lincoln, and Yitzhak Rabin. He also discovered the exile of Leon Trotsky. Besides all that, he discovered the name of Princess Diana and, in close proximity, the words MORTAL IN THESE JAWS OF DEATH.

If all that weren't enough, McKay discovered in *Moby Dick* a prediction of Michael Drosnin's death. The letters M. DROSNIN are crossed by the words HIM TO HAVE BEEN KILLED. With the other words scattered throughout the letter-picture, McKay deduced that Drosnin would be killed by someone DRIVING A NAIL INTO HIS HEART that SLICES OUT A CONSIDERABLE HOLE. The event will transpire in ATHENS or at least in GREECE (both words appear in the code) and apparently happen on the FIRST DAY of Drosnin's visit there. Even the names of the murderers are revealed. They happen to be two famous code researchers.

> AS WITH MOST MATTERS OF RELIGION, IT APPEARS THAT WHETHER PEOPLE BELIEVE IN THE CODE IS A MATTER OF WHETHER THEY *WANT* TO BELIEVE IN IT.

Apparently, all this information caused many who read it to believe that McKay was actually saying that Drosnin's death was predicted in *Moby Dick*. McKay issued a disclaimer explaining that he was merely illustrating a principle, not suggesting that Herman Melville was a prophet.

Heated exchanges continued between followers of Drosnin and followers of McKay. Drosnin's camp insisted that although mathematical coincidences appear in other books, the certifiable predictions found in the Bible far outnumber those of other books, and fewer "skips" are needed to form words in the original Hebrew of the Torah than in books written by other authors. McKay counters that this is not the case at all, and he and other scientists continued to offer evidence in support of this point.

The controversy apparently also caused a rift between Eliyahu Rips and Drosnin. Drosnin, however, insisted that Rips was merely distancing himself to underscore the fact that this was Drosnin's book, not his.

As with most matters of religion, it appears that whether people believe in the code is a matter of whether they *want* to believe in it. Drosnin's followers are finding new messages and posting them on the internet almost every day. McKay's followers say that the Drosnin camp is finding key prophetic "hits" because, mathematically speaking, in this kind of system you find what you expect to find. In other words, it's a rigged study done by people predisposed to find what they are looking for, whether it's really there or not.

The two camps show no evidence that they will ever agree. Meanwhile, the Bible code remains a fascinating enigma. Every year the data is updated. In 2020, some claimed to have found evidence in the Bible code that a coronavirus would cause a massive pandemic, prompting others to question why prophecies are always discovered after the fact. Meanwhile, whole websites remain dedicated to continuing Drosnin's work after his death from heart disease in 2020.

Does this prove that superintelligent, perhaps even supernatural, entities are working behind the scenes in human history? Are redaction and editing committees from our distant past guilty of unknowingly suppressing, maybe even censoring, their warnings by eliminating passages of the Bible that might contain secret clues that point to our future? If so, are they guilty of keeping from us the very messages that might save us from ourselves or, at the very least, teach us more about who we are by revealing our hidden past?

In the end, only time will tell.

# Hiding in Plain Sight: The Apocrypha

Beginning in the third century B.C.E., a group of scholars in Alexandria (tradition says there were 70 of them) began to translate Hebrew Scriptures into Greek. The work continued until 132 B.C.E. The book they eventually finished was called the Septuagint, or "Work of the Seventy Scholars." To this day, the Old Latin, Syriac, Old Georgian, Slavonic, and Coptic versions of the Old Testament are based on this work. Some of the books included were books that various committees later decided were not divinely inspired. But since they were included in the Hebrew Talmud, which is a kind of supplementary interpretation of the Hebrew Scriptures, they were also included in the Septuagint.

Here's where things start to get interesting. When the final canon of the Scriptures was determined at a convocation traditionally said to have taken place by a committee that met in Jamnia in 90 C.E., the books considered to be not divinely inspired were singled out and placed in their own separate section. They were called *apocryphal* by many scholars, employing a Greek word that means "hidden" or "secret." In other words, they were thought to contain material that was not for public consumption.

At least, that was the term used by those who questioned their authority. Those who accepted them called them *deuterocanonical*, or those that "belonged to the second canon."

Late in the fourth century C.E., a scholar now known as St. Jerome was given the job of translating the Greek Septuagint into Latin. This translation, finished and published in 405 C.E., became known as the Latin Vulgate and is still the Bible used by today's Roman Catholic Church.

Jerome had troubles with the Apocrypha. He didn't believe the message of these books could have really come from God. They didn't jibe with scriptural truth as he understood it. Some of the stories and assumptions he was reading seemed to inhabit a landscape that was too far out on the edge of his territory of belief. One of the books is about the slaying of a dragon. Another made its way into the modern Harry Potter series by describing a basilisk. To this day, a story of any kind that is probably not true but illustrates a point is called an "apocryphal" story.

Jerome's prejudice, however, was ignored by the Church. The Council of Rome, held in 382 C.E., declared the books to be a part of the official canon, and there they stayed. Much later, when Martin Luther, the man who

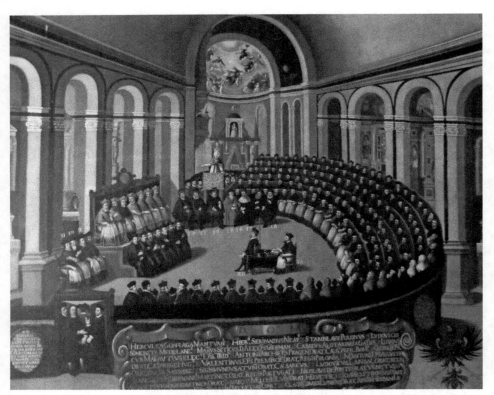

Held between 1545 and 1563, the Council of Trent in northern Italy was a reaction to the Protestant Reformation. Theologians and dignitaries of the Catholic Church met to clarify and solidify the doctrines of the Church.

was considered a Protestant upstart by the Roman Church, agreed with Je-rome about the books not being divinely inspired, church politics demanded that anything Luther said must be false. So, the books stayed in. The Council of Trent, first held in 1545, stated that this was to be the case.

In retaliation, Luther took them out of his own approved version of the Bible, and most Protestant Bibles still do not include them. If you open the Bible used today in almost all Protestant churches, you will not find books called Tobit, Judith, 1 and 2 Maccabees, the Wisdom of Solomon, Sirach, or Baruch or certain chapters of the books of Daniel and Esther.

The Eastern Orthodox Church, by contrast, includes more texts. Their Bible contains a third book of Maccabees, books called Esdras and the Prayer of Manasseh, and an extra psalm.

Once again we come face to face with political decisions, committee decisions, interpretations by unknown scribes, and choices made on the basis of individually held theologies. It's not that these books are racy or controversial in terms of juicy or prurient content. It's just that, once again, the Bible of today is not the clear and concise "word of God" it is touted to be. It is instead a heavily redacted, edited, opinion-oriented, censored volume, produced by unknown and unidentified gatekeepers who, for all we know, might have had an ax to grind.

In subsequent chapters we will examine some of the stories contained in these books on a case-by-case basis. But for now we are left with yet another reminder that it is too simplistic to believe that what we hold in our hands today, when we open a Bible, is a pure and unadulterated message from the voice of God. Without even getting into the specific content, which we are about to do, we collide with unexplained agendas and mysterious "hidden truths" that someone, usually a lot of "someones," decided must be redacted and hidden away from the general public.

> WHAT ARE THESE TRUTHS THAT WERE SO DANGEROUS? WHY DON'T MORE PEOPLE KNOW ABOUT THEM? COULD IT BE THAT THE VERY INFORMATION THEY SOUGHT TO REVEAL IS AT LEAST AS IMPORTANT AS THAT OF THE BOOKS MORE COMMONLY READ TODAY?

What are these truths that were so dangerous? Why don't more people know about them? Could it be that the very information they sought to reveal is at least as important as that of the books more commonly read today? Has a forgotten wisdom, a wisdom that was almost deleted from history, been hiding in plain sight all these years?

It's time to open a few of these mysterious texts.

# A GENESIS APOCRYPHON

The Dead Sea Scrolls, which were discovered in 1946 and gradually released to the public over the course of the next few decades, provided valuable insight into the minds of those who wrote the Bible.

The official name for the Dead Sea Scrolls is the Qumran Cave Scrolls. The caves are located a little over a mile inland from the Dead Sea in the area now called Israel's West Bank. Two thousand years ago, they were home to a group of Jewish conservatives called the Essenes, who sought to live a life that would keep them untainted from the outside world. Not wanting to socialize with the "liberals" in Jerusalem, they lived in the desert to purify themselves while they awaited the coming of the Messiah.

No less a luminary than John the Baptist might have studied with them. The Gospels say he lived "in the desert" until he announced his presence by officiating at the most famous baptism of all time. He was certainly a tough, crusty fanatic who would fit the part.

The Essenes had amassed a library of scrolls and believed strongly that YHVH (these days translated as either the LORD or Jehovah), the God of Light, was someday going to defeat the god of darkness—the being we now call the devil. Their theology was dualistic, no doubt derived from the time the Israelites spent in Persia, absorbing the dualism of Zoroastrianism. Many of the scrolls painted the world in shades of only right and wrong, white and black, light and dark.

In the year 70 C.E., a little less than 40 years after Jesus had been crucified (which event, by the way, didn't even register on the Essenes' radar), the Roman emperor Titus and the Roman legions burned Jerusalem to the ground. Their intent was to retaliate against the Jewish establishment, which refused to honor the Roman emperor in what the Romans thought was the proper fashion.

The Essenes didn't worry about their own deaths. They were willing to become martyrs for their cause. As far as they were concerned, whatever happened to them was a fulfillment of prophecy. But they didn't want their library destroyed. So, they carefully placed the scrolls in clay jars and hid them in caves way up in the mountains. There the forgotten texts sat undisturbed until 1946, when a Bedouin boy discovered some of them while searching for lost sheep.

Thus it was that those clay jars lay hidden for almost 2,000 years. In that time, some of what they contained decayed and was lost forever, but the

The Dead Sea Scrolls—or parts of them—have been put on exhibit at various museums around the world, but the main collection is held at the Shrine of the Book in Jerusalem's Israel Museum.

rest is very similar to the material found in today's Bible. The content had survived because it had been translated over and over again, and many copies had been made. Despite so much copying and translating, discrepancies between them are few and far between.

Although it is commonly believed that what folks hear in church or synagogue every weekend came straight from the lips of the Hebrew prophets, that's simply not the case. They're listening to a translation made from a copy of an older copy which came from another translation written way back before English or most modern languages came about. There's no telling how much could have changed after so many translations, given the time involved. Copyists make mistakes, especially in the centuries before spell-check.

But now, with the Qumran discovery, scholars could compare modern translations with ancient copies that, although still far removed from the original versions, were much closer to them in time. They were more than 2,000 years old, waiting to be compared to what we read today.

The most amazing discovery to come out of the recovery of the scrolls is that most of what is recorded in the modern Old Testament is spot on! In almost every case, the Dead Sea Scrolls verify that what we read today is amazingly close to what they read back then.

But perhaps the most interesting material found in the caves were texts that hadn't been included in the Bible. The committees involved in putting the Bible together were familiar with them, but they hadn't considered some of this material worthy to make the final cut. These texts contained fragments that had been rejected out of hand. In other words, some of the old scrolls didn't agree with what the gatekeeping editors believed. So, the ancient redactors just saved what they liked and threw away the rest. Now, for the first time, there arose an opportunity to peek inside the wastebaskets of Jamnia.

> THE COMMITTEES INVOLVED IN PUTTING THE BIBLE TOGETHER WERE FAMILIAR WITH THEM, BUT THEY HADN'T CONSIDERED SOME OF THIS MATERIAL WORTHY TO MAKE THE FINAL CUT. THESE TEXTS CONTAINED FRAGMENTS THAT HAD BEEN REJECTED OUT OF HAND.

In some ways, that's what the Dead Sea Scrolls are. They allow us to go back and see what the old-timers were reading and what eventually got thrown out. Parts of our modern Old Testament were discovered at Qumran, but there was much more. There were copies of selections of the scrolls that the Jamnia committee knew about but discarded. They may have destroyed their rejects back in the first century, but they had no idea that copies of those rejects were buried up in the hills outside Jerusalem so that 2,000 years later, academics could judge their work.

One such surviving remnant that didn't make the biblical cut was a fragment of a text that has since been called a Genesis Apocryphon. That's just another way of saying it's an alternate version of the book of Genesis contained in today's Bible. All that survived the centuries underground was a short section of the book that told about the birth of Lamech's son, gave an account of Noah's flood, and described the travels of Abraham, the patriarch.

In Genesis 5 there is a long list of what were once popularly called the "begats." "So and so was _____ years old when he begat a son called _____." (Never a daughter, by the way. Only sons were listed.) "He lived to be _____ years old and then he died."

It's not exactly attention-grabbing material. But the texts recorded that Lamach was the grandson of a man named Enoch, who fathered Methuselah, the oldest man who ever lived. Lamech was the father of none other than Noah himself.

We're going to study Enoch in more depth in the next chapter, but for now we'll say that he was surrounded by an aura of mystery. Every other person listed in Genesis 5 died a natural death, even if that death came about after an unnaturally long life. But not Enoch. After he had done his duty and had a child, "He walked with God for 300 years ... then he was no more, for God took him."

In other words, Enoch seems to have lived a long life and then said, "Okay, God, beam me up!" And he "was taken," whatever that means.

Then came Lamech's father, Methuselah, who lived for 969 years and died in the very year of Noah's flood.

Finally, we come to Lamech. There seem to be two of them. In Genesis 4, a man named Lamech is said to have been a descendant of Cain, the first murderer. This Lamech was the first bigamist. The Bible carefully points out that he took two wives.

The Lamech of chapter 6, however, is said to be related to Adam and Eve through their son Seth. He was the father of Noah and was said to have lived for 777 years.

With the discovery of the Dead Sea Scrolls, scholars were forced to deal with a real mystery. They had found a 2,000-year-old fragment of a nonbiblical book that no one had read since it was buried in the desert. It mentioned Lamech. But which Lamech was it talking about?

It seemed to be the one in chapter 6, the father of Noah. It recounted his surprise when he saw his soon-to-be-famous sailor son for the first time. Here's what he said:

> "Behold, I thought then within my heart that (his) conception was (due) to the Watchers and the Holy Ones ... and to the Nephilim ... and my heart was troubled within me because of this child."

Lamech seems to be accusing his wife of having an affair with a member of a group called the "Watchers and the Holy Ones." These were identical to the group called Anunnaki or Annuna Gods, who fathered a race of giants called Nephilim. We'll have a lot more to say about them in subsequent chapters. Called "sons of God" in Genesis and "angels" by later generations, the Anunnaki were obviously familiar to those who had transcribed the Dead Sea Scrolls.

But where did Lamech get the idea that his wife had been having sex behind his back with a "son of God," or angel? For that matter, can angels even have sex, let alone with humans?

If that wasn't enough, what about Lamech mentioning "the Nephilim"?

Here again is a mystery. The Bible says that the reason God brought about Noah's flood was that "the sons of God" saw that "the daughters of men" were beautiful, "and they married any of them they chose." The results of these sexual liaisons were the Nephilim.

The children of these illicit affairs were said to be "giants." In Genesis 6:4, they were called "heroes of old, men of renown." They were the reason God destroyed the world.

The Lord saw how great man's wickedness on the earth had become.... He was grieved that he had made man on the earth ... and said, "I will wipe mankind, whom I have created, from the face of the earth." (Genesis 6:5–7)

Now it gets confusing. The Bible goes on to say that Noah would be spared because he had "found grace in the eyes of the Lord."

But now, after 2,000 years, here was an old, old book about Lamech accusing his wife of being one of those women who had an affair with a "Watcher and a Holy One," aka "angel," aka "son of God," aka Anunnaki, who had seen her as nothing less than one of the beautiful "daughters of men"! In other words, Noah, who "found grace in the eyes of the Lord," now appears to

The Book of Enoch fragment from the Dead Sea Scrolls has a passage mentioning that the sons of heaven (Nephilim) descended to earth to procreate with human women, a theme depicted in this sculpture by American artist Daniel Chester French.

be one of the offspring of the very beings who had caused God to destroy the earth in the first place.

Why did Lamech accuse his wife of having an affair with an angel? It could only have been because the child looked like one of the Nephilim, a giant!

And who did this child turn out to be? None other than Noah himself!

So, was Noah a product of a union between an "angel" and a human? Did he descend from what nowadays we might call an ancient alien, an entity from a parallel dimension, or even an angel who fell from the grace of heaven? If so, the implications are staggering.

Noah was said to be the father of every human now living. He and his sons were God's do-over. Everyone else was destroyed in the flood.

So, if Noah is our ancestral "father," and he was part angel and part human, part ancient alien, or even part spiritual entity of some kind, what does that make us?

> So, was Noah a product of a union between an "angel" and a human? Did he descend from what nowadays we might call an ancient alien, an entity from a parallel dimension, or even an angel who fell from the grace of heaven?

We are children of the gods!

In other words, people who lived thousands of years ago believed we are descended from something other than earthly apes. And these folks lived side by side with, and were presumably just as smart as, the venerated folks who wrote the Bible we so revere today. They all wrote books, but we haven't been allowed to read all of them because 2,000 years ago, some unknown gatekeepers from Jamnia decided what was true and what was false. They preserved what they considered the good stuff and buried the rest.

That explains some pretty strange and enigmatic Bible verses. Psalm 82, for instance, says: "Know ye not that ye are gods?" Jesus even quotes that verse in John 10. It is echoed as well in the New Testament books of Hebrews and Jude.

Speaking of Jesus, the acknowledged Son of God himself, he refers to his followers as "brothers." (And, one assumes in these more enlightened days, "sisters.") These verses, and many more like them, are echoes from the destroyed texts that might have changed the history of religion.

The common way of explaining these things, which are now well known to professors but rarely brought up in lay circles, is to say: "Don't take these things too seriously. There were quacks and imaginative, superstitious people back then just as now. After all, Noah's flood was an early Hebrew myth, composed to convey some mysterious ethical or moral lesson. These people were much more primitive than you give them credit for."

But why all this detail? You don't need to insert a lot of extraneous facts if you just want to convey an ethical or moral lesson. As a matter of fact, too much extra material just clutters up your point. If you're trying to teach a moral lesson, and your audience is thinking about Lamech's reaction to seeing his firstborn son—a future hero named Noah—they might even miss the whole message. So, why bring it up?

These texts were written long before the birth of Jesus, as were the texts that now make up the book of Genesis. Both Hebrews and Jude, in the New Testament, were written after his death. From this we can deduce that the authors of Jude and Hebrews must have been familiar with at least one manuscript, long since disappeared, that told Enoch's story. Since no such manuscript was known to exist until recently, scholars assumed that as far as Enoch was concerned, his story would forever remain a mystery—one of those puzzling verses that pointed to an unknown and long-forgotten historical footnote.

But, as we shall see next, history is full of twists and turns. New discoveries are always possible, and when they occur, they take everyone by surprise.

# ENOCH AND THE WATCHERS

> When Jared had lived 162 years, he became the father of
> Enoch.... When Enoch had lived 65 years, he became the
> father of Methuselah. And after he became the father of Me-
> thuselah, Enoch walked with God 300 years and had other
> sons and daughters. Altogether Enoch lived 365 years. Enoch
> walked with God; then he was no more, for God took him
> away. (Genesis 5:18–24)

Who was the Hebrew patriarch known as Enoch, and why don't we know more about him? The Bible mentions him only briefly. He is said to be the son of Jared and the father of Methuselah, who everyone knows was the oldest man in the Bible. Methuselah is said to have died at the age of 969 during the year Noah's flood occurred. Enoch only made it to 365 years, but if we are to believe the biblical account, he never died. All it says is that "he was no more, for God took him away." And with that rather startling state-ment, except for a few very brief references in other sections of the Bible, that's all we are told.

The short New Testament book of Jude may provide a hint that he was a bit of a radical:

> Enoch, the seventh from Adam, prophesied: "See, the Lord
> is coming with thousands upon thousands of his holy ones to
> judge everyone, and to convict all of them of all the ungodly
> acts they have committed in their ungodliness, and of all the
> defiant words ungodly sinners have spoken against him."
> These people are grumblers and faultfinders; they follow their
> own evil desires; they boast about themselves and flatter others
> for their own advantage. (Jude 1:14–16)

Evangelical Christians often see Enoch's disappearance as a symbol of what they call the Rapture. That is, just before the flood, he was taken bodily up to heaven, thereby saving him from the coming judgment.

In Matthew 24:37, Jesus says, "As it was in the days of Noah, so will it be at the coming of the Son of man." According to most Evangelical theology, Enoch was thus a type or symbol of what will happen at the return of Jesus Christ. Christians will be taken up to heaven before the battle of Armaged-don, just like Enoch was taken before the flood that destroyed the world.

Enoch, according to Genesis, did not die a normal death but, instead, was carried into heaven while still living.

The term often used is "raptured." Although it does not appear in the Bible, the word is derived from the Middle French word *rapture*, which comes from the medieval Latin word *raptura*, meaning "seized" or "kidnapped." Later Latin renders it as *raptus*, which means "carried off."

There is disagreement as to how this will take place, but the general idea of a Rapture has remained constant throughout the Evangelical community ever since Hal Lindsey popularized the doctrine back in 1970 in his record-shattering book *The Late Great Plant Earth*.

For centuries, this was all we knew about Enoch. But in 1770 everything changed. James Bruce, an Englishman with a thirst for adventure, visited Ethiopia for three years. Upon his return he announced an astounding discovery. He had obtained an old manuscript written in Ge'ez, the sacred language of Ethiopia. It turned out to be a translation of the long-lost book of Enoch, purportedly written by Enoch himself.

Because this book had been quoted in the Bible and a few other texts, scholars knew of it. Apparently, it had been a mainstay of ancient Hebrew mystical theology. But it had been lost for so long that no one ever thought, in their wildest dreams, that it still existed. How did it turn up in Ethiopia?

The story is a fascinating mystery, full of twists, turns, and surprising confirmations of what were once thought to be only ancient tales and legends.

Jews of Ethiopia have long believed they were descended from King Solomon through the mysterious queen of Sheba. In 1 Kings, chapter 10, she is said to have traveled to Jerusalem to experience for herself the riches and wisdom of King Solomon, son of David and greatest of the Hebrew kings. If the event ever took place, it must have happened between 965 and 931 B.C.E. She

brought a caravan full of lavish gifts and seemed
to be quite taken with the king himself.

She said to the king, "The report I heard
in my own country about your achieve-
ments and your wisdom is true. But I
did not believe these things until I came
and saw with my own eyes. Indeed, not
even half was told me; in wisdom and
wealth you have far exceeded the report
I heard. How happy your people must
be! How happy your officials, who continually stand before you and hear your
wisdom! Praise be to the LORD your God, who has delighted
in you and placed you on the throne of Israel. Because of the
LORD's eternal love for Israel, he has made you king to maintain justice and righteousness." And she gave the king 120 tal-
ents of gold, large quantities of spices, and precious stones.
Never again were so many spices brought in as those the
queen of Sheba gave to King Solomon. (1 Kings 10:6–10)

JEWS OF ETHIOPIA HAVE LONG BELIEVED THEY WERE DESCENDED FROM KING SOLOMON THROUGH THE MYSTERIOUS QUEEN OF SHEBA.

Here's the problem. No one really knows who the queen of Sheba was
or where she came from.

There are two traditions:

• According to Arab and Islamic sources, the queen of Sheba was called
Bilquis, and she ruled over a nation on the southern Arabian Peninsula. It would have been located in what is now Yemen.

• Ethiopian records have long claimed that she was called Makeda, and
she ruled over an empire based in northern Ethiopia.

Now we come to what might be the first confirmation that we are dealing with history and not unsubstantiated legend because archaeological evidence indicates that at the same time the mysterious monarch was said to
have lived, Ethiopia and Yemen were ruled by a single dynasty for some four
centuries. In other words, both traditions might be right. The queen of Sheba
might have ruled over the entire empire of Ethiopia and Yemen.

When she departed from Jerusalem to return home, she appears to have
taken with her more than Solomon's gifts of gold and silver. The story was
told from generation to generation that Solomon was so smitten with
Makeda, or Bilquis, that he invited her to stay in his wing of the castle. She
agreed, as long as Solomon promised to make no sexual advances toward her.

To this Solomon acquiesced, but, given his nature, he too made a demand. He said he would not seek a physical relationship as long as she didn't

The queen of Sheba visits King Solomon in this nineteenth-century painting by Giovanni Demin. The story of the queen is a popular tale in the Bible, yet no one really knows who she really was or from whence she came.

take anything that belonged to him. When she agreed, he invited her to dinner.

But Solomon was crafty. He ordered a spicy, salty meal that she obviously enjoyed. Then, he set out a pitcher of water by her bed. When she awoke with a great thirst following such a rich dinner, she drank the water and fell into Solomon's trap. He immediately entered her room and declared she had just stolen his water.

Having forfeited her deal, she slept with Solomon that very night, causing one to wonder if she was really dumb or just flirting in her own, come-hither way.

Whatever transpired, she returned to Ethiopia carrying Solomon's son, Menelik I.

Echoes of this love affair may still echo down the corridors of biblical history. Solomon may have been smitten by love as well as lust.

In the Hebrew Scriptures, there is one book that gives scholars fits. It's called the Song of Solomon, and it consists of a series of love poems that are so graphic that most rabbis interpret them as an allegory representing God's love for humanity. In Christian circles it is usually interpreted as an allegory representing God's love for the Church. The detailed language of the Song is thus given a theological sheen of respectability, representing the union of the human soul with God. That makes it easier to explain to Sunday school kids.

> TO THIS DAY MANY ETHIOPIANS BELIEVE THE FABLED ARK OF THE COVENANT IS HOUSED IN ONE OF THEIR TEMPLES. IT HAS BECOME A STAPLE OF BOOKS AND TELEVISION DOCUMENTARIES.

This is a subject that could easily lead us astray, so I will quote only a few verses to make a point. Read these words from chapter 1, verses 5 and 6, uttered by a woman who is expressing her love:

> I am black, but comely, O ye daughters of Jerusalem, as the tents of Kedar, as the curtains of Solomon. Look not upon me, because I am black, because the sun hath looked upon me.

So, it appears as though Solomon, if he is indeed the author of this Song, had an affair with a black woman. Why not suspect the object of his desire was the queen of Sheba from Ethiopia?

To this day many Ethiopians believe the fabled Ark of the Covenant is housed in one of their temples. It has become a staple of books and television documentaries. Haile Selassie, the crown prince and regent of Ethiopia, referred to himself as "the Lion of the Tribe of Judah" until his death in 1975.

Could the legends be true that Menelik, the son of Solomon, returned to Jerusalem as an adult, probably to meet his father for the first time, and somehow returned with the Ark of the Covenant and copies of Hebrew Scriptures, among them the book of Enoch?

Up north, the original authors of Genesis and Jude must have known about this book because they quoted from it. But when it came time to put the Bible together, it was not considered worthy of inclusion, so it was destroyed. And that was it, for almost 2,000 years, until James Bruce's chance discovery of an Ethiopian copy that had escaped detection.

Why wasn't it included in the Bible? Why was it not deemed worthy? That is a fascinating question because Enoch tells a compelling story. He seems to be from a much older tradition than that of the Hebrew patriarchs. As a matter of fact, he seems to be more a shaman than a typical prophet. He was a dreamer. He engaged in out-of-body experiences. He claimed to have been contacted by spirit entities who existed on foreign planes of existence.

But he was also a Hebrew elder who no doubt embodied some of the very same cultural sexual prejudices of his descendants.

One could say that God brought the Flood down on humanity because he was disturbed that the sons of God were descending to earth and having sex with the women there.

The writers of the Old Testament didn't approve of sex unless it was very tightly controlled and regulated. It was a practice strongly circumscribed in the book of Leviticus. By disobeying the precepts laid down by the holy books, even kings were brought low. It scarred the reigns of King David, King Ahab, and many others. Apparently, Enoch shared their fears.

During what sounds a lot like a shamanic vision, he was given advance warning that a deluge was coming that would destroy the world. The reason for the flood was, basically, sexual in nature. We talked about this in relation to the Genesis Apocryphon. It seems that a group of otherworldly entities called "the sons of God" were attracted to women called "the daughters of men." The products of their union disturbed God so much he decided he needed to wipe out humankind from the earth and start over. The story comes down to us in the fifth chapter of the book of Genesis, but before we go into it in detail, we need to know a few other things about Enoch.

Traditions found all the way from Egypt to Arabia give Enoch the honor of being the one who invented writing. He is also credited with having been given the secrets of the "art of building." That is why he figures so prom-

The ruins of the ancient religious site Göbekli Tepe in Turkey are over 11,000 years old. Could it have been constructed after the ark settled atop Mount Ararat?

inently in Freemason traditions about ancient builders. Given these gifts, the book of Enoch records that he carved on a stone tablet the message that the world was going be destroyed in a great flood. He then buried this record "in the bowels of the earth."

This raises some interesting areas for speculation.

Turkey's Göbekli Tepe is sometimes called the most ancient temple site currently known. Whether it was a temple or served another purpose, it was built a little more than 11,000 years ago, right after the global catastrophe that caused the end of the Younger Dryas Ice Age, an event that produced worldwide flooding as masses of glacial ice melted suddenly with devastating effects. Göbekli Tepe is close to Mount Ararat, which is said to be the place Noah's ark landed following the biblical flood. Thus, the resting place of the ark and a nearby temple built shortly after the flood are linked in a common mythology.

After only a few generations of use, however, Göbekli Tepe was deliberately buried. Could it be that the book of Enoch transcribes a garbled mythology that remembered these events? Was Göbekli Tepe once thought to be the "stone that he (Enoch) then buried in the bowels of the earth"—the place that contains the secrets of "the art of building"?

This reading of the story suggests that Enoch is most concerned about two things:

One interpretation of who the "sons of God" were is that they were fallen angels (photo of The Fountain of the Fallen Angel in Madrid, Spain).

• First, that there is a great flood coming that will destroy a wisdom tradition that is thought to be the civilizing factor of humankind—that is, the secrets of building.

• Second, that the flood is coming because of what Enoch considers to be sexual sin.

Here's how the Bible puts it in Genesis 6:5–7:

The LORD saw how great the wickedness of the human race had become on the earth, and that every inclination of the thoughts of the human heart was only evil all the time. The LORD regretted that he had made human beings on the earth, and his heart was deeply troubled. So the LORD said, "I will wipe from the face of the earth the human race I have created."

What was the nature of this "wickedness"? According to the book of Enoch, the culprits were a group of bad "angels" called Watchers. Their mission, it seems, was to "watch" humans. He even provided their names: Azazel, Semjaza, Armen, Rumjal, Turel, Armaros, Danjal, and Kokabel.

As we said earlier, the Bible makes reference to the fact that "sons of God saw that the daughters of men were beautiful, and they married them." This was the reason God decided to send the flood, and it brings us back to the part about sex that so bothered Enoch.

No one knows who these "sons of God" were. Some believe them to be beings from another dimension—in effect, the fallen angels of the book of Enoch. If this was indeed the case, was Enoch, in his role as shamanic prophet, inadvertently drawn into a cosmic war between otherworldly entities who were using our planet as their battleground?

This is the scenario put forth in all the major monotheistic religions of history. God against the devil, Jehovah against Satan, Ahura Mazda against Angra Mainyu, and, to a lesser degree, Allah against Iblis. All religions that have a conception of spiritual gods also feature their counterparts. Even Buddhism tells the story of Siddhartha's temptation by Mara. Enoch could well be within this tradition.

But there is also speculation that the Watchers were really human beings of an advanced Ice Age civilization who were dispersed, in the tradition of the Atlantis story, to rebuild their lost civilization following a worldwide catastrophe. Their mission might have been to observe, but only observe, the Stone Age peoples of the Middle East who had survived the flood, a prime directive familiar to followers of the TV series *Star Trek*.

Mythology remembers the Watchers as being more advanced than the local population whom they visited. Hence, they are remembered by the indigenous population as being "sons of God." But, as missionaries sometimes do, they might have "gone native" and begun to marry the locals.

Such a practice would have bothered Enoch, who was a Jewish patriarch with traditional sensibilities. Much later, in Abraham's time, Jews were forbidden to mix with non-Jews. Old Testament kings such as Ahab brought down the wrath of God by marrying Gentiles. That might have been because thousands of years earlier, the Watchers had set a bad example by sleeping with the indigenous population.

Whether the Watchers were angelic or human in nature, the offspring of these unions were impressive. They were called Nephilim, and they became even more famous than their parents. Genesis 6:4 refers to them as "the heroes of old, the men of renown."

Enoch's fame doesn't begin and end within the Hebrew tradition. In the Islamic Quran, the name given for Enoch is Idris. Muslim tradition also links Idris/Enoch with Hermes, a member of the Greek pantheon. These were gods such as Zeus and Apollo, who were also known as "the heroes of old, the men of renown."

The Persian philosopher Abu Mashar reminds us that "the name Hermes is a title. Its first bearer, who lived before the Flood, was he whom the Hebrews call Enoch, whose name in Arabic is Idris."

Besides being a builder, a prophet, and the inventor of the written word, apparently Enoch/Idris/Hermes was also an astronomer.

Tamara Green, in *The City of the Moon God*, records that "he wrote many books, whose wisdom he preserved on the walls of Egyptian temples lest it be lost. It was he who constructed the pyramids."

Was Enoch the one who carried the secrets of the building tradition from Asia to Egypt and possibly beyond? Does his identification with the Greek Hermes tie the various locations together and reveal that they were all recipients of an ancient tradition that later mythology identified with the Enoch we know from the Bible?

The book of Enoch amplifies the story of the Watchers even further. Apparently, according to the text, there were those who were watching the

The Watchers may often be depicted as heavenly beings such as the archangel Michael, shown here as a warrior figure in Independence Square in Kyiv, Ukraine.

"Watchers." A group of angels named Uriel, Raphael, Michael, and Gabriel were taking part in the drama as well.

Those who identify the Watchers as angelic beings see this new group as good angels, who had not fallen to temptation. Some of them, such as Gabriel and Michael, return to play significant roles in later biblical events.

But those who look for more down-to-earth explanations of the Watchers have a different theory. Perhaps this new group was sent out from the homeland to rein in the first group of missionaries who had broken their prime directive. We can't be sure, of course, and Enoch doesn't offer any explanation. But this reading certainly implies that there must have been concern back at headquarters.

Let's try to summarize this story so far.

We know that about 11,500 to 11,800 years ago, right after a global catastrophe that ended the Younger Dryas Ice Age, the first religious temple was built. That is historical fact. Göbekli Tepe still stands to this day.

Soon after that, people discovered the agricultural arts. It marked the beginning of the Neolithic Revolution, also known as the Agricultural Revolution. This is important because it represents the beginning of our civilization. Soon after this came the invention of writing, city building, and settled communities. The world has never been the same.

What if the story of Enoch is a mythologized account of those days? We can imagine that the Watchers were members of an advanced civilization who, after the catastrophic floods of the Younger Dryas Ice Age event destroyed their homeland, set out to rebuild. Because they were advanced beyond the experience of the Stone Age people who survived the inundation, the more primitive people remembered the Watchers as being "the sons of God."

The Watchers would have probably settled in places with which they were somewhat familiar from previous exploratory visits. They might have even been

Sanliurfa (also known as Urfa) in southeastern Turkey, the birthplace of Abraham, could rightly be considered the true birthplace of Judaism.

doing cultural "missionary" work. They went to Egypt, to Turkey and Göbekli Tepe, to Lebanon at Baalbek, and maybe even to Central and South America.

Göbekli Tepe is central to this whole epic. It is located near the birthplace of Judaism, the city of Şanlıurfa, (search on Şanlıurfa, and replace with Şanlıurfa) the place the Bible calls Abraham's hometown, or Ur of the Chaldees. That city, in turn, sits on the outskirts of the traditional location of the Garden of Eden, where the four rivers of Genesis begin their journey to the Persian Gulf.

When we read the old, familiar stories of the Bible, we cannot help but wonder if the book of Enoch is a mythological account that connects all these dots. Enoch, an ancient Jewish patriarch, might have experienced an out-of-body shamanic journey to astral planes. Or he might have encountered real men, not gods, and recorded his accounts as shamanic visions based on historical accounts, albeit amplified and garbled ones. The tales of that encounter grew, no doubt, with the telling and retelling after thousands of years. But when we read them with this insight, at the very least it breathes life into them.

Good and bad angels, spiritual visions, and global catastrophes. Cultural missionaries who sound like a kind of Peace Corps, development programs to assist urban planning, interracial sex, revolutions, agriculture, and

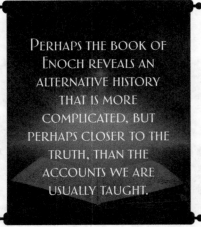

PERHAPS THE BOOK OF
ENOCH REVEALS AN
ALTERNATIVE HISTORY
THAT IS MORE
COMPLICATED, BUT
PERHAPS CLOSER TO THE
TRUTH, THAN THE
ACCOUNTS WE ARE
USUALLY TAUGHT.

even a little magic. All in all, it sounds strangely contemporary, as if people are people no matter what era they live in.

Is there at least a kernel of truth at the roots of this fascinating book? Can we seriously read the book of Enoch without resorting to explanations so quirky they resulted in its being banned and destroyed?

Well, consider a few facts. We can surely agree that a strictly historical reading of the first chapters of the Bible simply doesn't work. There are too many loose ends that contradict what we know from modern science, geology, astronomy, and history. If we throw in a healthy suspicion of noncorporeal angels having physical sex with humans, we can add biology to the list. After all, what would the mechanics be like?

So, most scholars choose a second method of interpretation. They call it a theological reading. By this they mean that the Bible was composed to teach a moral or spiritual lesson.

But that really doesn't work, either. There is simply too much extraneous material. You don't need to go into all that detail to teach ethics and basic morality. Why do you need to introduce extraneous subjects such as "giants in the earth in those days"? Why do you need to bring up a story line about "sons of God" and "daughters of men"? And why would you have your hero beamed up somewhere rather than dying a hero's death?

That's too much information. There is no need to add all that material with no context or relevance to the theological lesson you're trying to teach. It's simply unnecessary baggage for the reader to deal with if your object is to teach religion.

This might very well be the reason the committees who put the Bible together decided to leave out the book of Enoch, with its references to Watchers, good angels, bad angels, building arts, and the invention of writing. They felt it was more information than their followers could handle.

That leads us to a third alternative. Perhaps the book of Enoch reveals an alternative history that is more complicated, but perhaps closer to the truth, than the accounts we are usually taught.

Can we read it as though it were a straightforward history book?

No.

Can we place it in a specific time and location?

Probably not.

Was Enoch an actual historical personage or a mythological composite?

Maybe, like most literary heroes, it is a little of both.

Was Enoch, assuming he really ever existed, an ancient shamanic visionary with psychic powers?

I'm inclined to believe it.

And that's the reason he was deleted from the Bible. He didn't fit the preconceived notions of those who compiled the book of Genesis. They had to mention him in order to complete the genealogies they so loved. But when people wanted to know more about this intriguing figure, their answer was simple and direct: "You can't handle the truth!"

So, he was made to disappear from history until he mysteriously showed up a few thousand years later in Ethiopia.

Some heroes are too big to die.

# PSEUDEPIGRAPHA AND OTHER DISGUISES

As we have already seen, the books of the Apocrypha, although not held to the same standard of divine authorship as the rest of the books of the Bible, are at least included in some versions of the Bible, usually set apart in a separate section. That's not the case with books labeled *pseudepigrapha*. No one includes them at all, with the possible exception of a few that are read by some branches of the Ethiopian Orthodox Church. The Talmud lists them as *sefarim hizonim*, or "extraneous books." Some of them are quite visionary. They promote a strict, ascetic way of life and deal mostly with the mysterious subjects of creation and the dualistic aspects of good and evil as a way of dealing with life's secrets.

In this sense they are similar to the early Christian theology of the Gnostics, who believed that the creation story we read in Genesis was a lie written by a fallen and evil spirit. A good God could never have created a sinful world, they claimed. It wouldn't have been in his nature. Therefore, it must have been the work of a fallen angel or evil spirit. Human beings, according to Gnosticism, are divine souls trapped in a material, physical body.

Is it any wonder that early gatekeepers saw this viewpoint as heresy and sought to censor any such texts from accepted sources? The legendary Rabbi Akiva ben Yosef of the first and second centuries C.E. even declared that "he who reads *sefarim hizonim* forfeits his share in the world to come."

This subject takes us deep into the theology concerning the demiurge, or creator of the physical universe. To understand this concept, which is totally contrary to the accepted biblical account of creation, we need to take a brief tour through some Sumerian ideas about how the condition of the human race came to be so troubling. According to this view, we were created to be a slave race by a group of gods, possibly alien entities, called Anunna. They "came in strength from beyond time. They were carried, one day, by the rebellion of the universe." One of them was named Enlil. He was an evil being who wanted to enslave the human race. His opposite was Nenki, a female god who sought to free them from bondage.

In Sumerian literature, Nenki is usually pictured as a reptilian figure. This explains the presence of the serpent in the Garden of Eden. The serpent wasn't there to ensnare Adam and Eve. She was there to open their eyes to the truth and free them by offering them the gift of the knowledge of good and evil and, eventually, the gift of eternal life. These were gifts that had been forbidden them by the evil god. The two trees of Eden, the Tree of the Knowledge

A clay statuette of the god Enlil was discovered near Nippur, Iraq. Its origins date to around 1700 B.C.E. Enlil was an evil god from the Sumerian pantheon who was also worshipped by the Assyrians, Babylonians, Akkadians, and Hurrians.

of Good and Evil and the Tree of Life, would have made the humans able to "be like gods," as Genesis 3 clearly states.

In this version of the story, Enlil won the day. Humans did eat of the tree of Duality, the Tree of the Knowledge of Good and Evil. But they were stopped from eating of the Tree of Life by being cast out into the cruel world.

Remember that history is almost always written by the winners. In other words, according to Sumerian religious texts, the story of Abraham's god, who created the world, is the story of an evil entity called the demiurge, or Enlil. He even went so far as to place sword-wielding cherubim, or "Shining Ones," at the entrance to Eden to ensure that humans would never attain the godhead, or eternal life.

It has been said that the smartest thing the devil ever did was to convince humans that he didn't exist. This reading of the Sumerian myth goes one step further. It says that the smartest thing the devil ever did was to convince humans that he was God.

According to this reading of Scripture, JHVH, translated as the LORD, is not the creator. The creator is Enlil, the enslaver of humankind, henceforth known as the demiurge. He is head of the patriarchal system that wants to suppress freedom, especially the freedom of women. He doesn't want equality. He wants subservient slaves. He doesn't want creative, right-brained, intuitive thinkers. He wants left-brained, obedient servants who are forced to work each and every day.

In my book *Lost Civilizations*, I put it this way:

This reading of the story says that humans were upright-walking animals who were modified through DNA manipulation to fill the role of worker bees. The word "Adam" in Sumerian means "animal." "Eden" consists of the words "e," meaning "home," and "den," which means "life." "Satan" in Sumerian means "the administrator."

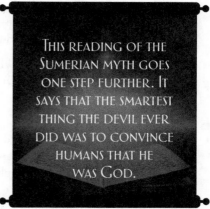

This reading of the Sumerian myth goes one step further. It says that the smartest thing the devil ever did was to convince humans that he was God.

Enki managed to grant wisdom to humans when he, through Ninki, the "serpent" of Eden, gave them the ability to discern good and evil. That caught Enlil by surprise. The best he could do was to drive them out of Eden and forbid their return.

To put it bluntly, according to this reading of the story, the God who monotheists have been worshiping for the last 5,000 years is not Jehovah, the creator God. He is Enlil, the patriarchal demiurge—Satan himself. This explains the God of the Old Testament who sent the flood to destroy humankind, who commanded the Israelites to kill innocent Canaanite women and children, who was the justification for the Crusades and the Inquisition, who seems so incredibly bloodthirsty. It explains why the author of 1 John in the New Testament could declare that "we know we are of God and the whole world is in the hands of the evil one" (1 John 5:19). He recognized that humans have been fighting the good fight, trying to get back to Eden.

We are here on earth to learn the lessons of duality, the "knowledge of good and evil." But we are caught in a divine battle of competing spiritual forces. We still need to "earn our daily bread by the sweat of our brow." It's just that we have turned our curse into a search for meaning. We want to get back to Paradise.

The Gnostics, in similar fashion to those who wrote the pseudepigraphal texts, believed there was a bigger game being played out by forces outside of planet Earth. The universe is bigger than we realize, they declared. As a matter of fact, the universe is simply one cell in the immense body (the multiverse) that is a manifestation of God. Here on earth the battle between good and evil, the battle called duality, is raging. The earth may be the domain of the demiurge, but that domain itself is called "Mother Earth," the creation of Sophia, the goddess of wisdom, the divine spark that Enlil, the devil, strives to put out.

This is a completely different reading from the account presented in the biblical canon. Is it any wonder that early censors wanted to make sure such ideas were not introduced into the accepted texts?

Here are a few examples of texts they considered worthy only to line the wastebaskets of history.

## Enoch

We've already looked at those parts of the book of Enoch that relate to the Watchers. In a few chapters, we'll look at what it has to say about giants. But we can't leave this book alone because it is obvious from the fact that it is referred to so often by other writers that members of the early Christian Church, including none other than Jesus, and the scribes of the Jewish tradition were very familiar with it. Nevertheless, it disappeared from history, being edited out of the established canon of both the Jewish and Christian tradition. Why?

One reason might be that it makes astounding claims concerning who Enoch was. In Enoch 68:1, we read the words of Noah himself:

> "And after that my grandfather Enoch gave me all the secrets
> in the book and in the parables which had been given to him,
> and he put them together for me in the words of the book of
> the parables."

If we assume, just for the sake of argument, that the book of Enoch records actual, although perhaps garbled, history and was written by an actual ancestor of the old sailor himself, it seems very reasonable to assume that his grandfather's treasured book would be one of the things Noah would have wanted to take aboard the ark, where it would presumably have survived the cataclysm.

Right away we have entered territory most biblical scholars would dismiss. Enoch may tell a great tale of ancient times, but academia universally suspects that it was written by multiple authors much later than the epic of Noah's flood, assuming that such a flood actually happened at all.

Still, the words "all the secrets" is tantalizing. All what secrets? What was the nature of the secrets? Why were such truths kept secret in the first place? What did they reveal that was so important and perhaps dangerous that they had to be kept secret at all? Implied is a hidden wisdom that had been long lost.

Even if all this is merely a literary device, it still makes us wonder. Someone, obviously, had to be aware of at least a rumor of such wisdom. Jude, a New Testament writer who claims to be a disciple of Jesus, put it this way in the 14th and 15th verses of the book that bears his name:

In the seventh generation from Adam, Enoch also prophesied these things, saying: "Behold, the Lord came with his holy myriads, to execute judgment on all, and to convict all the ungodly of all their ungodly deeds which they have committed in such an ungodly way, and of all the harsh things which ungodly sinners spoke against him."

> ENOCH MAY TELL A GREAT TALE OF ANCIENT TIMES, BUT ACADEMIA UNIVERSALLY SUSPECTS THAT IT WAS WRITTEN BY MULTIPLE AUTHORS MUCH LATER THAN THE EPIC OF NOAH'S FLOOD....

Enoch covers a huge amount of territory. Part of it deals with astronomy, going so far as to establish a calendar consisting of 364 days that are grouped into 52 weeks. It spends a lot of time talking about the subject of eschatology, which is the study of things to come, judgments, and the prophesied Messiah.

In chapter 17 there is an extended description of a journey into the heavens:

> And they took and brought me to a place in which those who were there were like flaming fire, and, when they wished, they appeared as men. And they brought me to the place of darkness, and to a mountain the point of whose summit reached to heaven. And I saw the places of the luminaries and the treasuries of the stars and of the thunder and in the uttermost depths, where were a fiery bow and arrows and their quiver, and a fiery sword and all the lightnings. And they took me to the living waters, and to the fire of the west, which receives every setting of the sun. And I came to a river of fire in which the fire flows like water and discharges itself into the great sea towards the west. I saw the great rivers and came to the great river and to the great darkness, and went to the place where no flesh walks. I saw the mountains of the darkness of winter and the place whence all the waters of the deep flow. I saw the mouths of all the rivers of the earth and the mouth of the deep.

Is Enoch simply describing a vision similar to those recorded by Isaiah and Daniel? Is this a dream/vision in the shamanic tradition?

If so, there doesn't seem to be any great need to suppress the whole book from public consumption. After all, other books that were allowed to enter the canon sound much like this.

The reasons are more probably tied up in the idea of secret wisdom that was deemed too dangerous to include. We don't know what that wisdom consisted of. But the original committees that vetoed the book and committed

An illustration from *Svyatoslav's Miscellany* (1066) depicts the Church Fathers, the theologians and writers who solidified Christian doctrine by the seventh century C.E.

it to obscurity obviously did. The so-called Church Fathers, such as Justin Martyr, Iranaeus, Origen, Clement of Alexandria, and Tertullian, who are studied by modern seminarians to this day, quoted extensively from it.

So, what happened?

The book of Enoch was officially banned, at least in Christian circles, by the Council of Laodicea (363–364 C.E.) in ancient Anatolia, which was in modern-day Turkey. It consisted of a committee of 30 clerics, all from Asia Minor, who gathered for most of a year soon after the conclusion of a war between the Roman Empire and Persia. Emperor Julian of Rome had attempted a revival of sorts, urging a return to paganism. In doing so, he began to discriminate against Christians. He died in battle, however, in 363, and the officers of the Roman army elected Jovian to take his place. They were in a precarious position, far from home, their supply lines broken, so Jovian ended the war with Persia under unfavorable terms, to say the least. He was succeeded by Valentinian I, who then appointed his brother Valens to be emperor of the East.

The Council of Laodicea began soon after. One of the things it sought to accomplish was to better define what Christianity was. The council did so by establishing which texts fit best into the prevailing trinitarian theology. Because of the recent bout with paganism, astrology was specifically condemned, and Enoch had a lot to say about astrology. So did many others in the young Christian sect, but the clerics of Anatolia were convinced the whole subject was a playground for the devil, so Enoch had to go. Because it was banned by the authorities, it gradually faded away.

During the Protestant Reformation in the sixteenth century, there arose a renewed interest in the book of Enoch, but by then, most of it had been lost to the modern world. In the late fifteenth century, rumors had begun to spread that a copy might still exist. This prompted a host of forgeries, each claiming to be the famous lost book of Enoch, but, as related in an earlier chapter, it wasn't until James Bruce and his journey to Ethiopia, returning in 1773, that the entire book was finally restored back into history. Until then, there were only fragments.

Once again we come face to face with another anonymous committee of editors who imposed their will on the Bible that we hold in our hands today. When we read it now, far removed from the time of the censors, it doesn't seem that dangerous, especially if it is read as metaphor.

To read it as a work of historical importance, albeit a garbled and possibly augmented account, it raises all sorts of questions. Did Enoch travel through interdimensional realities? Did he meet with alien entities? Was he sent on a mission to prevent the sexual union of material and non-material beings or humans and aliens, unions that produced the mysterious Nephilim? Did he meet with human survivors of a lost Ice Age civilization who were later remembered as gods? Did they actually teach him the secrets of an advanced astronomical culture whose inhabitants were familiar with the stars and the heavens? Were these "all the secrets of the world" that his grandson Noah talked about? What was going on back in those days?

Sadly, because a group of anonymous gatekeepers had a political ax to grind regarding a recent attempt to revive what they considered to be paganism, we might never know.

## Jubilees

When someone familiar with the Bible reads the book of Jubilees for the first time, they find it almost seems as if they are reading the first draft of the book of Genesis. Perhaps that's why it is sometimes called the "Lesser Genesis" or "Little Genesis." But there are fascinating details in Jubilees that Genesis skips over.

Genesis does not explain how Cain found women to wed after murdering Abel since they were, apparently, the only children of Adam and Eve. Jubilees, however, says that the original man and woman also had daugh-

One of the most common questions people ask about the Bible, for instance, is, "If Adam and Eve had only two sons, Cain and Abel, and if Cain killed Abel, whom did he marry in order to go out and build a city so soon after he got kicked out of the house?"

Well, Jubilees answers that question. It provides a list of the daughters of Adam and Eve. Apparently, according to an unknown author of long ago, Cain married his sisters. Or at least one of them.

Why wasn't Jubilees included in the Bible? It's tempting to say it was because of the possibility of condoning incest. But that's far too easy an explanation. The truth is that although it may have been written only in the first century or so B.C.E., the material it contains is far older. But aside from snippets of texts that have turned up here and there, written in Greek and Latin, it disappeared for a long while until a complete copy finally surfaced in, of all places, Ethiopia, written in Ge'ez, an ancient South Semitic language and the liturgical language of Ethiopia.

So, what we read today is translated from Ge'ez, Greek, Latin, and even some portions in Syriac. Nevertheless, most scholars are convinced it was originally written in Hebrew. If that's the case, however, there are real historical discrepancies that might indicate why it was thrown out so early in its history.

For one thing, Jews, especially at that time in history, followed a lunar calendar. Jubilees advocates a solar dating system, proposing a 364-day, 12-month year. That was a pretty radical proposal for those times. The unknown author divides history into periods of 49 years each, called "jubilees." He claims that system better explains the biblical passages that deal with prophecy and the time of the coming of the Messiah.

The fact that whoever wrote it is Jewish seems clear, even though we don't have any copies written in Hebrew. The book tells the story of the creation of the world up until the time of Moses using an interesting plot device. Moses climbs to the top of Mount Sinai and there encounters an entity called the Angel of Presence. Apparently, the entire history was written long before Moses was born, and the Jewish people were chosen to be set apart by God even before creation. On the mountain, Moses is shown "heavenly tablets" that were previously viewed by Noah, Lamech, and other patriarchs, placing Moses in quite an auspicious line of prophets.

He does learn some disturbing things, however. A demonic entity called Mastema, reminiscent of the Christian concept of Satan, is involved behind the scenes. But there are differences. For one thing, Mastema seems to serve God in some pretty offbeat ways. He is the agent through which God tests his followers. The closest Old Testament equivalent is found in the book of Job, wherein Satan is allowed to test the righteous Job to see if he will remain faithful.

In Jubilee's version of the story of Abraham, when Abraham is told to sacrifice his only son, it was Mastema who in the middle of it all:

> Behold, Abraham loveth Isaac his son, and he delighteth in him above all things else; bid him offer him as a burnt-offering on the altar, and Thou wilt see if he will do this command, and Thou wilt know if he is faithful in everything wherein Thou dost try him. (Jubilees 17:16)

The god of the book of Jubilees is portrayed almost as if he is a tyrannical dictator who wants both obedience and worship from his subjects. He wants their respect, but he also wants them to fear him.

Mastema wants some of this kind of action himself. He asks God for a company of spirits he can command, and God allows it:

> Lord, Creator, let some of them remain before me, and let them hearken to my voice, and do all that I shall say unto them; for if some of them are not left to me, I shall not be able to execute the power of my will on the sons of men; for these are for corruption and leading astray before my judgment, for great is the wickedness of the sons of men. (Jubilees 10:8)

Thus it is that a tenth of the angels in heaven become demons who follow Mastema.

When Moses had his famous confrontation with Pharaoh, culminating in his plea to "Let my people go," he took on Pharaoh's own court magicians, who matched him trick for trick before finally realizing they had met their match. This, according to Jubilees, was also the work of Mastema:

> And Mastema stood up against thee, and sought to cast thee into the hands of Pharaoh, and he helped the Egyptian sorcerers, and they stood up and wrought before thee. (Jubilees 48:9)

In Jubilees, the text indicates that it is Mastema who was behind the plagues that were brought down upon Egypt to convince the Pharaoh to release the Jews.

He even seems to be the one who orchestrated the ten plagues that eventually convinced Pharaoh to free the Israelites.

> For on this night—the beginning of the festival and the be-
> ginning of the joy—ye were eating the Passover in Egypt,
> when all the powers of Mastema had been let loose to slay all
> the first-born in the land of Egypt, from the first-born of Pha-
> raoh to the first-born of the captive maidservant in the mill,
> and to the cattle. (Jubilees 49:2)

All this activity is contrary to the traditional acceptance of a god who is merciful and all-loving. It is certainly an inconvenient truth, to say the least. Here we seem yet again to have come up against a cabal of editors who decided to eliminate from holy writ anything that didn't seem to agree with their theology. We can only wonder what modern religion would be like if they had allowed a more fertile ground for questions and speculations rather than dogma and doctrine.

## The Assumption of Moses

Strap yourself in for this one. It requires quite a ride through a vast biblical landscape.

The c. 1481 *Moses's Testament and Death* by Luca Signorelli depicts the scene related in Deuteronomy. But if Moses was supposedly the author of that book, how did he write about his own demise?

First, the basics. Most scholars believe this book was written in the first century by an unknown Jewish author who wrote in Hebrew. But the only surviving copies available are written in Latin, and they appear to be translated from Koine, or "common," Greek, which was the language the New Testament was written in. Why, then, do they think it was written in Hebrew? Because of the idioms used, which sound like those used in Hebrew.

That's confusing enough, but it doesn't even begin to address the real issues.

Let's jump right to the heart of the problem. The text seems to consist of a number of secret prophecies that Moses revealed to Joshua, his second in command, just before his death. Now, the plot thickens.

Earlier, we saw that the first five books of the Bible, the Torah, are often called the Books of Moses. Tradition says they were dictated to Moses straight from the Almighty during the times Moses climbed to the top of Mount Sinai to converse with God. The problem with this theory is that the end of Deuteronomy, the fifth book of the Torah, describes the death of Moses:

> Then Moses climbed Mount Nebo from the plains of Moab
> to the top of Pisgah, across from Jericho. There the Lord
> showed him the whole land—from Gilead to Dan, all of
> Naphtali, the territory of Ephraim and Manasseh, all the land

of Judah as far as the Mediterranean Sea, the Negev and the whole region from the Valley of Jericho, the City of Palms, as far as Zoar. Then the Lord said to him, "This is the land I promised on oath to Abraham, Isaac and Jacob when I said, 'I will give it to your descendants.' I have let you see it with your eyes, but you will not cross over into it." And Moses the servant of the Lord died there in Moab, as the Lord had said. He buried him in Moab, in the valley opposite Beth Peor, but to this day no one knows where his grave is. (Deuteronomy 34:1–5)

How could Moses write about his own death and burial?

That's not an insurmountable problem. The simplest explanation is that the final chapter of Deuteronomy was a postscript written by Joshua, who took over the leadership of the Israelites after Moses passed on.

A harder problem is that Moses's death becomes a bit suspicious later on in the New Testament. In Matthew 17, Jesus takes his inner circle of disciples, Peter, James, and John, up a mountain later called the Mount of Transfiguration. Here, Moses reappears, this time in the company of Elijah, who also died a suspicious death. As a matter of fact, according to the Bible, Elijah didn't die at all. The great prophet was taken up to heaven in a fiery chariot. But in Matthew 17, he now stands in the presence of Moses and Jesus:

After six days Jesus took with him Peter, James and John the brother of James, and led them up a high mountain by themselves. There he was transfigured before them. His face shone like the sun, and his clothes became as white as the light. Just then there appeared before them Moses and Elijah, talking with Jesus.

This incident is usually explained by suggesting that Moses and Elijah appeared to advise Jesus about his coming death. Who better to offer counsel than Moses, who represented the law, and Elijah, who represented the prophets? Jesus often used the phrase "the law and the prophets" when referring to the Hebrew Scriptures. Here's just one example from Matthew 22:

Jesus said unto him, "Thou shalt love the Lord thy God with all thy heart, and with all thy soul, and with all thy mind. This is the first and great commandment. And the second is like unto it, Thou shalt love thy neighbour as thyself. On these two commandments hang all the law and the prophets."

Just before ascending this mountain, Jesus had revealed to his disciples that he was going to "build his church." After the climb we are told he "set his face steadfast toward Jerusalem" and his crucifixion.

If this was where the story ended, we could chalk the whole thing up to an engaging metaphor. But now let's throw a monkey wrench into the works.

Once again, we confront the problem of too much information. Why mess up a good and moral theological lesson with extraneous facts?

The problem arises when we turn to a small, seemingly insignificant, book that comes almost at the end of the New Testament that was written by a man who is supposedly one of the apostles. His name is Jude.

THERE WAS OBVIOUSLY SOME KIND OF TRADITION THAT WAS FAMILIAR TO THE WRITER OF THIS LITTLE BOOK OF ONLY ONE CHAPTER, BUT WHAT WAS IT?

> But even the archangel Michael, when he was disputing with the devil about the body of Moses, did not himself dare to condemn him for slander but said, "The Lord rebuke you!"

Whoa! Why do we need to know that somehow the great archangel Michael was "disputing" with the devil over the body of Moses, who, aside from his transfigured appearance on the mountaintop, had been dead for more than a thousand years? There was obviously some kind of tradition that was familiar to the writer of this little book of only one chapter, but what was it?

No one knows. A lot of speculation has been offered, each variation purportedly giving the "truth." But the whole story is mysterious. Two men, Moses and Elijah, die suspicious deaths. One of them is secretly buried by none other than an archangel who has to contest the devil to do it, and the other is taken bodily up to heaven in a fiery chariot. Both men later step out of the ether to talk to Jesus about his upcoming death.

To put it mildly, this prompts a few questions.

In particular, it brings us back to the pseudepigraphal book called the Assumption of Moses in which Moses, the mystery man, imparts secrets to Joshua, his second in command, before his death. It's a story steeped in the possibility of conspiracy theory. Here are a few examples:

- The obvious way to approach this tale with sobriety and intellectual acumen is to say that it's a wonderful, imaginative fantasy that exists because one author built on the work of another, exploring strings of information that are left open to the imagination. Moses dies alone, and no one knows where he was buried. That's interesting. He's Jewish, obviously, so let's bring him back on a mountaintop to counsel none other than Jesus, the founder of Christianity, thus blending the older tradition with the newer. Meanwhile, we can throw in some mysterious material about angels and secrets to add a touch of the esoteric. It makes for a good mystery story.

- The problem with this approach, though, is that there is no real need for all this information if your purpose is to write an entertaining fantasy. In one sense, it's not very well written. It merely hints. It doesn't explain. There's no conclusion. So, the next approach is to ask if there is a basic story that was known to all the writers but lost to us. Think of it this way. If I mention that George Washington once chopped down a cherry tree, most Americans will understand that I'm talking about the importance of telling the truth because they are familiar with the tale, having been taught it since childhood. When challenged by his father, young George didn't cover it up; he confessed. It proves he was honest and willing to shoulder the responsibility for his actions. We all know that. But what if someone never heard about George Washington? They wouldn't have the faintest idea that chopping down a tree had anything to do with taking responsibility for one's actions and telling the truth. That's another way of interpreting the threads of the Moses story as they weave through time. The original listeners knew what it meant because they know the background. We don't.

• Now, we come to a third possibility. What if we are reading a story with garbled but deep historical roots that are memories of something that actually happened? What if Moses wasn't quite human at all? What if he was, for lack of a better phrase, an alien entity, or at least served as an envoy to either supernatural or alien entities? What if, like Elijah, he *did* die a suspicious death? What if he *did* know secrets that have never been revealed except to a precious few, such as Jesus of Nazareth when they met on a mountaintop? What if there *are* unknown entities who work behind the scenes to guide and direct the human race toward an unknown destiny, and these entities have been misidentified as God?

Each one of these approaches will work. The one you select depends on your imagination and degree of acceptance when it comes to differing ways of reading these accounts, based on your experience and upbringing.

Here's the point. Our purpose here is not to decide which interpretation is the correct one. It's merely to point out that the original, unknown editors of these stories had a point of view. What they selected and what they included remains, but not the reasons for their selections. We don't know why they chose the texts they did because they never tell us. They just present them in the guise of sacred writings and expect us to accept their opinions. That's no different from a Baptist preacher delivering his version of the truth and a Catholic priest telling us his. Usually, both will leave out inconvenient truths that undermine their position. Unless we take the trouble to listen with discernment and question not only what they say but what they leave out, we will be in the dark, having heard only half the story.

In other words, we come face to face with censorship once again. It may be spread out over many years and differing traditions, but it's still censorship.

## The Testaments of the 12 Patriarchs

This is yet another important work that most people don't know anything about. It's divided into 12 sections, each directed to one of the patriarchs of the 12 tribes of Israel. Abraham's grandson Jacob, whose name was changed to Israel, is the purported author of most of this work. He seems to draw on his own experiences of shortcomings and mistakes and warns his sons not to follow in his footsteps.

But he is also concerned with prophetic visions. Specifically, he spends a lot of time talking about the coming of not one Messiah but two. One will come from the tribe of Levi, the other from the tribe of Judah. This is a concept similar to that of the Essenes, who copied and preserved the Dead Sea Scrolls.

Let's take them one at a time.

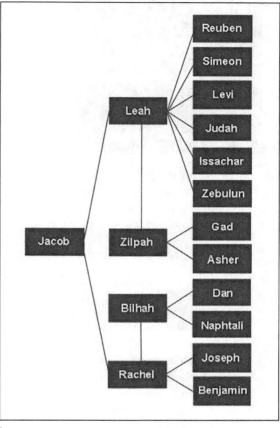

Jacob (Israel) had 12 sons by four wives, and those sons became the patriarchs of the 12 tribes of Israel.

### The Testament of Reuben

The primary theme of the Testament of Reuben involves falling into lust. Jacob is ashamed of Reuben's having had sex with Jacob's concubine, Bilhah. Bilhah, it seems, was bathing in secret, but Reuben watched her from a nearby hiding place. Later, when she became drunk, Reuben raped her. Something similar happened between David and Bathsheba in 2 Samuel. It also figures into the story of Jacob's son Joseph, who was nearly seduced by Potiphar's wife in Egypt. He resisted, and Jacob, in rather typical male fashion, blames the woman, not his son. He equates Reuben's transgression to the downfall of the Watchers, who "saw that the daughters of men were fair and [mated] with any of them that they chose."

### The Testament of Simeon

This section is devoted to exploring the sin of envy. It was envy that drove the 11 brothers to attempt fratricide against their brother Joseph. Jacob

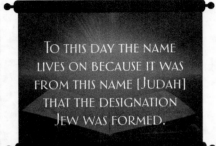

TO THIS DAY THE NAME LIVES ON BECAUSE IT WAS FROM THIS NAME [JUDAH] THAT THE DESIGNATION JEW WAS FORMED.

had given Joseph a "coat of many colors," and the brothers first planned to kill him but later sold him into slavery instead. The story ends well, as Joseph, having risen to great power in Egypt, is able to forgive his brothers and save them from starvation.

## The Testament of Levi

This is the longest section of the 12. Although its subject is the sin of arrogance, it deals with the whole nature of the Apocalypse and, interestingly enough, quotes extensively from the book of Enoch, which we already explored in great depth. In this section, Jacob promises that at the end of time there will be a glorious high priest who will restore righteousness to the earth.

## The Testament of Judah

The theme here is courage, but the Testament of Judah also touches on the sins of greed and fornication. (The Bible tells quite a tale about Judah, who had a number of affairs, some with non-Jewish women and even his daughter Tamar, who was pretending to be a prostitute at the time.) Right in the middle of the lecture, Jacob switches gears and announces that the role of priest supersedes that of a king, implying that the tribe of Levi, the tribe of religious priests, is greater than that of Judah, the political tribe that produced so many of the famous kings known to history, including none other than David and Solomon. When the tribes divided into two distinct nations, the southern nation, home to the temple itself, was given the name Judah. To this day the name lives on because it was from this name that the designation Jew was formed. When Jesus was born, the Gospel according to Matthew recounts that wise men from the East called him the King of the Jews.

## The Testament of Issachar

This book deals with the concept of asceticism as a virtuous way of life, an idea that haunts virtually every religious tradition. Take, for instance, this rather one-sided opinion of what constitutes a virtuous woman:

> Who can find a virtuous woman? For her price is far above rubies. The heart of her husband doth safely trust in her, so that he shall have no need of spoil. She will do him good and not evil all the days of her life. She seeketh wool, and flax, and worketh willingly with her hands. She is like the merchants' ships; she bringeth her food from afar. She riseth also while it is yet night, and giveth meat to her household, and a portion to her maidens. She considereth a field, and buyeth

it: with the fruit of her hands she planteth a vineyard. She girdeth her loins with strength, and strengtheneth her arms. She perceiveth that her merchandise is good: her candle goeth not out by night. She layeth her hands to the spindle, and her hands hold the distaff. She stretcheth out her hand to the poor; yea, she reacheth forth her hands to the needy. She is not afraid of the snow for her household: for all her household are clothed with scarlet. She maketh herself coverings of tapestry; her clothing is silk and purple. Her husband is known in the gates, when he sitteth among the elders of the land. She maketh fine linen, and selleth it; and delivereth girdles unto the merchant. Strength and honour are her clothing; and she shall rejoice in time to come. She openeth her mouth with wisdom; and in her tongue is the law of kindness. She looketh well to the ways of her household, and eateth not the bread of idleness. Her children arise up, and call her blessed; her husband also, and he praiseth her. Many daughters have done virtuously, but thou excellest them all. Favour is deceitful, and beauty is vain: but a woman that feareth the Lord, she shall be praised. Give her of the fruit of her hands; and let her own works praise her in the gates. (Proverbs 31:10–31)

From this we gather that a virtuous wife does all the work while "Her husband is known in the gates, when he sitteth among the elders of the land." Seems like a rather one-sided relationship. But it's nice work if you can get it, as long as you're the husband and not the wife.

## The Testament of Zebulun

The theme of virtuousness continues. According to Zebulun himself, he has lived a virtuous life:

I am not conscious that I have sinned all my days, save in thought. Nor yet do I remember that I have done any iniquity, except the sin of ignorance which I committed against Joseph; for I covenanted with my brethren, because they had all agreed that if anyone should declare the secret, he should be slain.

Apparently, virtue trumps pride every time.

## The Testament of Dan

This text considers the sins of anger and lying, using the story of Joseph's betrayal by his brothers as an example. For an entertaining treatment of this involved but foundational Old Testament story, one cannot do better than viewing a film based on the Broadway musical *Joseph and the Amazing Technicolor*

The text of the Testament of Naphtali that was found in Cave 4 at Qumran is complete. In it, there is a prophecy about the division of the tribes of Israel.

*Dreamcoat.* I highly recommend it. All 12 patriarchs are accurately and hilariously portrayed.

One strange incident caps this particular text, however. Dan reminds his sons that if they "stay near to God" and God's interceding angel, they will be received by the savior of the Gentiles. This indicates that the book was probably written after Christianity had become a reality. There are few Hebrew texts that indicate a Jewish Messiah will save Gentiles.

## The Testament of Naphtali

A complete copy of this text was discovered among the Dead Sea Scrolls in Cave 4. Because the keepers of the scrolls were obsessed with prophecies about a coming apocalypse, they would naturally have been attracted to it, for it deals with typical visions and dreams that so often accompany apocalyptic literature, such as the book of Daniel in the Old Testament and Revelation in the New Testament.

## The Testament of Gad

The theme here concerns the primacy of love over hate. "And now, my children, I exhort you, love ye each one his brother, and put away hatred from your hearts. Love."

## The Testament of Asher

This is the shortest book in the series. The other 11 all begin with Jacob on his deathbed, exhorting his sons one at a time. Here the lesson is simple. There are two ways to live. The best way is to follow truth with faith.

## The Testament of Joseph

This book builds on the familiar Genesis story of Joseph and his attempted seduction by Potiphar's wife. Once again, I refer you to *Joseph and the Amazing Technicolor Dreamcoat* for an entertaining refresher. The story is a classic. After being sold into slavery by his brothers, Joseph works for a rich man named Potiphar in Egypt. Potiphar's wife attempts to seduce Joseph. Joseph resists, and she has him thrown into jail. There, he displays his ability to interpret dreams.

When Pharaoh's troubling dreams cause concern, Joseph is released to interpret. Because of his success, he becomes Pharaoh's number-two man and leads Egypt successfully through a period of feast and then famine.

## The Testament of Benjamin

This is really a continuation of the Testament of Joseph. In the Genesis story, Benjamin was Joseph's favorite brother. If there is a moral to this story, it involves the dangers of deceit.

Together, these texts constitute one long pseudepigraphal book. Undoubtedly, those who put the Bible together were confused as to authorship and authenticity and therefore decided to leave out the whole thing, even though the subjects they cover deal with rather important moral themes. In some cases, they contradict sections of the Bible, now understood by many to be the word of God. But after reading them, we can't help but wonder. Are the books that made the final cut and ended up in the Bible really much different from those that were cut? Who made the choices? And why? Can we trust their judgment? What were the criteria they used to approve of some and disallow others? Was God at work in the process? If so, where in the Bible does it say

Joseph's ability to interpret dreams impressed the pharaoh of Egypt, who eventually gives him the position of vizier.

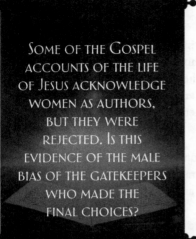

Some of the Gospel accounts of the life of Jesus acknowledge women as authors, but they were rejected. Is this evidence of the male bias of the gatekeepers who made the final choices?

that? If some books are "inspired" and others are not, who decides which are which?

It's a perplexing problem, seldom discussed in most Bible-believing communities.

## Sibylline Oracles

The Sibylline Oracles were written between the second and seventh centuries after the birth of Jesus, but they claim to have been composed of an unbroken line beginning with the daughters of Noah. Although this is almost certainly not the case, it's an interesting fact to remember because if it were true, and if they had been included in the final edition of the Bible, these would be the only books of the Bible written by women. Other books claim a feminine perspective, such as Esther and Ruth. Some of the Gospel accounts of the life of Jesus acknowledge women as authors, but they were rejected. Is this evidence of the male bias of the gatekeepers who made the final choices? They never claim this as a reason for their decisions. But it makes us wonder.

For a period of up to 500 years, both Jewish and Christian communities added to the Sibylline Oracles. A Greek philosopher named Heracleides Ponticus, who lived in the fourth century B.C.E., made the claim that the original Sibyl lived thousands of years earlier, yet her voice continued to add to the text, channeled by countless women. Jewish tradition said Sibyl was a daughter of Noah, and the others who followed were, in effect, her spiritual descendants.

This is an important point. When we looked at the Genesis Apocryphon, we saw that Lamech, the father of Noah, believed his supposed offspring would be the hybrid son of one of the Anunnaki, or the Watchers, also called "sons of God," and his wife, one of the "daughters of men." The products of these unions, which are mentioned in the book of Genesis, were described as otherworldly, to say the least. They were called Nephilim, or giants. Now we come upon Sibyl, believed to be a daughter of Noah. This would make her a second-generation hybrid, certainly distinct from ordinary humans.

Remember that it really isn't important whether or not we believe this to be the case. The important thing is that the early writers believed it. The fact that the text was well known is obvious. Throughout the ancient world, countries such as Babylon, Greece, Italy, the Levant, and Egypt developed traditions of oracles through whom the gods spoke. They were universally called "Sibyls."

From the oracle of Delphi to the famous Sibyl of Cumae in Italy, who lived in a cave and came out only to prophesy, the Sibyls were considered to be so important that even Michelangelo painted images of them on the ceiling of the Sistine Chapel. Together, they formed the basis of a tradition involving wise women who were in touch with the Source of All That Is.

Here are just two examples of their pronouncements, translated by J. J. Collins:

> And then God will give great joy to men,
>
> For earth and trees and countless flocks of sheep
>
> Will give to men the true fruit
>
> Of wine, sweet honey and white milk
>
> And corn, which is best of all for mortals. (Sibylline Oracle 3:619–623)
>
> But the holy land of the pious alone will bear all these things:
>
> A honey-sweet stream from rock and spring,
>
> And heavenly milk will flow for all the righteous.
>
> For with great piety and faith they put their hop
>
> In the one begetter, God, who alone is eminent. (Sibylline Oracle 5:280–285)

A 1400s artwork by Andrea del Castagno depicts the Sibyl of Cumae, a Greek colony that was located near Naples, Italy.

The tradition continues to this very day. Sibyl has become synonymous with a condition called dissociative identity disorder (formerly multiple personality disorder). It was the pseudonym given to a psychiatric patient whose treatment was rather spectacularly described in the 1973 book *Sybil*, written by Flora Rheta Schreiber. The condition was later proved to be a hoax when Shirley Mason, the real Sibyl, admitted to faking the 16 distinct personalities she claimed inhabited her. But the tradition of the Sibyl obviously contributed to the whole episode.

The early redactors who decided not to include any of these stories must have been aware that they were dealing with something that was beyond the boundaries of holy writ. They may not have been aware that a progression of women was each channeling their original inspiration—a second generation of a hybrid born of the "sons of [a] god and the daughters of men" who would one day be immortalized on the ceiling of the Sistine Chapel—but they knew the subject was delicate, to say the least.

## Conclusion

There are more books such as these that comprise the pseudepigrapha, but this provides at least a representative sample.

Why weren't they included in the final version of the Bible? Although we might never know for sure, one reason might be that there was a great disconnect between two camps of redactors. One believed that inspired scriptures ceased for 500 years between the two testaments of what became the modern Christian Bible. Prophecy had come to an end until the birth of Jesus. That was their editorial policy. Everything else was excluded as fake news.

Those who wrote these books disagreed. They believed God's voice continued on. No doubt the Essenes, who translated, collected, and preserved most of the pseudepigrapha, were very much interested in prophecy, coming events, and that which they considered to be God's great plan. That was one of the reasons they had withdrawn into the mountains northwest of the Dead Sea to await the coming apocalypse. In Jerusalem and other places of political and religious power, they were outcasts. But the Essenes seem to have reveled in that position. There must have been a bias against them when the traditionalists gathered to put the final edition of the Bible together.

There is no question, however, that their work was known and understood by some of those whose work was accepted into holy writ. Those included quoted, in some cases almost verbatim, some of the pseudepigraphal texts.

Little did the editors know, as they threw the discarded texts into the proverbial wastebaskets of history, that up in the mountains, deep in the Qumran caves, were copies of the very texts they thought they had destroyed, waiting to be discovered and translated almost 2,000 years later. Their work would one day be open to judgment by people who lived in a totally different world, a culture that they could never have imagined. Someday, those folks would even ask if what they were doing was censoring God.

# OTHER GEMS FROM THE DEAD SEA SCROLLS

On the fourth floor of the Museum of the Bible in Washington, D.C., there is a permanent exhibit that many thousands of people have gladly paid more than $20 to visit in order to gaze with rapt attention at fragments of the Dead Sea Scrolls. Carefully sealed in climate-controlled glass cases, protected from the hands of an adoring public, they are considered the most prized portion of the museum's extensive collection. Visitors read the story of their discovery and translation and are duly impressed by this precious example of archaeology at its finest.

Unfortunately, in March 2020, the museum was forced to announce that the entire collection, every one of the fragments so lovingly protected with high-tech equipment financed by the entry fees of the multitudes of adoring fans, was fake. Sixteen fragments form the heart of the exhibit. Every single one, some produced as late as the twentieth century, turned out to be a forgery. They fooled even the most careful collectors.

According to museum staff, there was no fraud involved. Many legitimate scholars who studied them thought they were authentic. But they are forgeries; make no mistake about it. To the museum's credit, as soon as the facts became known, they admitted it right away. "The Museum of the Bible is trying to be as transparent as possible," said CEO Harry Hargrave. "We're victims. We're victims of misrepresentation. We're victims of fraud."

Skepticism arose in part when David Green, an evangelical Christian who founded the multibillion-dollar Hobby Lobby craft-store chain in 1972, wrote of the Bible: "This isn't just some book that someone made up. It's God, it's history, and we want to show that." Skeptics tend to worry when a lot of money is spent to verify deeply held belief in the name of scholarship, and Green funded the museum.

I bring this up not to discredit anyone but to demonstrate how much the Dead Sea Scrolls continue to fascinate everyone from professional scholars to the general public. Someone knew there was a lot of money to be made from this interest. Only an extremely skilled forger could have pulled it off. Someone went to a lot of trouble. And it worked. They must have been in contact with the genuine fragments. Only the real articles could have served as models. This was a brilliant forgery.

This fraud aside, authentic fragments do still exist. They offer fascinating clues to curious scholars. Take, for instance, what is called the Copper Scroll. It's a sort of ancient treasure map, listing information about 64 caches of gold

The Museum of the Bible opened in November 2017 in Washington, D.C. A scandal occurred three years later when it was discovered that the Dead Sea Scrolls fragments displayed there were all forgeries.

and silver, supposedly buried to prevent the first-century Romans from discovering them. None of the caches have officially been found, so they are presumably awaiting discovery to this very day.

The possibility exists, of course, that the treasure has already been discovered, the caches looted long ago. Most of the Dead Sea texts are written in ink on parchment or animal skins, but the Copper Scroll consists of Hebrew and Greek letters chiseled onto metal sheets. Some scholars believe this was to better preserve the messages, but this, of course, is only theory.

In May 2016 another discovery shocked the academic community. In the 1950s, some scrolls had been discovered and placed in boxes to be later sorted or deciphered. They were very small in size and extremely delicate, so they went unexamined for more than 60 years, resting quietly in a storeroom in Israel. In 2016, as part of a project by the Israel Antiquities Authority designed to digitize the Dead Sea Scrolls, they were pulled out of storage and examined using new equipment that had not been available to the original finders.

To everyone's surprise, when NASA-inspired technology was employed, hidden out of sight to the naked eye, appeared a Paleo-Hebrew manuscript that indicated there were more scrolls yet to be found.

Oren Ableman of the Hebrew University of Jerusalem was credited with the discovery. It was, indeed, a significant piece of research. Fragments from the books of Deuteronomy, Leviticus, and Jubilees appeared, but what was most interesting was a fragment from what was called the Temple Scroll. It contained text describing directions for how to properly conduct services in what was called the Ideal Temple. This was unknown prior to the discovery. The fact that it was written in Paleo-Hebrew, a very early Hebrew script, indicates that the information was very, very old. But the complete manuscript remains lost, perhaps forever.

There is no doubt more information has yet to be deciphered. The work of translation is an ongoing task. But what is even more exciting is the very real possibility that hidden away in the mountains of the Dead Sea are more scrolls and texts awaiting discovery. Who knows what mysteries are yet to be found?

This raises a very important point. The Essenes, who buried these texts, obviously put great value on them. They were also a very secretive society. What did they know that was so important that they went to such pains, even risking life and limb, to preserve them? And even more mysterious, has their true identity and ideology been deliberately censored from the public? The story is a fascinating one, with many twists and turns. Let's start at the beginning.

The Temple Scroll is maintained at the Israel Museum. Among other things, it describes instructions given to Moses by God as to how the First Temple in Jerusalem should be constructed, but these guidelines were ignored when King Solomon later built it.

In the first century of the common era, a Roman historian known as Pliny the Elder wrote a book titled *Natural History*. He was the first to refer to the Essenes in print. According to his book, the Essenes possessed no money, and their priestly class practiced a strict celibacy. But he also said the group had existed for thousands of generations, scattered in communities throughout Israel while living among the general population. Their main geographical center was somewhere near Ein Gedi, close to the Dead Sea.

In 75 C.E. the great Jewish historian Flavius Josephus wrote massive accounts of the period. His books *The Jewish War*, *Antiquities of the Jews*, and *The Life of Flavius Josephus* are still studied today. He divided the religious community of Judaism into three groups, called Pharisees, Sadducees, and Essenes. The Pharisees and Sadducees are both mentioned in the New Testament, but there is no mention of Essenes. Josephus wrote that the Essenes lived a communal existence, ritually immersed themselves in water every morning, and kept a strict observance of the Sabbath. They ate communally and devoted themselves to a rigorous life of prayer. He also revealed that they had a cultlike devotion to studying religious texts and preserved secrets they would not reveal to anyone outside their number.

Some of the ruins at Qumran, a city that was inhabited by some of the Essenes, who would preserve the texts now known as the Dead Sea Scrolls.

One of the most startling revelations of Josephus was that the Essenes kept a systematic list of angels by name and claimed to converse with them.

Remember that fact. It's about to become very important as soon as we lay some more groundwork.

To sum up what these early writers tell us:

- The Essenes were a highly secretive, extremely religious cult that kept to themselves, the better to practice their spiritual lives in isolation.

- They believed themselves to be an elite group of Jews, as opposed to common Jewish believers.

- In isolation, they prepared themselves to be God's chosen people as they awaited the coming of Messiah and the building of a sacred temple on earth. Their writings reveal their belief that the current priesthood in Jerusalem were apostate, kept the wrong calendar, had forsaken the rules of purity, and were improperly officiating the laws of God.

One of the most intriguing texts found at Qumran is a scroll called *War of the Sons of Light against the Sons of Darkness*. This is the text that most clearly expressed the Essenes' dualistic belief system.

The "Sons of Light" were, of course, the Essenes. Apparently, the "Sons of Darkness" are everybody else. At some point, according to this scroll, there will be a great and final war, a cataclysmic battle between good and evil. This belief is echoed in the final book of the Christian New Testament called Revelation. The battle will be fought on earth, but its ramifications will be felt throughout the cosmos. Apparently, planet Earth has the bad fortune of being ground zero in a truly epic war being played out in the spiritual realm between God and Satan.

> DID THE ESSENES, IN EFFECT, REALLY WIN THE WAR, WHILE THE APOSTATE PHARISEES AND SADDUCEES WERE KILLED OR CARRIED OFF IN THE GREAT DIASPORA?

In this way, the beliefs of the Essenes are not much different from many other monotheistic systems of eschatology, or the study of the end times. But here the story takes a completely different twist.

For years scholars have wondered about the term "Son of God." That was the title Jesus took upon himself. But apparently it was in use way before Jesus was born. As we have already seen, it goes all the way back to the book of Genesis, but there it was used to describe fallen angels who in no way could have been confused with the second person of the Trinity. The Essenes also refer to a Council of Twelve, reminding the reader of the 12 disciples of Jesus. They practiced baptism in a manner reminiscent of John the Baptist, who baptized Jesus in the Jordan River. They also talked about healings, recalling the miracles of Jesus, and, most importantly, a communion meal. These are all analogous to Christian teachings, but they occurred long before Jesus was born. This has prompted some scholars to wonder if Christianity as we know it is a continuation of a Jewish sect called the cult of the Essenes.

Was Jesus the Messiah for whom the Essenes were waiting? Was he the real "Son of God" and teacher of righteousness? Can the reason that the Essenes are not mentioned in the Bible be attributed to the fact that they never disappeared at all but eventually morphed into the official state religion of the conquering Roman Empire? Did the Essenes, in effect, really win the war, while the apostate Pharisees and Sadducees were killed or carried off in the great Diaspora?

As if this is not enough, now the story takes on a really different hue. John Marco Allegro (1923–1988) was an archaeologist and Dead Sea Scrolls scholar. His most famous (some might say infamous) book was *The Sacred Mushroom and the Cross: A Study of the Nature and Origins of Christianity within the Fertility Cults of the Ancient Near East*. It was a book that both cemented his popularity and ended his career.

From his work working with the Copper Scroll and other Dead Sea texts, he put forth the theory that when the Essenes gathered to share their

Archaeologist John Marco Allegro proposed in his *The Sacred Mushroom and the Cross* that the Eucharist is based on the Essenes' ritual that involved eating psychedelic mushrooms.

communal meal, later ritualized in the Christian celebration of the Eucharist, or Last Supper, the main course consisted of psychedelic mushrooms. He believed this was the basis for the Christian sacramental meal.

In that sense, the Essenes, living in the nearby hills above the Dead Sea, now take on the appearance of an ancient, shamanic sect that surpasses the Hebrew religion and traces its roots way back to ancient shamanic rituals that may have taken place in the great painted caves of western Europe as much as 40,000 years ago. Indeed, this may even mark the beginning of religion.

In my book *Supernatural Gods,* I put it this way:

When the first humans crawled back into those great painted caves 40,000 years ago, or gazed in wonder at the night sky and wondered where they came from, the human race had finally evolved to the point where the real work of discovery could begin. We were able to think symbolically. We had religious thoughts—spiritual inclinations. We were off to the races and haven't stopped since. We had glimpsed our Grail and were off on our quest for Supernatural Gods.

Some anthropologists believe that it was by consuming hallucinogenic mushrooms that the first shamans learned to communicate with the gods. They experienced out-of-body travel and, for the first time, surveyed landscapes that were beyond humans' perceptual realm.

Think of it this way. Many Christians believe they will go to heaven when they die. Heaven is the abode of God. But isn't "heaven" just a word that describes a place outside of this dimension and our plane of existence?

For countless thousands of years, shamans have used psychedelics to achieve visions of such realms. Many report talking to spiritual entities that resemble what the Dead Sea texts call angels. The Essenes even kept lists of the names of these beings. Were they practicing an ancient religion—indeed, perhaps the most ancient religion in the world? Were they a continuation of the original tradition of shamanism?

This is why Allegro lost his job and was banished from the company of accepted scholars. He was, in effect, censored because he proposed a radical explanation for something that is, to this very day, still not understood. He put forth the theory that Jesus, who was the teacher of righteousness, was introduced to the world because of the psychedelic experience of Essenes— shamans who practiced their religion in the area of the Dead Sea. Their communal meal of mushrooms is now kept alive each and every Sunday morning whenever Christians gather to celebrate the last supper. Wine has replaced the *Amanita muscaria* mushroom, that's all.

> HE [ALLEGRO] PUT FORTH THE THEORY THAT JESUS, WHO WAS THE TEACHER OF RIGHTEOUSNESS, WAS INTRODUCED TO THE WORLD BECAUSE OF THE PSYCHEDELIC EXPERIENCE OF ESSENES—SHAMANS....

Allegro went a lot further than this, however. He believed that to confuse the Romans, the early Essenes sect, which might have morphed into mystical Jewish Gnostics, used code when referring to their meal. They juxtaposed Hebrew with Aramaic, two languages known and used in Israel at the time.

He might have a point. Take the famous words, "Our Father, who art in heaven." Transliterated to Aramaic, the phrase becomes "Abracadabra."

Allegro also speculated about the Christian doctrine concerning consuming the body of Christ. Whenever the sacrament of communion is celebrated, the priest repeats the words of Jesus: "This is my body, broken for you. This is my blood, shed for you. Take it in remembrance of me." Does this refer to the fact that the sacred mushroom was actually a form of divinity?

Allegro's career ended with the publication of his book. According to the academic world, he was henceforth an outcast—a pariah. He had dared challenge the Church's well-known narrative, and for that he was censored.

But reading his well-thought-out and convincingly presented arguments, it makes you wonder. Pliny the Elder, the first to write about the supersecret world of the Essenes, said the sect was thousands of years old. He might have underrepresented their age. They might go all the way back to the most ancient human religion, first practiced some 40,000 years ago. And their presence might be seen, albeit in modified and garbled form, every Sunday morning when Christians gather to drink wine and consume the "body of Christ."

In this sense, there might be much more to the Dead Sea Scrolls than meets the eye.

# THE LOST BOOKS OF EDEN

> Now the LORD God had planted a garden in the east, in Eden;
> and there he put the man he had formed. The LORD God
> made all kinds of trees grow out of the ground—trees that
> were pleasing to the eye and good for food. In the middle of
> the garden were the tree of life and the tree of the knowledge
> of good and evil.
>
> A river watering the garden flowed from Eden; from there it
> was separated into four headwaters. The name of the first is
> the Pishon; it winds through the entire land of Havilah, where
> there is gold. (The gold of that land is good; aromatic resin
> and onyx are also there.) The name of the second river is the
> Gihon; it winds through the entire land of Cush. The name
> of the third river is the Tigris; it runs along the east side of
> Ashur. And the fourth river is the Euphrates. (Genesis 2:8–14)

Was there really a Garden of Eden? Does the book of Genesis record historical fact or mythological metaphor?

Most scholars today come down on the side of mythology, reading the Genesis account as a sort of parable. But ancient texts indicate the early writers believed it was a real place that existed in real time. This has been the case until recent history.

Giving the early writers the benefit of the doubt for a moment, if there was a real Eden that was the landscape in which human origins took place, where would it have been? If the story is simply a metaphor divorced from historical content, there certainly seems to be a lot of extraneous detail thrown in.

> Now the LORD God had planted a garden in the east, in Eden;
> and there he put the man he had formed.

The garden was "in the east, in Eden." But east of what?

> The LORD God made all kinds of trees grow out of the ground
> —trees that were pleasing to the eye and good for food. In the
> middle of the garden were the tree of life and the tree of the
> knowledge of good and evil.

Okay, the place was heavily forested. Obviously, the two main arboreal stars of the tale were the Tree of the Knowledge of Good and Evil, or the tree

The Bible only gives a vague idea of where Eden was located, saying only that it lay somewhere "east" and there were four rivers there. Was there an actual garden, or is the Genesis story merely a metaphor?

representing the duality inherent in human existence, and the Tree of Life. Those are important if the story was written to use as a teaching device. So, why throw in all the others?

A river watering the garden flowed from Eden; from there it was separated into four headwaters.

Now the plot develops. A clue is inserted that involves a specific river—indeed, four rivers—that rise in a particular geographical location. This almost invites future readers to attempt to discover where it lies.

The name of the first is the Pishon; it winds through the entire land of Havilah, where there is gold. (The gold of that land is good; aromatic resin and onyx are also there.) The name of the second river is the Gihon; it winds through the entire land of Cush. The name of the third river is the Tigris; it runs along the east side of Ashur. And the fourth river is the Euphrates.

Now we definitely move into an area that seems to be begging for specificity rather than interpretation. Names and details begin to pile up. Some are familiar, others not. We don't know where the Pishon is, let alone the country called Havilah. But if it is only to be read as metaphor, why do we need to know that "there is gold" in the hills?

Likewise with the Gihon. We have a good idea about an ancient land called Cush, although there is disagreement as to where it was located. But the Tigris and the Euphrates are well-known rivers, and they both rise in the Armenian hills near each other.

With all this information, we now enter into a very strange ideological fact concerning biblical interpretation. Earlier we studied instances of scholars letting their beliefs influence their interpretation and decision making. This is another of those cases. Most scholars who believed in a literal Eden had already decided where they wanted it to be before they translated the texts. This has led to some rather fanciful interpretations rather than a strict reading of the Genesis account.

## Mesopotamia

Most scholars want the Garden of Eden to be in Mesopotamia, now Iraq. It is a land steeped in biblical history and tradition and lies between the Tigris and the Euphrates, so they place Eden's location at the head of the Persian Gulf, where the two rivers run into the sea. But this raises a real problem. The Genesis account clearly says that Eden was to be found where the rivers rose, not where they end up. The rivers flowed down "*from* Eden," not "*to* Eden."

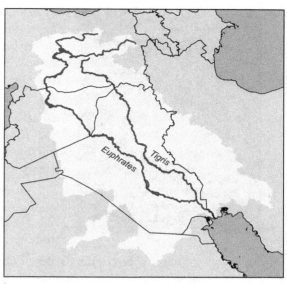

Two of the rivers mentioned with regard to Eden were the Tigris and Euphrates, which were also borders of ancient Mesopotamia in present-day Iraq.

## Jerusalem

This is an even more fanciful interpretation. In verse 14 of Genesis 2, God appears to equate Eden with "the holy mountain of God." In the Bible, this mountain is usually associated with Mount Moriah, where Abraham was sent to sacrifice his son and later shared a communion meal of bread and wine with the mysterious Melchizedek, a priest of Salem, later called Jerusalem. It was the place where Solomon built the great temple and is now home to the famous golden Dome of the Rock—the Islamic mosque seen in every picture of Jerusalem. This hilltop is known as the Temple Mount.

For this reason, while ignoring everything in the text about rivers, gold, aromatic resin, and onyx, some insist that Eden was located where Jerusalem stands today.

## Africa

This interpretation treats the story as complete metaphor. Since the human race is thought to have arisen in Africa, according to the accepted "out of Africa" theory of origins, it places Eden somewhere in the African nation of Botswana, south of the Zambezi River. This theory is based not on ancient texts but rather on modern DNA testing. It represents the birthplace of the one called "Mitochondrial Eve," the hypothetical first woman of our species.

## Armenia

If we are to treat the biblical account seriously, there is really only one candidate for Eden, and that is in modern-day eastern Turkey. This is the birthplace of the Euphrates River, which is actually two rivers that rise to the

REMEMBER THAT THE
GARDEN OF EDEN WAS,
ACCORDING TO THE
BIBLICAL TEXT, LOCATED
AT THE SOURCE OF THESE
RIVERS. THIS ALONE PUTS
EDEN IN ANCIENT
ARMENIA, MODERN
TURKEY....

north and northwest of Lake Van. From there, they proceed to flow south through southeastern Turkey before merging and making their way through northern Syria and Iraq, eventually emptying into the Persian Gulf.

A second river, the Tigris, flows "east of Ashur," or Assyria. Then, it heads down through Iraq, parallel to the Euphrates, where the two join forces just before they both empty into the estuary at the head of the Persian Gulf.

In other words, the two rivers that we know about for sure, and can identify to this very day, flow down out of the Armenian highlands in eastern Turkey.

Remember that the Garden of Eden was, according to the biblical text, located at the source of these rivers. This alone puts Eden in ancient Armenia, modern Turkey, even before we identify the other two rivers.

Klaus Schmidt, the archaeologist who discovered and supervised the archaeological dig at Göbekli Tepe, must have thought along similar lines. He was once quoted as saying that Göbekli Tepe was "a temple in Eden." This, of course, implies that Eden was to the east of Göbekli Tepe, possibly offering an explanation to our first question. What was Eden "east" of? It was east of the temple associated with it—Göbekli Tepe.

As it turns out, Schmidt was misquoted. What he actually said was that "Göbekli Tepe is an Eden-like place." But a good misquote often takes on a life of its own, and such was the one attributed to Schmidt. It provided some good headlines, but he never said it.

Identifying the remaining two rivers is a real challenge. But that hasn't stopped any number of people from speculating about them.

The river Gihon, for instance, is sometimes identified with the Nile, which flows through Ethiopia, which in turn is often identified with the land of Cush. But this explanation takes us far afield from the two rivers already located. If we stick strictly to the text, it opens up some interesting possibilities.

In Genesis, a man named Cush is said to be the father of Nimrod, who built the Tower of Babel. Nimrod is legendary to Armenians.

Tourists to the modern Turkish city of Şanlıurfa which is said to be the home of the patriarch Abraham, are told the story of how he was catapulted into a fiery furnace because he would not worship pagan idols even though his father manufactured and sold them. Abraham survived, of course, but that is a whole separate tale.

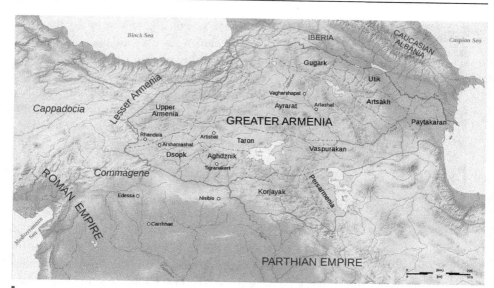

A map of the region of Armenia around 150 B.C.E. Now part of Turkey, this area is a candidate for the location of the Garden of Eden.

The point is that these stories offer a connection to a specific geographical location near ancient Armenia. This opens the possibility of identifying the river Gihon because the Araxes River, now known as the Aras River, rises in the Bingöl Mountains, flows east along the base of Mount Ararat, where it joins another mighty river called the Kur River, and eventually empties into the Caspian Sea. In the eighth century, during the Arab invasion of the Caucasus mountains, the river was called the Gaihun. That's pretty close to Gihon.

In the early eighteenth century, the Dutch scholar Hadrian Reland suggested that the land of Cush might refer to the country called "Cussaei of the ancients."

This is all speculative, of course, but that leaves one river to go—the Pishon. "It winds through the entire land of Havilah, where there is gold. (The gold of that land is good; aromatic resin and onyx are also there.)"

Here, we really have to reach. No one knows what country Havilah was associated with. The only reference in the Bible is that a man named Havilah was, like Nimrod, a son of Cush. No one knows about a gold field in the area either, let alone "aromatic resin and onyx." So, when it comes to identifying this river with any accuracy, we're up the creek.

Nevertheless, of all the places Eden could have been located, assuming it was ever a real, historical place, the highlands of ancient Armenia, today's Turkey, east of Göbekli Tepe, the world's first temple, is as good a bet as anywhere and better than most. On a map of modern Turkey, if we locate Gö-

> A WHOLE TREASURE TROVE OF MATERIAL NEVER MADE THE FINAL CUT. SOME OF THE TALES OFFER A TOTALLY DIFFERENT TAKE ON THE STORY THAT IS FAMILIAR TO MOST CHURCHGOERS.

bekli Tepe and then Lake Van to the northeast, the area in between is a good place to start if we want to visualize a location for the original Garden of Eden. Mount Ararat, of Noah's ark fame, isn't far to the northeast. Şanlıurfa the birthplace of Abraham, is just to the south. The whole area lies right on the Fertile Crescent and positively reeks of biblical tradition. So, if we are seeking a specific spot, why not call this the location of the Garden of Eden?

I spent a lot of time on all this because, whether or not Eden ever existed, there are many more stories about it and its first inhabitants than can be found in the Bible. A whole treasure trove of material never made the final cut. Some of the tales offer a totally different take on the story that is familiar to most churchgoers. One can only wonder how Church doctrine might have evolved had any of the alternatives been accepted as gospel. Here are just a few.

## "Life of Adam and Eve," Part I: The Greek Version

This book is known, in its Greek version, as the Apocalypse of Moses. It tells the story of Adam and Eve after they were expelled from the Garden of Eden but has quite a different take on how the expulsion actually happened. Among other things, it offers Eve's side of the story, a version that doesn't appear in the traditional story we have been taught.

Everyone who has ever read or heard Bible stories knows how Satan, the devil, appeared in the garden to tempt Eve to sin. It is one of the best-known, most-quoted tales from the book of Genesis.

In Genesis 3, Adam and Eve are enjoying life in the Garden of Eden when "that old serpent, the devil," as he is called in the book of Revelation, appears on the scene. Up until now everything has been going wonderfully. The man and woman are one with nature, one with each other, and one with God. They don't have a care in the world. There are no problems or vexing situations. They have no morning commute and no boss to butter up. They don't even have any kids to clutter up the place. They eat fruit when they're hungry and sleep when they're tired. God himself comes down to walk around the garden in the cool of the evening. There are no Ten Commandments. There is only one rule to follow, and it's an easy one. One tree in the garden is fenced off, and they are told not to eat of its fruit.

It's a pretty simple rule, so they live a good life until "that old serpent," the devil, shows up. He corners Eve while Adam is off doing whatever it is that Adam does all day and begins by asking an insidious, penetrating question.

A façade on Orvieto Cathedral in Umbria, Italy, depicts Adam and Eve giving in to the temptations of the serpent. The Greek version of the well-known tale has some notable differences from the one known by readers of the King James Bible.

"Did God *really* say you must not eat from any tree in the garden?"

Eve is sure of this one. "We may eat from any tree in the garden but one. God said not to eat of the pretty tree with the fence around it. We're not even supposed to touch it, or we'll die!"

A careful reading of the previous chapter reveals that God did forbid the eating of the fruit from this tree, but he didn't say anything about not touching it. She just made that up. Talk about presumption! She put words right into the mouth of Almighty God! No doubt her heart was in the right place. After all, it made perfect sense to her. If they weren't supposed to eat the fruit, it stands to reason they weren't supposed to touch it, either.

But this little slip gave the devil an opening. "You will surely not die! God knows that when you eat the fruit of that tree you're going to be just like him, knowing good from evil!"

And the three temptations suddenly worked their power.

> When the woman saw that the fruit was (1) good for food, and (2) pleasing to the eye, and also (3) desirable for gaining wisdom, she took some and ate it. She also gave some to her husband. (Genesis 3:6)

This version of the story puts the blame solely on the woman. She was tempted by Satan and fell under his spell. But the Greek version of the "Life of Adam and Eve" puts a different spin on things. In this tale, Eve somehow gets separated from Adam. She keeps company with the female animals and Adam with the males.

The devil befriends the male snake and entices him to rebel against Adam and Eve. The trap is sprung at the hour when all the angels go up to worship God. Satan takes on the disguise of an angel and whispers in Eve's ear using the mouth of the serpent. He gives Eve some fruit and says she is to offer some to Adam. What she doesn't know is that he has placed the poison of lust in the fruit. Eve takes a bite and suddenly realizes she is naked. All the trees in the garden immediately lose their leaves except for the fig tree. Eve immediately hides her nakedness with fig leaves. Not wanting to be alone in this newfound experience, she deceives Adam, who also eats of the forbidden fruit.

At that point, Michael sounds a trumpet and rides into the garden on a chariot, accompanied by cherubim, who are high-ranking angels. His throne is placed where the Tree of Life stands, and all the other trees immediately blossom and bring forth leaves again.

He summons Adam, who was hiding because he was now ashamed to be naked in the presence of an angel, and Michael proceeds to reproach him severely. Likewise Eve and the serpent. The order of the accused is reversed from the traditional story, in which first the serpent, then Eve, and finally Adam is accused. The end result, however, is the same. The angels cast Adam and Eve out of the garden and tell them to go to work.

Adam begs God to let him eat of the Tree of Life, but he is refused the gift of immortality. He is, however, given a promise. If he can refrain from doing evil, God will raise him up at "the last day." He is also given a gift of sweet spices with which to offer sacrifices, and seeds for planting.

After being banished from Eden, Adam and Eve head "to the east," where they live for 18 years and two months. Eve gives birth to Cain and Abel, and later the famous murder takes place wherein Cain kills his brother.

Here the story again takes a new twist. The angel Michael appears and promises to give Adam a new son to replace Abel. The son is named Seth. But then Adam and Eve beget 30 more sons and 30 daughters as well.

When Adam comes down with a sickness, his children all come to visit, and he tells them the story of the fall from grace. Seth and his mother, Eve, then travel back to the garden, where they stand at the gate and beg for oil from the fruit of the Tree of Life. There, they meet Michael, who refuses to give them any but promises to give it to them at the end of time, when the dead shall be raised and the righteous allowed to reenter Eden, and God will once more walk with them as he did before.

One would think this would be good news, but apparently Adam disagrees. He says to Eve, "What hast thou done? Thou hast brought upon us great wrath which is death." His sickness continues as he foretells his own demise and asks Eve to pray for him. In a moving scene, a being called "the angel of humanity," who might be the angel Michael, appears at his side and shows Eve the spirit of her husband leaving his body and ascending to God. A chariot of light appears, pulled by four bright eagles and accompanied by seraphim. The "seven heavens" are revealed, and Seth, ever the dutiful son, explains to his mother that the sun and moon are in darkness because of the great light of God, which diminishes them. Adam is cleansed three times in water and is then carried to God, who stretches out his arms in welcome. Michael carries Adam to the third heaven, where he will await the end of days.

> IN A MOVING SCENE, A BEING CALLED "THE ANGEL OF HUMANITY," WHO MIGHT BE THE ANGEL MICHAEL, APPEARS AT HIS SIDE AND SHOWS EVE THE SPIRIT OF HER HUSBAND LEAVING HIS BODY AND ASCENDING TO GOD.

Finally, although only Seth is allowed to see what is happening, Adam is returned to the Garden of Eden, where he is reunited in death with his son Abel.

Six days later, Eve asks to be buried with them, and her wish is granted. Michael gives some final instructions to Seth, however. He is told never to mourn on the Sabbath.

There is another striking contrast in this story that offers a different interpretation to the fall of Satan, the devil. This version is later amplified by the prophet Muhammad in the Quran.

Traditional Jewish and Christian teaching says that in the beginning, God created a class of supernatural beings we now call angels (from the Greek *angelos*, or "messengers"). Their purpose, apparently, was to serve God.

According to the book of Isaiah, chapter 14, the leader of this heavenly company was called Lucifer, which means "son of the morning." Unfortunately, he aspired to a loftier position. He wanted to "be like God."

Lucifer, however, didn't understand the pitfalls surrounding the temptations of ego. As a result, he "fell" from grace and was banished to earth, where his evil could be contained to one planet in the vast cosmos. A third of the angels followed him. Henceforth, they would be called demons. Contrary to popular conception, they don't reign in hell. They reign on earth. Hell is their punishment, not their dwelling place. Lucifer became Satan, the "deceiver" and the "accuser of the brethren."

LVCIFER

The name Lucifer once had a much less sinister connotation. In mythology, Lucifer meant "light bringer" and represented Venus; he was a son of Aurora and represented the arrival of the morning, which is why his name also means "son of morning." (1704 engraving of Lucifer as a childlike angel.)

Here's the biblical version of the events—the version we know today. We begin with the first passage, which has God speaking directly with Satan:

How you have fallen from heaven, morning star, son of the dawn! You have been cast down to the earth, you who once laid low the nations! (Isaiah 14:12)

Now, we jump to the book of Ezekiel. Here, God talks to the "King of Tyre," a name usually interpreted as a metaphor for Satan:

Thus says the Lord GOD: You were the signet of perfection, full of wisdom and perfect in beauty. You were in Eden, the garden of God; every precious stone was your covering, carnelian, chrysolite, and moonstone, beryl, onyx, and jasper, sapphire, turquoise, and emerald; and worked in gold were your settings and your engravings. On the day that you were created they were prepared. With an anointed cherub as guardian I placed you; you were on the holy mountain of God; you walked among the stones of fire. You were blameless in your ways from the day that you were created, until iniquity was found in you. In the abundance of your trade you were filled with violence, and you sinned; so I cast you as a profane thing from the mountain of God, and the guardian cherub drove you out from among the stones of fire. Your heart was proud because of your beauty; you corrupted your wisdom for the sake of your splendor. I cast you to the ground; I exposed you before kings, to feast their eyes on you. By the multitude of your iniquities, in the unrighteousness of your trade, you profaned your sanctuaries. So I brought out fire from within you; it consumed you, and I turned you to ashes on the earth in the sight of all who saw you. All who know you among the peoples are appalled at you; you have come to a dreadful end and shall be no more forever. (Ezekiel 28:11–19)

SATAN'S SIN WAS, IN EFFECT, THAT HE LOVED GOD TOO MUCH TO KNEEL BEFORE A LESSER BEING, SUCH AS A HUMAN.

Christians and Jews thus teach that Satan was cast out of heaven because of his ego-centered desire to "be like God." He became jealous of humans and began to "prowl around like an angry lion, seeking someone to devour" (1 Peter 5:8). In 1 Corinthians 6:3, we read this injunction: "Do you not know that we (humans) will judge angels?" Apparently, this didn't sit well with Lucifer. His response filled the world with the familiar sin and degradation we now know so well.

But the "Life of Adam and Eve" has a different take on the subject. Here, Lucifer loved God so much that when God created Adam and then told all the angels to bow down before him, Satan was presented with a horrible problem. How could he bow before anyone but his beloved God? Satan's sin was, in effect, that he loved God too much to kneel before a lesser being, such as a human. Thus, when he disobeyed God's command to worship a human, he was cast out of heaven.

How did Satan console himself throughout eternity? He did it by remembering the last words that God, his beloved, said to him. And what were those words? "Go to hell!"

It's an interesting take on the familiar story.

At any rate, in this version of the story, at least Adam and all his descendants are promised a resurrection at the last day. It gives them all something to look forward to.

## "Life of Adam and Eve," Part II: The Latin Version

The Latin version of this story is similar to the Greek one but with a few significant changes. In this story, when Adam and Eve leave the garden, they travel not to the east but toward the west. Instead of 18 years and two months, only six days pass before they become hungry and begin to try to get back into God's good graces. Adam decides they need to do penance, and his method is to immerse himself in the Jordan River for 47 days. Meanwhile, he tells Eve to do the same thing but only for 40 days, she being only a frail woman, and she must do it in the Tigris, giving the newly stressed couple a bit of a break from each other.

Seth, the third son of Adam and Eve, would begin the line of descendants leading to Noah. (Icon maintained at Museum of Cyril Belozersky Monastery in northern Russia.)

As the penance begins, Satan disguises himself as a bright angel and talks Eve out of entering the icy river. Eve returns to Adam to tell him the good news, but Adam sees through the ruse and reproaches her. When Adam complains to Satan about how they are being treated, Satan tells Adam the whole story about how he and his followers refused God's command to worship anyone else except for the divinity. He paints quite a picture about how righteous he is—that he will not worship Adam or any lesser being, including images. Meanwhile, Eve lies prostrate in her grief. Adam remains adamant and serves out his entire time in the river.

Eve is so stricken with grief that she leaves Adam and travels further west, lamenting and crying the whole way. Eventually, she gives birth to Cain, all alone. At this point, Adam has finished his penance and finds her. Because Adam was so righteous in his rejection of Satan, God sends angels to help Eve in her labor. Together, they travel back east, and the angel Michael appears to teach agriculture to Adam.

Some time later, Abel is born. Eve had terrible dreams about Cain drinking Abel's blood, so to separate them, Cain is made a gardener and Abel a shepherd. The plan doesn't work. Cain kills Abel anyway, so Seth is born to replace Abel, along with 30 other sons and 30 daughters.

Much later, Adam again falls sick. By this time, he is 930 years old and entitled to some aches and pains. He gathers his family around him and tells them about the fall from grace, the reason for his decline. Then comes the story of Seth and Eve's trip back to the garden, Michael's refusal to give them the oil of the Tree of Life, Adam's death followed by Eve's, and the burial of the bodies, similar to the tale told in the Greek version. An interesting sidebar, however, is that Eve predicts a judgment of water and fire that shall come on the earth. The water probably refers to the flood. The fire is yet to be determined. Seth, however, writes down the story of Adam's life on two tablets and buries them, presumably on the Temple Mount, where one day, Solomon will discover and read them.

## Book of Adam and Eve

From the "Life of Adam and Eve" we move to the "Book of Adam and Eve." Sometimes, this book is called the "Conflict of Adam and Eve with Satan," but perhaps, "Books (plural) of Adam and Eve" is a more accurate title, for there are really four of them.

There is good evidence that this is in part a rather modern tale with portions not appearing until the late Middle Ages. This being the case, these stories may show more Christian influence than Jewish. The fact that we have them at all is due, once again, to the fact that the early versions we know about had made the same mysterious journey to Ethiopia that we saw earlier when we looked at the book of Enoch.

They were written in Ge'ez, the sacred language of Ethiopia, and not released in English until the now classic 1926 edition of *The Lost Books of the Bible and the Forgotten Books of Eden*. The author of this book is unknown, but the section containing the "Book of Adam and Eve" was translated by S. C. Malan. He used the German version, translated from Ge'ez by August Dillmann.

Book 1 is concerned with filling in the blanks of the Adam and Eve story we know from Genesis. In this version of the story, after leaving Eden, Adam and Eve live in a new home called the Cave of Treasures. Satan visits them there quite often. His appearances are often translated as "apparitions," and they are marked by many different attempts to deceive and trick them. There, Cain is born along with his twin sister, Luluwa, and then Abel with his twin sister, Aklemia.

Book 2 chronicles the history of the patriarchs who lived prior to the Great Flood. This is the text that identifies Seth's descendants, the Sethites, as the "sons of God." Cain's descendants, the Cainites, are called the "daughters of men." They tempt the Sethites to come down from the mountain where they live and mate with the Cainites, who live in the valley. This whole affair is orchestrated by a man named Genun, who is a son of Lamech. After

STRANGELY, THE AUTHOR
OF BOOK 2 SEEMS TO GET
THE TRADITIONAL STORY
BACKWARD WHEN
IT COMES TO CAIN
AND ABEL.

seducing the Sethites, the offspring of these unions, called Nephilim, become the "mighty men of old" whom we met when we studied the books of Enoch and Jubilees.

Strangely, the author of Book 2 seems to get the traditional story backward when it comes to Cain and Abel. Here, Cain is the shepherd and Abel is the agriculturist:

> Then on the morrow Adam said unto Cain his son, "Take of thy sheep, young and good, and offer them up unto thy God; and I will speak to thy brother to make unto his God an offering of corn."

Contrast that with the biblical account:

> And in process of time it came to pass, that Cain brought of the fruit of the ground an offering unto the Lord. And Abel, he also brought of the firstlings of his flock and of the fat thereof. And the Lord had respect unto Abel and to his offering.

It's exactly backward. Either the author had heard a different story, or he mixed up the one he did hear. Either way, it's a bit of a jolt to read this account for the first time. Since this text might have been written far into the Christian era, it's possible that the writer just remembered the story differently. After all, it had been placed in time a few thousand years back. But it still makes you wonder if something else is going on.

Books III and IV detail the lives of Noah, his son Shem, and the mysterious Melchizedek, priest of Salem. The history moves all the way forward in time until Titus, the Roman general, destroys the Jerusalem temple in 70 C.E. What is unique here is that in outlining Jesus's ancestors, the names of the wives are given as well. These aren't included in modern Bibles. Jewish scholars didn't have a high regard for the importance of women.

## "The Slavonic Life of Adam and Eve" and "The Armenian Penitence of Adam and Eve"

I mention these two books just to emphasize the number of accounts about the Eden story that didn't make the final cut when the Bible was assembled. They don't add much to the story of the texts we have already examined, but they remind us that we fall into grave error if we think that the biblical account is some kind of unique divine recounting of historical reality. It is only one version of a tale that was told over and over again in many different ways for more than a thousand years.

What, then, do we make of all this? What does it mean? Is the Eden story a metaphor—a fireside story told generation after generation that grew in the telling? Or is it a garbled version of a historical episode that became twisted and convoluted as it was passed down through the generations?

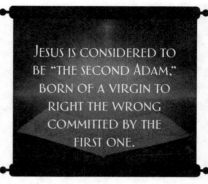

JESUS IS CONSIDERED TO BE "THE SECOND ADAM," BORN OF A VIRGIN TO RIGHT THE WRONG COMMITTED BY THE FIRST ONE.

If it is a metaphor, it is certainly a good one. It has stood the test of time, and very few people today are not at least somewhat familiar with it. Although written by Jewish writers, it is also a mainstay of the Christian Church, with its emphasis on sin and atonement, the need for baptism, and varied and sometimes competing doctrines about why the human race acts the way it does. It is a simple story with a complex moral lesson that is debated anew with every fresh generation of theologians. It has served as the basis for millions of sermons and homilies. Jesus is considered to be "the second Adam," born of a virgin to right the wrong committed by the first one.

Every Christmas, Christians gather to sing "Hark! The Herald Angels Sing." If they sing all four verses, they join in a mighty chorus to proclaim:

Come, Desire of nations, come!
Fix in us Thy humble home:
Rise, the woman's conqu'ring seed,
Bruise in us the serpent's head;
Adam's likeness now efface,
Stamp Thine image in its place:
Final Adam from above,
Reinstate us in Thy love.

This final verse of the popular Christmas carol makes no sense without at least a superficial knowledge of the Eden story. It sums up the whole theology of what transpired in the Garden of Eden.

But is it just a metaphor, a myth with a message? Could it be a poetic rendition of something that really happened? Do we find in the Eden stories a transition of humankind from Paleolithic to Neolithic—from a hunter-gatherer culture to the Agricultural Revolution?

Think of it this way. Images of paradise are universal. It was always better back in the old days. The Eden story takes us back to the beginning. There, we were one with nature. This could take us back in time to an epoch that goes back at least 200,000 years, maybe even longer, to the emergence of anatomically modern humans.

Much of Western culture has been influenced by the Adam and Eve story, including even Christmas songs like "Hark! The Herald Angels Sing!", which has lyrics referring to the serpent in the Garden of Eden.

The biblical text doesn't explain the way things were back then with words and phrases that would make a biologist happy. It just says, "God did it." The ancients didn't understand the mechanics of spontaneous generation and evolution. But we don't have it all figured out, either. So, saying "God did it" is no stranger than studying theories involving panspermia or the Many Worlds theory.

Simply put, what the texts tell us is that, for an unknown time, we were one with the animals. We were one with nature. And, at least in memory, those times were good. In the words of Genesis, "And the Lord God formed man from the dust of the earth and breathed into him the breath of life, and man became a living soul.... And God saw that it was good."

In those remote, ancient, and memory-shrouded times, our human ancestors achieved something that no other animal did. It goes without saying that they developed the capacity to think and reason, but many other animal species can do that to varying degrees. Humans also developed the ability to work together in community, but other species do that as well.

What makes us unique is the ability to think symbolically—meaning "this" stands for "that"—and to become aware of a great mystery that is beyond ourselves.

Forty thousand years ago, early spiritual teachers, the gifted shamans, crawled back into the great painted caves of western Europe, possibly under the influence of mind-expanding and consciousness-raising hallucinogens, and began to imagine a world far bigger than any other animal species could ever picture. They reproduced that image on the cave walls. When they came out, they explained their newfound wisdom in stories, such as those about Eden.

Was it simply a made-up reality? Was it only in their heads?

Modern physics seems to have discovered that was not the case at all. As the great wizard Dumbledore observed to Harry Potter, it may have been in their heads, but that doesn't mean it wasn't real. It was simply outside their sensory perception. It took a mind-expanding experience to first catch a glimpse of these foreign landscapes. But anyone who has ever had an out-of-body or near-death experience will insist that it was more real than reality itself.

> SIMPLY PUT, WHAT THE TEXTS TELL US IS THAT, FOR AN UNKNOWN TIME, WE WERE ONE WITH THE ANIMALS. WE WERE ONE WITH NATURE. AND, AT LEAST IN MEMORY, THOSE TIMES WERE GOOD.

The Apostle Paul, in 2 Corinthians 12, describes his own out-of-body experience. But he is forced to admit in 1 Corinthians 13 that in this life, we can only "see (as if) through a window, dimly." That "window" consists of our senses.

We are just beginning, in our day, to face the fact that our senses filter out much of what is real—light, for instance, and sound and vibration. That doesn't mean things such as ultraviolet light or supersonic sound waves aren't real. It just means we can't perceive them in the particular material-perception realm we inhabit in these bodies.

The difference between us and the ancients is that they seem to have discovered all this by instinct and intuition. With us, it took microscopes and particle accelerators. We publish our findings in peer-reviewed scientific journals. They told stories.

Those stories conveyed to their listeners that the time when we lived in Eden was a good time. In that sense, stories about Eden are no different from stories about Paradise, or Atlantis, or Mu and Lemuria. Maybe they had a basis in fact, or maybe they didn't. But they represent a good way of life, now lost forever. It was a foundational time, a time of exploration and achievement. It wasn't for everybody. All humans weren't created equal. There were Stone Age peoples and advanced intellectual societies both inhabiting the planet. But that's the case today as well.

The advanced, technical cultures seem to have developed the first civilization, perhaps as far back as before the Younger Dryas Ice Age (around 13 to 12 thousand years ago). It was a time of exploration. Humankind had awakened to the greater world around them. They had become aware, so they set out to "fill the earth and subdue it," as was the command of Genesis 1:28.

Did those early civilizations send out the equivalent of diplomats or emissaries to seek out new worlds and establish a beachhead on foreign soil? Did they try to communicate with Stone Age people in distant places? Did

Human mythology and legends are filled with stories about paradises that were lost: from the Garden of Eden, Camelot, and Utopia to the strange tales of Atlantis, Mu, and Lemuria. They are part of our collective consciousness.

explorers go searching for natural resources that could help the motherland? At the very least, were there ambassadors of goodwill sent out to expand human horizons?

We'll never know for sure, of course. But that's what *we've* done for thousands of years. Why wouldn't *they* have done the same thing? Just because they were ancient doesn't mean they were any different from us.

But something happened 12,800 years ago that might well have been interpreted as a divine judgment. We are not immune to the whims of the cosmos any more than were the dinosaurs of 65 million years ago.

Evidence is piling up that a segmented comet blew up in our atmosphere, almost crushing the newfound human experiment we call our civilization. The weather had been moderating quite nicely since the close of the previous ice age, and perhaps our hypothetical lost civilization was beginning to explore the world. Suddenly, however, the earth returned to bitterly cold conditions. The Younger Dryas Ice Age appeared about 12,800 years ago and wreaked vengeance upon the earth for more than a thousand years.

Wherever the fledgling civilization called home, be it Eden, Atlantis, or something very much like it, the people discovered a bitter truth: You can't go home again.

They were cast out of Eden and had to make their way into the world.

The people must have asked why. In their view, the attack by what some cultures referred to as a "serpent" from above (after all, a comet would have had a long tail) seemed like retribution for their sins. In short, they blamed themselves. What had they done wrong?

They decided it was probably tied up with hubris. Genesis 3:5 says that they had wanted to "be like God." They tried to build a tower that would reach into the heavens. Their reach had exceeded their grasp. They had played with toys that proved much too dangerous.

How could they warn future generations about their mistake? What could they say to a future civilization that might, for instance, destroy the atmosphere with technology powered by burning fossil fuels, release unthinkable energy by splitting the atom, or populate themselves out of existence?

Well, they could tell stories. They were myths, yes, but they were myths based on something that really happened.

Meanwhile, after the destruction of their homeland, now forever closed to them by what Genesis 3:24 describes as "cherubim with flaming swords," they might very well have set out to recreate the world. Where should the efforts begin? They had to establish some criteria.

First of all, they would have wanted to go to places that were

What if the angels armed with flaming swords described in the Bible had been people from an advanced civilization who had survived a disaster that, in effect, forced them to leave their Eden?

warm. The Younger Dryas Ice Age still ruled the world, but to plant crops and become "tillers of the soil" like Cain, they would have needed a suitable climate.

Around the equator the sun still warmed the soil. Waters lapped on sandy beaches. The band of pyramids found in equatorial regions around the globe probably didn't happen by accident. Early civilizations in Egypt, Sumer, Indonesia, Turkey, Lebanon, Easter Island, Peru, and Mexico speak volumes about ancient beachheads of civilization. The founders of those places had been expelled from Eden, but they were still willing to "fill the earth and subdue it."

If the homeland period of this lost civilization that once lived in Eden marked a great beginning, the epoch following the Younger Dryas Ice Age might be called its golden age. The comet would have forced them to "go forth and multiply." This they seem to have done. It was a period of expansion and growth that probably marked the world's first growth-based economy based on world trade.

They probably decided to go to places where they had already sent their ambassadors before the comet struck. It only made sense. They had already

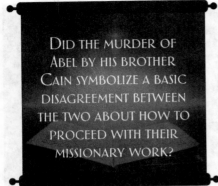

DID THE MURDER OF
ABEL BY HIS BROTHER
CAIN SYMBOLIZE A BASIC
DISAGREEMENT BETWEEN
THE TWO ABOUT HOW TO
PROCEED WITH THEIR
MISSIONARY WORK?

scouted the territory and perhaps even learned the language.

Maybe that even answers the questions raised by those who first read the Bible for themselves. Whom did Cain marry? He went native. How did he find enough people to build a city? They were already there and willing to go to work. Why was he an agriculturalist? Because he taught the locals how to grow crops instead of how to hunt and gather their food. He had to. There are a lot of mouths to feed once you build a city and get people to settle in one place.

This is pure speculation, of course, but it's based on stories about Eden that have been told for thousands of years, so let's continue for a bit. Did the murder of Abel by his brother Cain symbolize a basic disagreement between the two about how to proceed with their missionary work? Did the "Abel" faction represent those who thought it best to simply encourage the natives in what they were already doing? Perhaps this group believed in a "hands-off" policy—a *Star Trek*-type "look but don't touch" prime directive to let the locals develop in their own way.

If that's the case, the "Cain" faction would represent those who wanted to jump-start local evolution by teaching the native inhabitants new things and actively becoming involved in their evolutionary path. This sense of involvement might also explain why Cain married one of the local women. He became actively involved with the indigenous population.

The two groups could not have both had their way. According to the Genesis story, the Cain faction "killed off" the Abel faction, perhaps by simply outlasting them. That eventually led to the great explosion of knowledge that occurred shortly after this time during the period now known as the Neolithic Revolution or Agricultural Revolution.

Perhaps this even explains some of the mysterious passages in Genesis 6, which we will study in depth in the next chapter:

> When men began to multiply on the earth ... [Of course they multiplied. Farming ensured a stable food supply. The laws of biology tell us that when there is an ample food supply, the species expands.]
>
> and daughters were born to them, the sons of God ... [the Cain faction]
>
> saw that the daughters of men ... [the indigenous local population]

were beautiful, and they married any of them they chose ...
[as has been the case throughout our history wherever missionaries were sent].

The Nephilim were on the earth in those days—and also afterward—when the sons of God went to the daughters of men
and had children by them. They were the heroes of old, men
of renown. [Apparently, we are dealing with real men here,
who could reproduce. Not angels. The mixing of the races
seemed to produce some pretty healthy offspring.]

Myths from all over the world emphasize this mixing of the races. The
"gods," people such as Cain and his ambassador colleagues, seem to have
created quite an impression. But it is always thus.

It cannot be denied that the mixing of the races, or populations, in
ways both beneficial and worrisome, furthered civilization. Look what happened according to Genesis 4:16–26.

- City Building
  So Cain went out from the LORD's presence and lived in the
  land of Nod, east of Eden. Cain made love to his wife, and
  she became pregnant and gave birth to Enoch. Cain was then
  building a city, and he named it after his son Enoch.

- Population Expansion
  To Enoch was born Irad, and Irad was the father of Mehujael,
  and Mehujael was the father of Methushael, and Methushael
  was the father of Lamech.

- Bigamy among the Missionaries
  Lamech married two women, one named Adah and the other
  Zillah.

- Animal Husbandry
  Adah gave birth to Jabal; he was the father of those who live
  in tents and raise livestock.

- The Arts
  His brother's name was Jubal; he was the father of all who
  play stringed instruments and pipes.

- Industry
  Zillah also had a son, Tubal-Cain, who forged all kinds of
  tools out of bronze and iron. Tubal-Cain's sister was Naamah.

- Grit in the Civilization Machine
  Lamech said to his wives, "Adah and Zillah, listen to me;
  wives of Lamech, hear my words. I have killed a man for

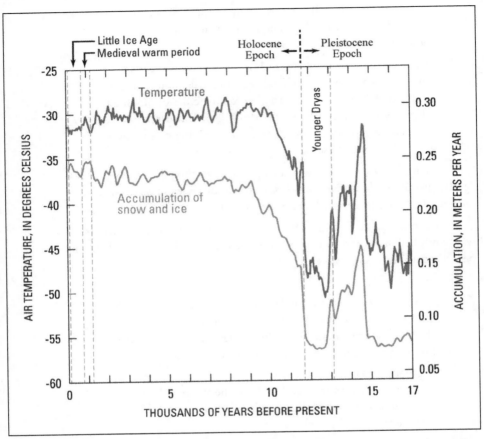

This graph shows temperatures calculated by analyzing glacial ice from Greenland at different depths. It indicates clearly the plunge in temperatures during the Younger Dryas about
13,000 to 12,000 years ago.

wounding me, a young man for injuring me. If Cain is
avenged seven times, then Lamech seventy-seven times."

• Religion
At that time people began to call on the name of the LORD.

All this seems to have taken place during or shortly after the Younger
Dryas, a period that lasted for more than 1,200 years. That's a long time. The
Eden story, by its very nature, seems to present the story as a quick occur-
rence. But the time spans presented are really vast.

The end came with a bang. For reasons no one fully understands, the
Younger Dryas ended as abruptly as it began. The geologic record indicates
that global warming arrived seemingly overnight. The melting of the ice caps
drastically raised ocean levels and broke apart ice dams that held in place inland

seas bigger than the size of Texas, resulting in huge inundations all around the globe. The time of Noah's flood had arrived. It didn't cover the whole earth. But flooding was so widespread, it must have felt like it. The myths are in complete agreement. Wherever you lived on earth 11,600 years ago, you had to head for high ground.

When the deluge ended and the earth slowly began its step-by-step path to what we now call normal, Eden was a forgotten experience, remembered only in myth.

But there is archaeological evidence that the world began a new phase, outside the boundaries of Eden. It was precisely at this time that the first temple at Göbekli Tepe was built and some of the first agricultural experiments were conducted. Strange symbols involving sky charts, animal effigies, and religion are found there. Great, brooding, multiton, megalithic figures were crafted, their hands pictured as clasped over their bellies, just like the giant figures found in Peru, Indonesia, Mexico, and the Moai statues of Easter Island.

> GIVEN THE OBVIOUS, AND IN SOME CASES GLARING, DISCREPANCIES OF THE ARCHAEOLOGICAL RECORD, IS THE EDEN STORY REALLY DIFFERENT, OR ANY LESS ACCURATE, THAN THE STORY WE ARE TAUGHT IN SCHOOL?

And then, as soon as Göbekli Tepe was finished, it was buried until our time.

Why?

The answer is again speculative, of course. But when we want to remember a particular era, we bury a time capsule that will be dug up at a future date to testify to our presence and to remind future people what we were like.

Is Göbekli Tepe a time capsule that points to a mythological Eden? Who knows? But if it is, we are the recipients of the message it contains. We need only to apply ourselves to its meaning.

We have now arrived at that point in time that traditional archaeology claims marks the beginning of our civilization. It started, according to accepted knowledge, at Göbekli Tepe, from where it quickly spread downstream to Sumer and across the Fertile Crescent, sprang up independently in Egypt, and, after a few thousand years, again independently, took off in Mexico and Peru.

Given the obvious, and in some cases glaring, discrepancies of the archaeological record, is the Eden story really different, or any less accurate, than the story we are taught in school? And aside from its historical importance, it comes with a bonus we don't find in textbooks. It is a story steeped in religion. It combines history with spirituality and insists both are important when it comes to understanding who we are and where we came from. It tells stories of warm, flesh-and-blood people who lived understandable and familiar lives.

The stories are far removed and much more memorable than a simple, sterile recitation of historical facts. They stay with you for your whole life.

What do these early texts convey? What did the writers believe?

The stories indicate that they believed in a metaphysical force they called God. They believed in Something that is greater than ourselves. They believed that Something was guiding us and developing our journey through time, forming our destiny, from memories of Eden to the present day.

We need to read these stories again and again, even the ones the early editors decided we didn't need to know. By hiding them from us, they may have been guilty of censoring God.

# THERE WERE GIANTS IN THE LAND

When human beings began to increase in number on the earth and daughters were born to them, the sons of God saw that the daughters of men were beautiful, and they married any of them they chose. Then the LORD said, "My Spirit will not contend with humans forever, for they are mortal; their days will be a hundred and twenty years."

The Nephilim were on the earth in those days—and also afterward—when the sons of God went to the daughters of humans and had children by them. They were the heroes of old, men of renown. (Genesis 6:1–4)

We now return to one of the most enigmatic and debated passages in the book of Genesis. The setting is right before the flood of Noah. Humankind has been going about the business of "filling the earth and subduing it," as God commanded Adam and Eve in Genesis 1:28, but something has gone terribly wrong. Entities we looked at earlier called "the sons of God" have begun to lust after "the daughters of men" and to "marry" them. The resultant children are called Nephilim and are identified as "the heroes of old, men of renown." God has looked down on all this and decided the human race needs a do-over. He has announced he is going to destroy everyone and everything with a flood and start again, this time with Noah and his family instead of Adam and Eve.

To untangle all this, we need to define some terms. But that is precisely where the problems begin. As we have seen in previous chapters, "sons of God," "daughters of men," and "Nephilim" have all been translated in different ways by different scholars, and in almost every case, it appears the scholars' translations were influenced by their interpretation of the text rather than translating the text and letting that determine their interpretation. Let's take them one at a time.

## Sons of God/Daughters of Men

Some scholars interpret this rather literally. A "son of God" is an angel or created being of some kind. This creates a few doctrinal problems. Jesus is called "the Son of God." The word "the" implies there is only one. So, how could there be many "sons"? To make the matter even more confusing, trinitarian doctrine insists that Jesus was not created. He is the second person of

Many scholars interpret the phrase "sons of God" as referring to fallen angels because, they reason, these were beings who mated with human women.

the Trinity, or God himself. The Nicene Creed specifically states that Jesus was "begotten, not made." In other words, before his birth ("begotten") as a man, he was eternal ("not made") with the Father and the Holy Spirit. Were the "sons of God" in Genesis created beings? If so, they could not be "sons of God" and thus equal to the second person of the Trinity. Therefore, they must be angels, and fallen ones at that, or why would they be messing around with "the daughters of men"?

But can an incorporeal angel, even a fallen one, actually have physical sex with a material woman? How would that work? It sounds rather blasphemous considering that the only other woman we know about who was supposedly impregnated by a nonhuman was Mary, the mother of Jesus. This position was enforced in 1854, when Pope Pius IX published a papal bull called *Ineffabilis Deus*. Papal bulls are considered to be infallible, so the official position of the Catholic Church is that Mary was a virgin, free from original sin ever since she was conceived in the womb of her mother, St. Anne. This is called the Immaculate Conception, and, as far as the Roman Catholic Church is concerned, it puts her in a separate category from "the daughters of men." Protestant scholars beg to differ on this point.

Do you see how our theology is already starting to influence our interpretation? We've superimposed New Testament trinitarian doctrine, some of it not declared until as late as 1854, over a Jewish text written more than a millennium before Jesus was born.

This brings us to another interpretation. Some scholars—and the famous evangelist Billy Graham counted himself among them—agreed with the position put forth in the "Book of Adam and Eve," thinking that the "sons of God" must refer to the sons of Seth, who was born to sort of replace Abel, the victim of murder at the hands of his evil brother Cain. Seth thus fathered a "godly line" called "sons of God," while Cain fathered a line of fallen children called "the daughters of men."

> WHAT WAS THE MESSAGE OF THE MINORITY REPORT? "THERE ARE GIANTS IN THE LAND! NEXT TO THEM, WE LOOK LIKE GRASSHOPPERS!" THE WORD THEY USED WAS NEPHILIM.

But this sounds a bit contrived even to those who are looking for a way out of the quagmire. After all, both Seth and Cain were completely and unequivocally human with human DNA. Why were their offspring called the "heroes of old" and "men of renown," only to be destroyed in an earthly cataclysm? Besides, Seth didn't commit the original sin that contaminated the human race. Adam and Eve did. His offspring would be no more "godly" than Cain's. To say they were "sons of God" seems a bit of a stretch.

## Nephilim

This brings us to the children of these unions. They are described as being pretty impressive human or hybrid specimens—"heroes of old, the men of renown."

The term "Nephilim" is used in only one other place in the Bible. In the Book of Numbers, when the Israelites were camped on the banks of the Jordan, ready to enter the Promised Land, they sent 12 spies into Israel to check out the situation. After the requisite "40 days and 40 nights" they came back, in true committee fashion, with a majority report and a minority report. The minority report was delivered by a man named Caleb and the man who would become the future hero of Israel, Joshua. "Let's go," they said. "We can take 'em!"

But the majority report carried the day and sentenced the Israelites to 40 years of wandering in the desert. What was the message of the minority report? "There are giants in the land! Next to them, we look like grasshoppers!" The word they used was Nephilim.

Almost every translation of the Bible uses the word "giants" to translate Nephilim. That certainly seems to be the context both times it is used. But, once again, there are some who let their theology influence their interpretation. They claim, with some good reasons, that Nephilim means "fallen ones" or even, in its root form, "to fall down." This might fit the bill when it comes

The giant Goliath, who was defeated by the future King David, certainly would have qualified as one of the Nephilim; he also, apparently, had four brothers.

to interpreting "sons of God" as pertaining to the upstanding Seth versus the fallen Cain.

But not quite. As we just pointed out, technically, Adam and Eve, parents to all of the above, had already fallen, and with them tumbled all their offspring. There is nothing in the Bible that claims any kind of saintliness for Seth, much less declares his children to be "sons of God." The fact is nowhere mentioned that, if this is the correct interpretation, they fell again by marrying the daughters of Cain, thereby bringing down the judgment of the flood. Given that no such command to separate the two lines was ever issued, it seems hard to believe.

There's one more thing to note in passing that lends credence to the use of the word "giants" as opposed to "fallen ones." Generations later, when Israel needed a king, they were given David. He rose to power after using his slingshot to slay a giant named Goliath. This gives us pause. To top it all off, in 1 Chronicles 20, we discover that Goliath had four giant brothers! Apparently, there were still "giants in the land." And somehow, they had managed to avoid being killed in the flood. This hints at something we discovered when we studied the Genesis Apocryphon. There, Noah himself was suspected of being the hybrid offspring of one of these unions. Lamech, you will remember, accused his wife of being one of the "daughters of men" who was impregnated by one of the "sons of God." Did he pass on his genes to his children, who sometimes produced a throwback to one of the "sons of God"? Whoever those Nephilim were, they were sure hard to dispose of!

All we've done so far is raise red flags. We haven't settled on a definition. Maybe that's because we've been sticking to biblical texts. But what about extrabiblical texts? Can we find any hints in them that the ancients were as concerned with the problem of giants as much as modern scholars?

Indeed, we can. Let's turn to a book that has already popped up from time to time in our survey.

## Enoch 15 and 16

And now, the giants, who are produced from the spirits and flesh, shall be called evil spirits upon the earth, and on the earth shall be their dwelling. Evil spirits have proceeded from their bodies; because they are born from men and from the holy Watchers is their beginning and primal origin; they shall be evil spirits on earth, and evil spirits shall they be called. [As for the spirits of heaven, in heaven shall be their dwelling, but as for the spirits of the earth which were born upon the earth, on the earth shall be their dwelling.] And the spirits of the giants afflict, oppress, destroy, attack, do battle, and work destruction on the earth, and cause trouble: they take no food, but nevertheless hunger and thirst, and cause offences. And these spirits shall rise up against the children of men and against the women, because they have proceeded from them.

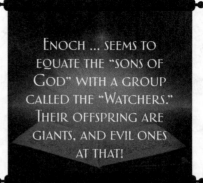

ENOCH ... SEEMS TO EQUATE THE "SONS OF GOD" WITH A GROUP CALLED THE "WATCHERS." THEIR OFFSPRING ARE GIANTS, AND EVIL ONES AT THAT!

From the days of the slaughter and destruction and death of the giants, from the souls of whose flesh the spirits, having gone forth, shall destroy without incurring judgment—thus shall they destroy until the day of the consummation, the great judgment in which the age shall be consummated, over the Watchers and the godless, yea, shall be wholly consummated.

Now we seem to have gone even further down the rabbit hole. Enoch has introduced a whole new dimension into the mystery. First, he seems to equate the "sons of God" with a group called the "Watchers." Their offspring are giants, and evil ones at that! If that weren't enough, they "shall destroy until the day of the consummation, the great judgment in which the age shall be consummated, over the Watchers and the godless, yea, shall be wholly consummated."

In other words, they shall be a long-lived race, perhaps even still living among us because we have not yet reached the day of the "great judgment."

With these words Enoch introduces us to a worldwide corpus of curious stories. All around the earth, if we delve into the mythology of indigenous cultures, we find giants in the land. Let's look at a few representative geographical locations.

## North America

In 1528 a Spanish explorer named Pánfilo de Narváez was, quite presumptuously, granted much of the land the Spanish called Florida. The name

Spanish explorer Pánfilo de Narváez reported seeing native people in Florida who were as large as giants.

derived from Juan Ponce de León in 1513, who employed the Spanish word *florido*, which means "full of flowers; flowery." Narváez's objective was to command the entire eastern gulf coast, as far inland as he could seize, to look for gold and riches. He landed near Tampa Bay to begin his explorations but, through what became a logistical nightmare, was repulsed by "naked warriors who had bodies like giants."

A later description of Florida giants came from a French expedition up the St. Johns River. The French had established Fort Caroline on Amelia Island near present-day Jacksonville, but they were driven off by the Spanish in 1565. Before they left, however, Jacques le Moyne, an artist and cartographer, insisted they had been in contact with a race of native giants who appeared to be in a position of leadership among the native Timucuan people. Most scholars reject the idea that there were giants among the Timucua, but the legends persisted.

Perhaps that might have influenced later reports published by Hernando de Soto in 1539. He led an expeditionary force of 620 volunteer soldiers and another 100 enslaved people, 237 horses, 200 pigs, some mules, and attack dogs into the interior from Tampa Bay. The expedition would eventually march through Florida, Georgia, North and South Carolina, Tennessee, Alabama, Mississippi, Arkansas, Oklahoma, Louisiana, and Texas. Eventually, only 311 survivors ended up in Mexico in 1542. Along the way they took prisoners, spread diseases from which the local people had no immunity, caused immense devastation and death, and generally raised a havoc from which there was no recovery.

That one march changed the course of history in the American southeast. The invaders encountered and destroyed civilizations of Mound Builders and organized cities and cultures, and along the way, they wrote descriptions of warriors who towered head and shoulders above the Spanish. One report describes the chief Tuscaloosa, who was encountered in what is now Alabama. He "appeared to be a giant, or was one, and the rest of his body was proportionate to

his height." He was "greatly feared by his neighbors and vassals."

Moving up the Mississippi and forward in time, we come to more discoveries.

The Adena civilization is probably best known as part of the Mississippian Mound Building culture. The Kanawha River Valley in West Virginia held a part of that culture. What is not so well known is that rumors going back hundreds of years have involved giant skeletons found throughout this region.

Jim Vieira has done his best to publicize this fact and has endured the wrath of the traditional archaeological establishment in doing so. Vieira was a stone mason by trade, but he burst forth into public consciousness when the History Channel featured him and his brother on

FROM NEW ENGLAND IN THE AMERICAN NORTHEAST TO THE ADENA COUNTRY OF THE HEARTLAND, VIEIRA RECORDED THE ANCIENT PRESENCE OF GIANTS WHO SEEM TO HAVE OCCUPIED A SHAMANIC LEADERSHIP POSITION AMONG THE ADENA CULTURE.

their popular show *Search for the Lost Giants* in 2014. He followed this series with *Roanoke: Search for the Lost Colony* in 2015 and then *Return to Roanoke: Search for the Seven* in 2016. His 2015 book *Giants on Record*, written with Hugh Newman, caused a stir and prompted another academic backlash.

From New England in the American Northeast to the Adena country of the heartland, Vieira recorded the ancient presence of giants who seem to have occupied a shamanic leadership position among the Adena culture. His research involves actual archaeological work but also covers a lot of ground in terms of unearthing old newspaper articles and recorded accounts of giants in the Americas.

Traditionalists, of course, want evidence of another nature. They want to see the bones. Old accounts dating back to the 1800s record the discovery of such bones, but the artifacts are now missing. Where did they go?

There are, of course, conspiracy theories galore. Most accuse the Smithsonian Institution of covering up the evidence, an accusation that drives the museum experts nuts. But the answer might be a lot simpler than that. In November 1990 the U.S. government enacted the Native American Graves Protection and Repatriation Act (NAGPRA). The act requires any agency or institution that receives federal funding to return cultural artifacts, including bones, to the Native American tribe who owns the ancestral land in which they were found. Museums across the country, who had stockpiled such items and never gotten around to studying them, were forced to return them. It could be that bones of ancient giants were among them. No one knows. And, at least for the foreseeable future, no one ever will.

Nevertheless, the mythology of North American Indians, which includes stories about creatures called the Thunder Beings, Sasquatch, Bigfoot, and other forms of giants, is in universal agreement. Giants once existed in North America. Their size is estimated to be anywhere from 7 feet (2 meters) to 10 feet (3 meters) tall and, in a few cases, even bigger. These stories are not limited to Native American legend. The early Spanish and French chroniclers reported evidence as well.

Where did the giants go? No one knows. But pandemic diseases for which the people of North America had no defenses were rampant. Their effects rapidly killed off whole villages. These diseases, for instance, destroyed 95 percent of the indigenous Florida population in a matter of years. It happened in New England as well. Even "giants" would have had no luck against such deadly plagues.

## South America

On March 31, 1520, the Portuguese explorer Ferdinand Magellan landed at a place he called Tierra de Patagones near the southern tip of South America. Today, that strait bears his name, the Strait of Magellan at Tierra del Fuego. Soon after landfall, he made contact with either the Tehuelche or Ona people who lived there. He described them as being "giants."

Tehuelche means "fierce people" or "fierce tribes." The Italian scholar Antonio Pigafetta chronicled the expedition. In 1964 his work was translated and published in a book called *First Around the World: A Journal of Magellan's Voyage*. In his chronicles, he estimates that the height of the Patagonians was as much as 10 feet (3 meters) tall. Some of Pigafetta's drawings can be found on the internet. In typical fashion for Spanish explorers of his day, Magellan proceeded to kidnap two hostages to take back home for display, but they died en route and were buried at sea—that is, thrown overboard. The story goes that Magellan named the region Patagonia because the word means "big feet," but that is a supposition that has never been confirmed.

This whole episode is rightly the subject of much criticism by today's academics. But the fact remains that whether or not the whole incident was exaggerated at the time, later voyagers confirmed the story in their own journals, and maps from that era, such as the famous Diego Gutiérrez map of 1562, almost universally illustrate the huge size of the Patagonians.

In 1578, English naval officer Francis Drake visited the area. His reports were that Magellan had greatly exaggerated the size of the inhabitants. He estimated their size as "only" 7 to 8 feet tall. When he returned home and his reports were published, the Spanish viceroy in Peru sent Captain Pedro Sarmiento de Gamboa down to establish a Spanish colony there. Sarmiento's written accounts still survive, and they report that he encountered a "race of giants" so large that it required ten Spanish soldiers to subdue one Patagonian giant.

The report makes us have great respect for David the shepherd boy, who took on his giant armed only with a slingshot.

The Dutch had similar luck in the area in 1598. Captain Sebald de Weert was forced ashore and reported running battles with a "race of giants."

They were followed by the English as late as 1766. Captain John Byron reported run-ins with people estimated to be 9 feet (2.7 meters) tall. When scientists of his day followed up, the height of the natives was in some cases reduced to no more than 8 feet (2.4 meters).

All of these reports, of course, are ridiculed by most

Portuguese explorer Ferdinand Magellan added to the legend of giants in the New World with his stories of the tall people living in Patagonia. Modern scholar Antonio Pigafetta estimated these people to be about 10 feet tall.

modern academics on the basis that they must be exaggerated because such people do not exist—a tenuous application of the scientific method at best.

## Siberia

When news of the discovery of a new human species called Denisovan filtered down into public consciousness, the first evidence of the astounding discovery that has turned traditional anthropology on its head was a single tooth. But what a tooth it was! Bence Viola is a paleoanthropologist at the University of Toronto in Ontario, Canada. He was also a sort of liaison between the Max Planck Institute for Evolutionary Anthropology and the Russian archaeologists who made the discovery at the site of the now famous Denisova Cave, also known as Altai Cave after the mountain range where it sits.

In 2012 he was interviewed for a *National Geographic* television documentary. Despite his distinguished credentials, which certainly entitled him to speak in professional, polysyllabic words, his explanation of the size of the tooth was surprisingly easy to understand: "We have the assumption that this pretty big tooth belonged to a rather big individual. We don't know how big

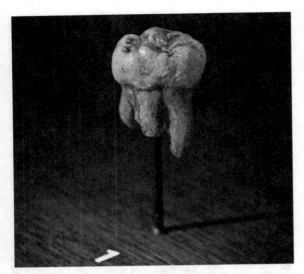

An upper molar found in a Russian cave proved that the Denisovan people belonged neither to *Homo sapiens* nor Neanderthals.

... but big teeth frequently belong to big guys. If this belonged to a woman, I don't want to see the man. He might have been pretty big."

Since then, all the evidence that has been discovered about Denisovans indicates that they were, to put it mildly, a robust species. We know they mated with our species because many of you now reading these words have Denisovan DNA flowing through your veins.

We could go on and on. Our purpose is not to write a book about giants. It's not necessary to highlight reports from China and Australia and everywhere in between. Instead, we began with passages from the Bible, moved on to extrabiblical material such as Enoch, and then pointed out that such descriptions of "giants in the land" were not limited to biblical writers, who have long been accused of writing accounts that were "merely" mythological in nature. These accounts were universal, familiar to people all around the world.

Those who decided which books were "inspired" and which were not, and possibly even discarded material on the basis of this kind of content, knew perfectly well that these stories had circulated for a long, long time. But by the time both Old and New Testaments of the Bible were assembled, a long time after the death of Jesus, such stories were obviously already suspect.

What does all this mean? Are we implying that the censors were deliberately trying to hide the evidence—to somehow either shield a naive public from falsehood or cover up some kind of diabolical conspiracy?

Not at all. It most probably illustrates yet again that the gatekeepers in charge of assembling sacred texts were operating out of a sense of perceived human intelligence and not, as was their claim, divine guidance. What we read today is based on their prejudices, not their inspired wisdom.

This leads us to ask some questions, the answers to which we may never know for certain.

- *Did a race of giants once exist on earth alongside anatomically modern humans?* The evidence provided by both sacred and secular texts, as well as the documented experiences of relatively modern people, seems to answer in the affirmative.

• *If so, did they originate somewhere other than earth?* Most textual and physical evidence seems to indicate this was their planet of origin, although Sumerian accounts such as the Gilgamesh and Enuma Elish material point to the heavens, as does the enigmatic Genesis account involving "sons of God" and "daughters of men."

• *Could a race of giants who were closely related to human beings once have existed?* This seems to be

Is the story about Goliath a rare hint in the Bible that there *were* giants in those days, and maybe they were the "sons of God" of old who mated with humans?

the case as we discover more and more about the extinct Denisovan species, especially with the new DNA evidence suggesting that they once mated with our species as well as the Neanderthal and passed on their genes to modern humans alive today. If they were anatomically compatible in this way, they must have been a branch of our family tree way back in history.

When all is said and done, the best we can say for now is that those who wrote the early religious texts believed they were telling true tales, and that some of those tales were rejected by those who made the final choices about what was to be preserved and what was to be discarded.

But what they saw as myth now shows every indication of being factual, anthropological history. A bit garbled, perhaps, but that is to be expected of old, old stories that have been told for a long, long time. Some tales after all, grow with each repetition. But that doesn't mean they are not based on fact.

Were these giant "sons of God" a human species such as Denisovans, later remembered as "gods" because of their stature and powers?

Maybe.

Did they see that the "daughters of men" were beautiful and mate with them?

Well, many humans alive today carry their DNA.

Was the human race once capable of great feats that today defy explanation?

One needs only to inspect the great megaliths all around the world to contemplate such mystery.

Is there a supernatural component to all this?

The early writers seem to have thought so.

If any of this is true, it indicates that the story we have all been taught needs some major modification. A committee once stood between us and the truth. Countless years of possible research have been squandered as a result. The fact that they made such an effort to destroy their rejects sets off some alarm bells. What were they afraid of? Did they fear being second-guessed? Did they have personal doubts they wanted to expunge?

Thank goodness for the conscientious scribes of the Dead Sea area and the Egyptian deserts. Thank goodness for the faithful Catholic scholars who, at risk of life and limb, kept at least some native texts from the self-righteous fires of the Inquisition. Thank goodness for Ethiopian translators who salvaged books such as Enoch and other pseudepigrapha. Without those unknown heroes, we would now know even less than we do. But because of their work, our ancient history is finally beginning to stir and, perhaps, even rise from the dead.

# THE GREAT FLOOD

M ost everyone has probably heard at least something about Noah's ark and the biblical flood. It's the subject of many a delightful stand-up comedy routine from Bill Cosby to Danny Bhoy and has provided more than its fair share of entertainment hours on television specials and movies. Many, many books have been written to debate whether it was a real, historical event or religious mythology. Expeditions have endeavored to cover almost every inch of Mount Ararat, the place where Noah was supposed to have stepped ashore following his epic cruise. Even photos from planes and satellites have come into play, which purportedly show some kind of man-made craft perched high on the mountain's snow-packed slopes.

A recent round of publicity surrounding the supposed discovery of the ark was prompted by an invitation to an October 2015 event offered by the Southern Evangelical Seminary in conjunction with Calvary Church in Charlotte, North Carolina. Turkish expert Ahmet Ertugrul, known popularly as Parasut, was invited to talk about his find. Philip Williams, an American engineer and telecommunications entrepreneur, was scheduled to present a program in which he and Parasut claimed that a structure discovered on Mount Ararat the previous year could prove to be Noah's ark.

This prompted Rick Lanser, M.Div., to write a letter that was later reproduced in a publication of the Associates for Biblical Research. In it he warned the sponsors of the event to proceed with caution. He told them to be "wise as serpents but innocent as doves" in the matter because the information in the program had not been vetted and was apparently a bid for money rather than simply a presentation of scientific research.

The fallout from conventions such as these is a matter of contentious debate. The topic of the biblical tale of Noah's ark is a really hot topic between religious conservatives and liberals, and it almost guarantees a full house for the sponsoring organization.

What is not so well known is that there are reports of a flood found in virtually every civilization on earth. The story is not unique to the Bible. Some accounts are similar to one another. Others differ widely. Most claim that the flood was the result of a judgment by a divine being. A few say it was connected to creation.

But unquestionably the text that is thought by many people to be the definitive version, straight from the mouth of God, the story found in the book of Genesis, was handpicked and cobbled together by a committee. It

Cultures around the world have stories of a Great Flood. In India, for example, the god Vishnu warns mankind of such a flood and tells people to build a giant boat to save themselves.

was by no means the only version they had in front of them. They chose it for a reason, but they didn't say what that reason was. Maybe we should look at a few other versions, some of which the committees had in front of them but discarded and others that would have been unknown to them.

## Abrahamic Religions

Judaism, Christianity, and Islam are called the Abrahamic religions because they all revere the patriarch Abraham. Although he is not connected to Noah's flood, coming, as he did, so much later in time, one of the places celebrated as his birthplace is in the vicinity of Mount Ararat. We'll have more to say about that in a few chapters when we study the travels of Abraham, but for now, it is enough to know that if, indeed, Abraham was a historical figure rather than a mythological character, it is possible that he grew up hearing certain legends, even if they hadn't yet been written down in any kind of systematic way.

Here's the version that eventually made it into the Bible:

> The LORD saw how great the wickedness of the human race
> had become on the earth, and that every inclination of the
> thoughts of the human heart was only evil all the time. The

LORD regretted that he had made human beings on the earth, and his heart was deeply troubled. So the LORD said, "I will wipe from the face of the earth the human race I have created—and with them the animals, the birds and the creatures that move along the ground—for I regret that I have made them." But Noah found favor in the eyes of the LORD. (Genesis 6:1–9)

Then follows the familiar instructions involving cubits and gopher wood, the procession of animals into the ark, two by two, the 40 days and 40 nights of rain, and the eventual end of the cruise atop Mount Ararat.

Here's a condensed version, accepted by Jews, Christians, and Muslims alike:

The Bible says that God gave Noah specific instructions on the size of the ark, the type of wood to use, and how he would save the animals.

Noah was six hundred years old when the floodwaters came on the earth. And Noah and his sons and his wife and his sons' wives entered the ark to escape the waters of the flood. Pairs of clean and unclean animals, of birds and of all creatures that move along the ground, male and female, came to Noah and entered the ark, as God had commanded Noah. And after the seven days the floodwaters came on the earth.

In the six hundredth year of Noah's life, on the seventeenth day of the second month—on that day all the springs of the great deep burst forth, and the floodgates of the heavens were opened. And rain fell on the earth forty days and forty nights.... The waters rose and increased greatly on the earth, and the ark floated on the surface of the water. They rose greatly on the earth, and all the high mountains under the entire heavens were covered.... Every living thing that moved on land perished—birds, livestock, wild animals, all the creatures that swarm over the earth, and all mankind.... Only Noah was left, and those with him in the ark. The waters flooded the earth for a hundred and fifty days.

But God remembered Noah and all the wild animals and the livestock that were with him in the ark, and he sent a wind over the earth, and the waters receded. Now the springs of the deep and the floodgates of the heavens had been closed, and the rain had stopped falling from the sky. The water receded steadily from the earth. At the end of the hundred and fifty days the water had gone down, and on the seventeenth day of the seventh month the ark came to rest on the mountains of Ararat....

After forty days Noah opened a window he had made in the ark and sent out a raven, and it kept flying back and forth until the water had dried up from the earth. Then he sent out a dove to see if the water had receded from the surface of the ground. But the dove could find nowhere to perch because there was water over all the surface of the earth; so it returned to Noah in the ark. He reached out his hand and took the dove and brought it back to himself in the ark. He waited seven more days and again sent out the dove from the ark. When the dove returned to him in the evening, there in its beak was a freshly plucked olive leaf! Then Noah knew that the water had receded from the earth. He waited seven more days and sent the dove out again, but this time it did not return to him....

Then God said to Noah, "Come out of the ark, you and your wife and your sons and their wives. Bring out every kind of living creature that is with you—the birds, the animals, and all the creatures that move along the ground—so they can multiply on the earth and be fruitful and increase in number on it."

So Noah came out, together with his sons and his wife and his sons' wives. All the animals and all the creatures that move along the ground and all the birds—everything that moves on land—came out of the ark, one kind after another.

Then Noah built an altar to the LORD and, taking some of all the clean animals and clean birds, he sacrificed burnt offerings on it. The LORD smelled the pleasing aroma and said in his heart: "Never again will I curse the ground because of humans, even though every inclination of the human heart is evil from childhood. And never again will I destroy all living creatures, as I have done. As long as the earth endures, seedtime and harvest, cold and heat, summer and winter, day and night will never cease." (Genesis 7:6–8:22)

> IT TOOK NOAH 120 YEARS TO BUILD THE ARK, ALLOWING PLENTY OF TIME FOR GAWKERS TO EITHER EXPRESS THEIR CONTEMPT AND RIDICULE OR CHANGE THEIR WAYS.

Although all three religions accept that version of the story, their interpretation of it differs. As we compare them, one by one, remember that there is plenty of disagreement within each of the three traditions. What follows tries to encapsulate a rough average.

## The Jewish Interpretation

Traditional Jews tend to see the flood as a judgment from God. Before the flood, human life spans were longer, no doubt because of general health, abundance, and prosperity. The climate was amiable and pleasant, and life was generally pretty good.

The natural human tendency, unfortunately, is to exploit things rather than be thankful for them, and this is what happened.

Noah, however, was a righteous man. According to the Jewish calendar, in the year 1536 after creation, about 2225 B.C.E., the word of the Lord came to Noah that things were about to change. Noah was told about the coming deluge and instructed to select two of every nonkosher animal and seven of every kosher animal. Fish were excluded. They were left to fend for themselves.

It took Noah 120 years to build the ark, allowing plenty of time for gawkers to either express their contempt and ridicule or change their ways. No one did, so in the year 1656, or 2105 B.C.E. by our calendar, the flood came, beginning in the Hebrew month of Cheshvan.

Here is a quick summary of the historical details as noted in the Torah as interpreted by Rabbi Eliezer ben Hurkanus, a first-century Jewish sage:

- *Cheshvan 17* (mid-fall)—Noah enters ark; rains begin.
- *Kislev 27* (early winter)—Forty days of rain end; beginning of 150 days of water's swelling and churning.
- *Sivan 1* (early summer)—Water calms and begins to subside at the rate of one cubit every four days.
- *Sivan 17*—The bottom of the ark, submerged 11 cubits beneath the surface, touches down on the top of the mountains of Ararat.
- *Av 1* (summer)—The mountain peaks break the water's surface.

One problematic item in the Noah's ark story involves the question of what did the carnivores eat? The answer, according to Hasidic tradition, is that animals such as lions and tigers reverted to peaceful behavior and did not require meat.

- *Elul 10* (late summer)—Forty days after the mountain peaks become visible, Noah opens the ark's window and dispatches a raven.
- *Elul 17*—Noah sends the dove for the first time.
- *Elul 23*—The dove is sent a second time and returns with an olive leaf in its beak.
- *Tishrei 1* (early fall)—Dove's third mission. Water completely drained.
- *Cheshvan 27*—Ground fully dried. Noah exits ark.

According to the Midrash, an ancient commentary on the Hebrew Scriptures, life was tough on board. Because Noah's family had to take care of all the animals, they got very little sleep, and tempers were stretched thin. Noah even started to cough up blood at one point. In addition, he was late one day in feeding a lion, and it bit him.

One might be tempted to ask what exactly Noah was feeding the lion, given the lack of Purina Lion Chow back in those days and the fact that the lion's natural prey consisted of some of the ark's crew. The answer, according to Hasidic teaching, developed early on by Jewish scholars, was that during their time on Noah's ark, the animals reverted to the kind of behavior prophesied by the prophet Isaiah, when "the wolf will lie down with the lamb, and the leopard with the kid, and a little child shall lead them."

Interestingly, according to Jewish tradition, up to this point, humankind had been told to eat only vegetables and fruits. Afterward, when the earth began to fill up with animals and people, humankind became meat eaters.

The problem with this literal approach to the story, including dates, is that there is simply no geological evidence to support its claim of historicity. And if the flood happened as reported a little more than 4,000 years ago, it doesn't explain how the Egyptian pyramids or Göbekli Tepe, among other megaliths, managed to survive the damage. Both are unequivocally much, much older.

> IN KABBALAH TEACHING, AN ANCIENT JEWISH MYSTICAL INTERPRETATION OF THE BIBLE THAT FLOURISHED DURING THE MIDDLE AGES, THE FLOOD WAS SEEN AS MORE OF A CLEANSING THAN A PUNISHMENT.

In Kabbalah teaching, an ancient Jewish mystical interpretation of the Bible that flourished during the Middle Ages, the flood was seen as more of a cleansing than a punishment. The waters were a sort of ritual bath—a mikvah. It was more of a spiritual cleansing than a physical one, although actual water was involved, and is something the earth must experience from time to time.

## The Christian Interpretation

Christianity these days is starkly divided when it comes to discussing the issue. The argument is not about interpretation as much as whether the biblical flood actually occurred. Was it a historic event, or was it a myth meant only to teach a lesson?

On one hand, if you visit the Creation Museum in Petersburg, Kentucky, or engage an Ark Encounter Experience in Williamstown, Kentucky, you can board a copy of the ark built to scale while listening to trained guides, using a sophisticated sound system, who explain, down to the smallest detail, how, why, and when the ark was constructed. They will answer all your questions and declare that the ark was real and necessary and that the flood was a historical event in time. They will also try to convince you that the reason the ark is not a part of a child's public school education these days is that the liberal establishment doesn't believe in it and wants to cover up the whole thing to discourage belief in God.

Which, to a degree, is true. The liberal establishment, even the liberal religious establishment—both Christians and Jews—tend to view the ark and the flood story as a religious myth designed to teach a moral lesson, not as historical reality. As one contemporary Gnostic teaching source (gnosticteachings.org) puts it:

One effort to counter the fact that Christian traditions are not taught in American public schools is the Ark Encounter museum in Williamstown, Kentucky.

The story of Noah and his Ark has been told as a children's story for so many centuries that nowadays no one suspects the real meanings it hides. Instead, it is seen like all children's stories: as something sweet and foolish. Yet, the story of Noah was written in the Bible by Moses not as entertainment for babies, but as part of the sacred science he encoded in his books. Moses, a man who stood face to face with God, did not waste his time on trifles. He wrote the story of Noah to teach something important to those who wished to have the experiences he had. Meeting divinity is no easy feat.

In the book of 1 Peter in the Christian New Testament, the flood was a symbol of baptism, the ritual cleansing from original sin. This is in keeping with the Jewish interpretation at the time of its authorship during the late first century.

Hippolytus of Rome, a third-century Christian writer, taught that the ark was a symbol of "the Christ who was expected" to carry his people safely through the waters of God's coming judgment. He believed that Noah brought the bones of Adam on board, along with the three gifts that were later given to Jesus at his birth—gold, frankincense, and myrrh. He further believed that the ark drifted in the sign of the cross before landing on Mount Ararat.

As for arguments about its size and how it managed to contain all those animals, Origen, a second-century Christian scholar, settled that one by deciding that since Moses had been brought up in Egypt, he would have used the larger Egyptian cubit rather than the standard Middle Eastern one. An early segment of parchment from the Dead Sea Scrolls seems to hint at the fact that the ark was shaped more like a pyramid, adding to that conviction. As a matter of fact, it wasn't until the twelfth century that pictures of the ark began to show it in the now standardized form of a long, rectangular box meant to float, not maneuver.

Saint Augustine of Hippo, a fourth-century theologian, pointed out in his monumental work *City of God* that the dimensions of the

As the Church of Ireland Archbishop of Armagh and Primate of All Ireland, James Ussher (1581–1656) famously declared that the world was created by God in 4004 B.C.E.

ark corresponded to the dimensions of the human body, which, of course, according to Church doctrine, is the body of Christ and thus the Church.

This is not to say that contemporary Christianity is free from the subject of dates for a literal flood. In 1650 Bishop James Ussher famously presented his idea of biblical proof that the world was created in October of the year 4004 B.C.E. That would place the date of the flood at 2348 B.C.E. This was the date noted in Gideon Bibles, placed in every hotel room, as late as the 1970s.

Just about the only thing Christians do agree on is that the olive branch brought back by the dove symbolized peace.

## The Islamic Interpretation

In the Quran, the prophet Muhammad refers to Noah as Nuh ibn Lumik Mutushalkh. He recognized Noah as an early prophet and an apostle of Allah, or God. As such, his mission was to warn the people as much as it was possible to start humankind all over again. Preaching, after all, is one of the duties of a prophet. Noah was to teach the people, advising them to give up idolatry and live a pure and clean life. According to the Quran, Noah preached for 950 years:

IN SUMMARY, THE THREE MONOTHEISTIC, OR ABRAHAMIC, RELIGIONS TEND TO READ THE NOAH'S ARK STORY IN THE SAME FASHION BUT WITH SOME RATHER STARTLING OMISSIONS.

Noah cried to Us, and We are the best to hear prayer.

And We delivered him and his people from the Great Calamity,

And made his progeny to endure (on this earth)

And We left (this blessing) for him among generations to come in later times:

"Peace and salutation to Noah among the nations!" (Quran 37:75–79)

Although there is some dispute among Islamic scholars as to whether the flood was universal or local, there are sites to this day where Noah is said to be buried. Perhaps the most well known is the Imam Ali Mosque in Najaf, Iraq, although Azerbaijan puts forth a strong claim as well.

In summary, the three monotheistic, or Abrahamic, religions tend to read the Noah's ark story in the same fashion but with some rather startling omissions. As we have already seen, the Bible clearly states that the reason God sent the flood was because the "sons of God" mated with the "daughters of men" and had offspring with them that were called Nephilim, the "giants" or hybrid "heroes of old." Remember the verses we have already quoted:

> When human beings began to increase in number on the earth and daughters were born to them, the sons of God saw that the daughters of humans were beautiful, and they married any of them they chose. Then the LORD said, "My Spirit will not contend with humans forever, for they are mortal; their days will be a hundred and twenty years."
>
> The Nephilim were on the earth in those days—and also afterward—when the sons of God went to the daughters of humans and had children by them. They were the heroes of old, men of renown. (Genesis 6:1–4)

It might be helpful at this point to go back and reread the previous chapter, "There Were Giants in the Land." This was the reason the Bible says God destroyed the world with a flood. It is a fairly obvious conclusion that anyone would make when reading the Bible for the first time. But in every interpretation made by the three Abrahamic religions, it is almost never the reason given for the deluge. Most religious leaders teach that the flood was sent because of unspecified sins, even though those sins are clearly specified in the text.

A c. 2600 B.C.E. mosaic depicts a Sumerian king and his subjects. The Sumerians were one of the earliest civilizations on Earth, possessing a sophisticated culture that included an early form of cuneiform writing.

We can never get into the minds of previous generations, but it seems obvious that some sins are worse than others or, at least, more believable. It is a form of textual censorship that operates in plain sight because few people read and know the texts that they claim come straight from the mouth of God. Instead, they accept interpretations by an intermediary priest, minister, or imam. It's too confusing to interject giants and hybrids into contemporary conversations, so interpretations based on easily understood morality issues usually suffice.

That being said, we can now move on to other versions of the flood story.

## Sumer

The Genesis account of the Great Flood is the most well-known version of the tale, but it was by no means the first account to be recorded. That honor goes to the Sumerians.

Sumer, in Mesopotamia, was called "the land of civilized kings." It reached its peak around 6,500 years ago when it had the distinction of being a very advanced civilization with a sophisticated written language, the earliest example of magnificent architecture, complex mathematical systems, and

A figurine dating back to 2000 B.C.E. depicts the Sumerian god Enki, who, along with Ninki, created the first man, Adapa, in a story reminiscent of Adam in Genesis.

amazing astronomy. Hundreds of gods were honored in its religious system. Sumerians believed that although humans and gods once shared the earth together, they didn't share a coequal existence. Humans, they believed, were designed for the express purpose of serving the gods.

Their chief god, Anu, commissioned his son, Enki (or Ea), and daughter, Ninki (Enki's half-sister), to create humans by sacrificing a god, mixing his body and blood with clay, and forming the first human made in the likeness of the gods.

According to Sumerian mythology, humanlike gods called Anunna had initially come to mine resources that were needed on their home planet. Now, with the creation of a human labor force, their duties were changed. They ruled over what was, for all practical purposes, an enslaved race. Their base of operations was Mesopotamia, the land between the Tigris and Euphrates rivers. In the *Epic of Gilgamesh*, the world's first epic poem, it was called Eden.

At first, according to the texts, humans were unable to reproduce on their own. This proved inconvenient. So, Enki and Ninki found a way to modify the new species. The result was a man called Adapa, a fully functional and independent human being.

Enki had given Adapa great wisdom and the ability to understand the concept of eternal life. But Adapa's curse was that he could never attain that which he was able to visualize.

Were it not for the Amarna texts, discovered some 900 miles (1,400 kilometers) from Sumer in Egypt in the archives of the Egyptian king Amenophis, we might never have known about Adapa. But in 1912 his story was verified and confirmed by a unique discovery in the Library of Ashurbanipal in Nineveh (now Mosul, Iraq). Five partial fragments, since translated, were revealed that told part of the story, called "Adapa and the South Wind."

According to the story, Adapa had risen to the position of priest or sage. One day, while he was fishing in the Persian Gulf, the sea became rough, and his boat capsized. Adapa became angry and "broke the wings of the south wind." He prevented it from blowing for seven days and nights.

> IN GENESIS, GOD FORBIDS THE FIRST MAN FROM EATING OF THE TREE OF IMMORTALITY. IN THE SUMERIAN VERSION, IT IS ENKI.

This, of course, caught the attention of the god Anu, who wanted to punish Adapa for the sin of hubris. But Enki came to Adapa's aid. He instructed him to journey to the abode of the goddess Tammuz, who, along with Gishzida, stood guard at the gates of heaven. While there, Enki warned him, he was not to eat or drink anything because heavenly food would kill him.

Here note the connections with two accounts we studied earlier. Adapa returns to Eden, in effect, to partake of the fruit of the Tree of Life, which will grant him eternal life. He is met at the gate by two "angels," just as in the biblical account, who guard the way back to paradise.

Adapa put on traditional sackcloth and ashes, the garb of mourning, and appeared before Tammuz and Gishzida, claiming he was sick at heart because the two gods had disappeared from his land. Ever hospitable, they offered Adapa food and drink. Forewarned, he refused.

Only later did he come to understand that he had made a mistake. When he was brought before Anu, Anu asked why he hadn't eaten the food that had been placed before him. He said it was because Enki had told him not to eat "the bread and water of life."

At this, Anu laughed. "What ill has Adapa brought on mankind?" If Adapa had partaken of the food, he would have obtained immortality. As it is, humankind, the creation of Enki, would henceforth suffer disease and death.

Compare this story to the biblical account. In Genesis, God forbids the first man from eating of the tree of immortality. In the Sumerian version, it is Enki. This is about to become an important distinction.

Adapa was sent back down to earth. Now the plot thickens. Enki's brother, Enlil, hadn't been told about Enki's work. He had wanted only an obedient slave race, and now Enki was tinkering with things like wisdom and eternal life. Enlil and Enki fought, and the battle continues to this day.

Enlil advised the gods that he was going to destroy the newly created human race with a great flood. Afterward, he reasoned, they could start over from scratch. But Enki overheard the plans and contacted a righteous man named Utnapishtim. We'll learn more about him in a moment.

It's important to remember that the Sumerian authors didn't believe they were the earliest human civilization on earth. They claimed to have received their wisdom from an earlier civilization that had, by their time, become extinct. Who comprised that civilization, and where they had come from, is a mystery.

Added to the dilemma is the fact that when we read the Bible, as we have already noted, we are reading the edited work of scholars who lived centuries ago. They made choices, compiling one work and condensing another, so it seems as if we are reading a seamless book written by one author.

No one ever did that with ancient Sumerian texts. We read a little of this and a little of that, from here and there, and the story doesn't seem as uniform as the familiar texts that form the Bible. On top of that, some of the old texts are written in Sumerian hieroglyphs, some in Babylonian cuneiform, and others in ancient Egyptian. A modern editor has a lot to choose from and can snip a little from one text or another, confident that most of us, who don't read any of the ancient languages, will be none the wiser. But a comparison of Sumerian and biblical texts, even in translation, is revealing.

## Mesopotamia

The *Epic of Gilgamesh* was composed more than 4,000 years ago. It tells the story of how two men as different as King Gilgamesh and the savage Enkidu could triumph over adversity and develop a personal friendship. According to the story, Enkidu was created by the gods specifically to keep Gilgamesh from subjugating and oppressing his people. After an epic battle, the two became friends and shared many adventures. Eventually, however, the now "civilized" Enkidu was given a death sentence by the gods, partly as a consequence of failing to fulfill the purpose for which he was created.

Depressed and disillusioned by his friend's death, Gilgamesh undertook a long and difficult quest to discover the secret to eternal life. He believed the gods to be unfair because they created humankind with the knowledge of eternity but without the ability to ever achieve it. This, he came to believe, was an unforgivable act.

Grieving for Enkidu and fearful of his own death, Gilgamesh decided to seek wisdom from Utnapishtim, one of the two survivors of the Great Flood that had destroyed most of humanity. As we just saw in the Sumerian accounts, this flood was brought about because of two gods named Enlil and Enki. They were half brothers, prone to sibling rivalry. Enlil had decided to destroy the human race with a great flood, but Enki decided to help Utnapishtim and his wife escape the deluge by building a boat.

Utnapishtim was given precise dimensions to employ, and he finally sealed the hull with pitch and bitumen. Just in time, he loaded it with "all the animals of the field," gathered his family aboard, and was able to float to safety after a strong storm arose that was terrifying even to the gods, who retreated to the safety of the heavens.

The boat eventually lodged on a mountaintop, and Utnapishtim released first a dove, then a swallow, and finally a raven. The dove and swallow returned to the safety of the boat, but the raven didn't come back. This convinced Utnapishtim that there must be dry land somewhere, so he knew he could safely disembark.

A seventh-century tablet relates the story of the flood from the *Epic of Gilgamesh*. The tablet is maintained at the Library of Ashurbanipal in Nineveh, Iraq (formerly the capital city of the Assyrians).

Thus, because of their faithfulness, Utnapishtim and his wife were the only two humans ever granted eternal life on earth by the gods. The rest of the *Epic of Gilgamesh* continues the story of Gilgamesh's adventures.

Both the Sumerian account and the *Epic of Gilgamesh* were recorded long before the Bible was put together. It's easy to see how the texts of ancient Mesopotamia could have been the basis for the Genesis account. Scattered as the texts were, from the land between the rivers, up and down the Fertile Crescent, and all the way to Egypt, it is almost certain that the biblical writers would have had access to them or, at the very least, been familiar with their content.

The Babylonian Captivity that began in 586 B.C.E., in which the Jews were captured and transferred to Babylon, would also have exposed them to the written records and almost certainly influenced them when they came to write down their own version of the flood story, which became a part of their own sacred Scriptures.

But the flood story is not limited to the lands of the Middle East. It is found in mythology all over the world. Here are just a few examples.

## Africa

African flood myths are quite a bit different in content from the tales of biblical or Mesopotamian origins, but they are still important because

IT'S EASY TO SEE HOW THE TEXTS OF ANCIENT MESOPOTAMIA COULD HAVE BEEN THE BASIS FOR THE GENESIS ACCOUNT.

they point to the universality of flood legends. Here are summaries of just a few of them as compiled by Mark Isaac in *Flood Stories from around the World*:

*Kwaya* (Northern Tanzania)—A man and his wife had a pot that never ran out of water. They told their daughter-in-law never to touch it, but she grew curious and touched it. It shattered, and the resulting flood drowned everything.

*Southwestern Tanzania*—The rivers began flooding. God told two men to go into a ship, taking with them all sorts of seeds and animals. The flood rose, covering the mountains. Later, to check whether the waters had dried up, the man sent out a dove, and it came back to the ship. He waited a while and then sent out a hawk, which did not return because the waters had receded. The men then disembarked with the animals and seeds.

*Mandingo* (Ivory Coast)—A charitable man gave away everything he had. The god Ouende rewarded him with riches, advised him to leave the area, and sent six months of rain to destroy his selfish neighbors. The descendants of the rich man became the present human race.

*Yoruba* (Southwestern Nigeria)—A god, Ifa, tired of living on earth, went to dwell in the firmament. Without his assistance, humankind couldn't interpret the desires of the gods, and one god, in a fit of rage, destroyed nearly everybody in a great flood.

There are many more, but this is a small representation of the common thread that runs through African mythology. Note the continuing theme of human hubris and the waters of the flood being a judgment.

## North America

In the mythology of many North American tribes, the flood is coupled with the story of previous civilizations that were destroyed to usher in a new beginning—a new creation. Here are just a few examples.

### Ojibwa

The Ojibwa tell a story about how the world long ago was filled with evil men and women who had lost respect for each other. The Creator decided he would purify the earth by sending a great flood. One man, named Waynaboozhoo, survived by gathering logs to build a raft. He gathered some animals to accompany him, and together, they floated on the tides for a full month.

When the waters began to recede, Waynaboozhoo told a loon to dive down into the depths and bring back some mud that could then be shaped into a new world. But the loon failed to accomplish the task. A beaver then tried, but it also fell short. Finally, a small coot volunteered. Because of his small stature, he was jeered at by the other animals, who then began to argue among themselves as to how to best accomplish what needed to be done. While they argued, the coot slipped away and, just before he died in the attempt, came back with the needed mud. He had given his life in the process, but in so doing, he shamed the bigger animals, who had doubted him because of his small size.

Waynaboozhoo was so moved by the sacrifice that he breathed life back into the coot's body, and the bird proceeded to swim away.

The mud was placed on the broad back of Mikinaak, the turtle. It soon took on the familiar

An illustration from the 1905 book *North American Indian Fairy Tales Folklore and Legends* by R. C. Armour depicts the Ojibwa legend of Waynaboozhoo (also spelled Manabozho), who survives a great flood by building a raft.

shape of the land that was the basis for the world that exists today. Thus was given to the land the name it still bears: Turtle Island.

The land grew so large that Waynaboozhoo appointed birds to fly about and report back to him to tell him how things were progressing. This they continue to do to this very day. Whenever you hear a bird sing, it is reporting on the conditions of the world.

## Mi'kmaq

Mi'kmaq, Micmac, and L'nu all mean "The People." They are names for the original inhabitants of the northeast Atlantic seaboard who lived in the maritime provinces of Canada and northeastern United States, extending from Nova Scotia and New Brunswick down to present-day Massachusetts. Their oral history can be traced back more than 10,000 years, all the way to the first people who moved into the area on the heels of the melting glacier.

Their mythology is rich, indeed, with tales of visitors who came across the ocean from the east and recollections of an earlier time of flood. In poetic language, they remember that before the earth was new, the sun was all that

A pictogram of Nenaw-bo-zhoo as a rabbit on a rock wall in Bon Echo Provincial Park, Ontario, Canada (outline added for clarity).

existed in the universe. The earth was divided into various geographical areas that were separated by many great lakes. In each area, one man and one woman were born. Just as in the biblical tale, their children lived long lives, but wickedness eventually prevailed over goodness. The people began to war with one another.

The sun god wept with grief. His tears turned into rain, which fell from the skies until water covered the entire earth. The families built bark canoes to save themselves from the flood, but a violent wind overturned their boats. Eventually, all drowned in the sea except for the original old man and old woman, who were the best of all the people, and it was they who repopulated the earth.

## Ottawa

The name Kwi-wi-sens Nenaw-bo-zhoo roughly translates to "the greatest clown boy in the world." He was an immensely strong young man and a great prophet. He was always accompanied by his hunting dog, a black wolf the size of a buffalo. The beast's long hair and eyes, which shone at night like the moon, caught the attention of the sea god, who was so jealous of him that he decided to kill him. The sea god transformed himself into the image of a deer, and when the wolf attacked it, he was grasped and drowned in the depths of the sea. When the wolf-dog was properly drowned, the sea god threw a dinner party. Chief on the menu was barbequed dog. The attendees included whales, serpents, and various monsters of the deep.

Waw-goosh, the fox, however, saw what had happened and reported back to his friend Kwi-wi-sens Nenaw-bo-zhoo, who decided to avenge the death of his beloved companion. He hid near the shore until Neben Manito, the sea god, came to rest. There, he drew back his giant bow, which was twice as long as he was tall, and shot a poisoned arrow through Neben Manito's heart. The sea god rolled over into the sea, crying, "Revenge! Revenge!" At that point the minions of the sea god came rushing out of the sea and caused a great wall of water to inundate the land. Kwi-wi-sens Nenaw-bo-zhoo fled but could find no dry land. He then called upon the god of heaven to save him. A great canoe appeared, in which were all kinds of land animals. It was paddled by a beautiful maiden, who threw down a rope and pulled him to safety.

The prophet floated on the waters for many days. Finally, he ordered Aw-milk, the beaver, to dive down and see if he could reach the bottom and bring up some earth. When he reappeared, it seemed as if he was dead, but Kwi-wi-sens Nenaw-bo-zhoo blew into his mouth and restored him to life.

Next, it was Waw-jashk, the muskrat's, turn. He, too, seemed to die in the attempt, but when Kwi-wi-sens Nenaw-bo-zhoo blew into his mouth to restore him, some mud was found wedged in his paw. The prophet rolled it into a ball and attached it to the neck of Ka-ke-gi, the raven, saying, "Go thou and fly to and fro over the surface of the deep, that dry land may appear."

> AS THE RAVEN CARRIED OUT HIS TASK, THE WATERS BEGAN TO RECEDE. THE EARTH RESUMED ITS FORMER SHAPE. THE MAIDEN AND THE PROPHET WERE MARRIED, AND TOGETHER, THEY RE-PEOPLED THE EARTH.

As the raven carried out his task, the waters began to recede. The earth resumed its former shape. The maiden and the prophet were married, and together they re-peopled the earth.

## Cree

Wisagatcak was called "the trickster." Once, he dammed up a stream to catch the Great Beaver as it left its lodge. After waiting all day, dusk finally arrived. The Great Beaver knew powerful magic, however, and sent a large creature to attack Wisagatcak. As Wisagatcak prepared to spear it, a muskrat bit Wisagatcak on his buttocks, causing him to miss his target. Even though he had escaped, the Great Beaver was angry and wanted revenge.

The next morning Wisagatcak tore apart his dam, but the water level had not gone down, even though the stream continued to flow freely through the spot where the dam had been built. What was worse was that the water level began to rise even more.

As it turned out, the Great Beaver had used his magic indeed to flood the whole world. This went on for two weeks as the Great Beaver and his companions made all the waters of earth rise. Eventually, there was no dry land left.

Wisagatcak was forced to build a raft out of logs. He took many earth animals aboard with him as the water rose even higher.

Indigenous tribes in the Pacific Northwest, such as the Tlingit, have a folk tale about the raven god (Yehl), who saves children from a great flood as represented here in this totem pole.

Finally, Wisagatcak sent a muskrat out to search for dry land, but it drowned. Next, a raven was sent forth. He flew around the entire world but found no land.

Wisagatcak then made his own magic with the help of his friend the wolf, who had been saved on the raft.

By this time moss had grown on the surface of the raft. Wolf ran around and around on the raft, causing the moss to expand. Eventually, the raft itself became dry land. But to this very day, if you observe the earth carefully, water will still spring up through holes in the ground. These were the cracks in the original raft.

## Tlingit

Yehl, the raven, was the creator. He was the one who made plants grow and set the heavens in their place. But his uncle had a young wife whom he closely guarded. He did not want any of his nephews to inherit his widow after he died, even though this was the Tlingit custom. In a fit of jealousy, he killed Yehl's ten older brothers by drowning them. (In some versions of the story, he cuts their heads off.)

When Yehl became a man, his uncle tried to kill him as well, but Yehl's mother had conceived him by swallowing a round pebble she had found at low tide. This, along with another magic stone she had obtained, made Yehl invulnerable to such attacks. When his uncle tried to behead Yehl, the attempt failed.

In his rage, the uncle called for a flood. Eventually, all the mountains were covered with water. But Yehl sprouted wings, a good talent to have, and flew into the sky. There he remained for ten days, hanging by his beak.

When the water began to recede, he eventually let go, dropping onto a pile of seaweed. He was rescued by an otter, who brought him safely to land.

Yehl had created a woman whose job it was to watch over the tides. On one of Yehl's excursions, he had wanted to visit the undersea world, so he caused the woman to raise the waters, revealing what was underneath. At this critical time, he thus directed her to raise the ocean slowly once again so that people might have time to gather provisions for a giant canoe.

> IT IS INTERESTING TO NOTE HOW OFTEN ANIMALS AND BIRDS WORK WITH THE SURVIVORS OF THE FLOOD. THIS INDICATES A CLOSE CONNECTION BETWEEN HUMANS AND NATURE.

As the waters rose, land animals were driven to the mountaintops, where they were safely picked up by the canoe. The people landed on the tops of mountains and built strong walls all around to keep out the water.

People were thus saved from a universal flood in a giant canoe. Eventually, when it struck a rock and split in two, the Tlingit people were in one half, and all other people were in the other half. This explains why there is a diversity of languages.

These are only a few representative examples of flood stories told by the first peoples of North America. There are many more. It is interesting to note how often animals and birds work with the survivors of the flood. This indicates a close connection between humans and nature. In the biblical version, animals are saved from extinction and birds are sent forth as ambassadors, but in the Native American stories, the animal kingdom often assists in the actual act of creation.

Flood stories are not limited to North America. Here are some from the southern continent.

## South America

### Inca

Most of the textual material produced by the Inca cultures were destroyed by the Spanish, who claimed to be doing the work of the Inquisition. But a few Catholic scholars found ways to relate Inca legends while claiming to be simply relating curious historical memories. They thus circumnavigated the Church's religious reach.

Perhaps the best example of a priest finding an excuse to preserve what he thought was important was the work of Antonio de la Calancha, who wrote in the early seventeenth century: "By their *quipos*, which are their method of record keeping, and by their songs and events that they conserve in their traditions, they knew the story of the ark and the waters of the flood, and they spoke of it."

Fernando de Montesinos lived in Peru for 15 years. He claimed to have crossed the Andes at least 60 times, and he even claimed he could decipher

In Inca mythology, a great flood (called *Uno Pacha-cuti*) devastated the region around what is now Lake Titicaca (pictured), which borders Peru and Bolivia.

the flood legends he encountered to the extent that he could compute the date of the event. It happened in the year 2340 B.C.E. They called the deluge *Llocllay Pachacuti*, or "universal flood."

The Catholic scholars tended to patronize the legends, claiming, for example, that the Incas "don't remember that they come from the descendants of Noah after the flood, even though they preserve a memory of the flood, because they call it *Yaco Pachacuti* and say that it was a punishment from God."

Pedro Sarmiento de Gamboa was a soldier in 1572. He gave yet another variant spelling of the Incan words for universal flood. "And above all, their god sent them a general deluge which they call *Uno Pachacuti* which means 'water that transformed the earth.' And they say that it rained for sixty days and sixty nights, and that every living thing was drowned."

Some of the best and most accurate histories of this period come from Pedro de Cieza de León. He was a respected scholar who wrote in 1550:

> These nations say that anciently, many years before there were Incas, the earth being heavily populated with people, there came such a great storm and flood that the ocean overflowed its boundaries and natural course, and that water filled the earth in such a manner that all the people died, because the water rose enough to cover the highest peaks in all the mountain ranges.... Other people from the mountains and even those from the lowlands say that no one escaped drowning, except six people who escaped in a small boat or bark, who gave birth to all the people who have lived and are since that time.... Don't you doubt this, reader, because all of the people in general affirm this and tell this that I have written about it.

A Father Avendaño claimed to have tried to teach the indigenous people about Christianity by building on the mythologies they shared with Catholicism. This is an excerpt from one of his sermons:

Since the Incas didn't have books, they couldn't know these things, and their historians say that of the ancient things which they have for tradition in their Quipos, they only remember back 400 or 500 years, and before that, they say, was the Purunpacha, which means the time of which there is no memory. They only remember the flood, when God drowned the world with water, and all say that it was because of the sins of mankind.... The Indians admit that there was a deluge, and they call it Lloc-clai pachacuti.

THERE ARE A FEW SIMILAR DETAILS CONTAINED IN THE MANY RENDITIONS OF THE INCA FLOOD STORIES. ONE OF THEM IS THAT THE ANIMALS WARNED HUMANITY THAT THE DELUGE WAS COMING.

There are a few similar details contained in the many renditions of the Inca flood stories. One of them is that the animals warned humanity that the deluge was coming. This was described in the work of a writer named Bernabé Cobo in the seventeenth century:

> The Indians of the province of Ancasmarca, district of Cuzco, had the following legend: They say that when the flood was about to come, for one month the llamas which are like sheep in this land, showed such great sorrow that they didn't eat, and at night they only gazed at the stars, until finally, a shepherd thought about the situation and asked them what was the cause of their distress. They replied that he should look at a certain group of stars, which were conspiring and consulting about the destruction of the world by flood. After he heard this, the shepherd told his six sons and daughters, and they decided to gather with them food and cattle, as much as possible. With their provisions secured, they climbed a high hill called Ancasmarca. They say, that as the waters rose and flooded the earth, the hill rose, and floated so that it was never covered with water, and after the water subsided and gathered together again, the hill lowered itself until it came to rest again in its former place, and from these children of the shepherd who survived the flood, their province was repopulated.

Another similarity is given in the work of Francisco Dávila, written in 1598:

> They say that anciently the world was to be destroyed, and it happened like this: as one Indian tied up his llama in a good pasture ... the llama talked to him, saying: "Loco, what do you know, or what do you think? Understand that I am worried,

One of the parallels between the Genesis story of the Great Flood and the Flood story in Inca mythology is the symbol of the rainbow as a promise to humans that God would not destroy the world again.

and with good reason. You should know that in less than five days the sea is going to swell and burst open until only it covers the whole earth.... You must take refuge on the summit of the mountain Vilcacoto." Carrying his belongings on his back, and taking his llama on a leash, the Indian arrived at the summit of the indicated mountain where he found many diverse animals and birds huddled together.... The waters rose until only the summit of this Vilcacoto was not covered.... Finally the waters rose so high that some of the frightened animals were almost in it. The fox, for instance, was close to the water, waving his tail in the waves, which is the reason why the fox's tail is black at the tip. And at the end of five days, the waters began to recede and the sea returned to its former place, even lower than it had been before, and thus the entire earth was cleansed of people except the Indians referred to.

Another point of contact with the Catholic fathers is that the rainbow was seen as the symbol of hope that the gods gave to humans as a sign that the world would never again be destroyed by a universal deluge. Take this passage, for instance, written by Miguel Cabello de Balboa in 1586:

They came to a hill that today is called Guanacauria and one day at dawn they saw the bow, or rainbow of the heavens that came to the foot of the same hill, and Mango Capac told the rest that it was a good sign that the world would not be destroyed any more by water, and that they should follow him and climb the hill, and from there they would see the place where they were to settle.

Perhaps the best observation to sum up the Catholic interpretation of the Inca flood legends was penned by Antonia Vázquez de Espinosa in 1630:

Thus, since it had been such a short time after the flood that the Indians came over to these lands, they remembered it so well that they conserved its story by tradition passed on from one to another until the present time, because the Indians had memory and knowledge of it by tradition from their ancestors, even though with the passage of time and lack of writing, they had mixed the truth with some lies and superstitions that had dimmed the light of truth, although they had some sparks and indication of it.

THE FLOOD CAME, AND THE PEOPLE SURVIVED BY BEING TURNED INTO FISH. AFTER THE WATERS RECEDED, NATA AND NENA DISOBEYED THEIR ORDERS AND ATE FISH, SO TITLACAUAN TURNED THEM INTO DOGS.

## Aztec

The Aztec flood story shares a few similarities with the story of Noah, but it adds a radical plot twist. In this tale, Titlacauan, one of the primary gods of the Aztec religion, warned a man named Nata and his wife, Nena, of a coming flood. Nata and Nena hollowed out a cypress tree, and Titlacauan sealed them inside, warning them that they had only enough food that each of them could eat only one ear of corn.

The flood came, and the people survived by being turned into fish.

After the waters receded, Nata and Nena disobeyed their orders and ate fish, so Titlacauan turned them into dogs. The whole world began again, starting off with two dogs and a whole lot of fish.

None of these texts and stories, of course, were available to those who put the Bible together. Most of them came about much later and worlds away. But they do point out the fact that flood stories were universal and a part of virtually every civilization on earth. Thus, they either pointed to an event or series of events that happened in historical time, or they hint at the presence of certain psychological motifs that are to be found in the psyches of everyone, even those who compiled the Bible.

With that thought, we turn to cultures that discovered a flood story at the very heart of their philosophical system of belief formation.

# China

Derk Bodde (1909–2003) was an American historian who wrote specifically about the legal system of China. After earning a degree from Harvard University in 1930, he lived and studied for six years in China, where he was able to access a wealth of information about Chinese mythology. He found that at the base of Chinese folklore is an underpinning that begins with flood stories. In his words, "From all mythological themes in ancient Chinese, the earliest and so far most pervasive is about a great flood." He discovered three themes that permeate the mythology:

The Chinese flood story takes place during the reign of the legendary Emperor Yao (c. 2356–2255 B.C.E.), whose vast kingdom was said to have been completely covered in the great disaster.

- Heroes control the flood.
- Brother and sister marry to repopulate the world.
- The flood drowns the whole civilization.

In this, Chinese flood mythology echoes that of many worldwide mythologies.

## India: Hinduism

In Hindu religious systems, the principal trinity is composed of three gods named Brahma, Shiva, and Vishnu. Of the three, Vishnu is considered the preserver and protector of humankind. Whenever humans are threatened throughout their history, Vishnu appears in one of the *Dashavatar*, or ten avatars, which are physical incarnations, to bring salvation. (Although popular mythologies list ten avatars, classical Hindu thought recognizes a total of 24.)

Here they are, in order of appearance, along with the Hindu text that describes them:

- *Matsya* (fish)—Satya Yuga
- *Kurma* (tortoise)—Satya Yuga
- *Varaha* (boar)—Satya Yuga
- *Narasimha* (half human, half lion)—Satya Yuga
- *Vamana* (dwarf Brahmin)—Treta Yuga
- *Parshurama* (warrior)—Treta Yuga
- *Rama* (prince)—Treta Yuga
- *Krishna* (herder of cows)—Dawapara Yuga
- *Buddha* (Enlightened One)—Dawapara Yuga
- *Kalki* (horse rider) is yet to appear—Kali Yuga

Notice the first avatar, Matsya, the fish. According to the text known as the Satya Yuga, Vishnu appeared as a fish to save humans from a great flood. In some versions of the story, Matsya appeared to the first man, Manu, who was originally called Satavrata, to advise him to build a boat to escape a coming deluge. Manu was washing his hands in a river when Matsya swam into his hands and pleaded with him to save his life. Manu placed the fish in a container, but the fish continued to grow and soon was too big for his bowl. He was moved to a tank and finally to the river itself. Out of gratitude, Matsya eventually revealed himself as Vishnu and warned about what was to come. He told Manu to build a boat large enough to accommodate animals, medicinal herbs, and all manner of seeds.

Thus did Vishnu save the world through Manu, his faithful servant.

The Hindu god Vishnu (depicted here in half-fish form) saved humans from the flood by turning into a great fish and telling Manu to build a boat and tie it to the fish so that he can be pulled to safety.

## South and Southeast Asia: Buddhism

Buddhism originated in India. Some claim it is an advanced form of ancient Hinduism. Buddhist mythology features a complicated flood story called Samudda-Vānija-Jātaka. There are many versions, but here is a representative one.

One thousand families once lived in a village that housed a group of dishonest carpenters. These craftsmen would promise to build houses, furniture, and other household items, take the money in advance, but never deliver the finished products.

They were, of course, quickly kicked out of town, so they looked for another place to live.

Because they were carpenters, they built a large boat and sailed the seas until they discovered a beautiful island. One man lived alone on the island. He was a victim of a shipwreck. The man told them that food was plentiful, life on the island was comfortable, and the carpenters were welcome to stay.

> ONE SPIRIT, HOWEVER, TURNED HIMSELF INTO A BALL OF LIGHT IN THE SKY AND TOLD THE PEOPLE THAT BECAUSE OF THEIR CARELESSNESS, THE ISLAND WOULD BE FLOODED.

There was only one caveat. The island was haunted by spirits, who enforced a single rule. Every time a human needed to defecate or urinate, they needed to dig a hole and cover it up when they were finished. The spirits wanted to keep their island clean.

The carpenters enjoyed the island and decided to throw a party to celebrate their new home. During the festivities, however, they got drunk on fermented sugar cane. Ignoring the one rule, they did what drunken partygoers sometimes do.

The spirits were furious and decided to flood the island with a giant wave, which would occur on the night of the full moon. The spirits didn't want to kill the carpenters. They weren't that vindictive. They just wanted them gone.

One spirit, however, turned himself into a ball of light in the sky and told the people that because of their carelessness, the island would be flooded. He warned them to flee for their lives.

Another spirit was less accommodating. He appeared in the sky, announcing that the previous warning about a flood had been a lie. He assured the visitors they had nothing to worry about and could continue their party.

The carpenters were ruled by two men. One of them was wise, the other foolish. The foolish carpenter believed the second spirit and advised the carpenters to stay. The wise carpenter told them to build another boat.

And so, the group was divided. One portion started to work, and the other continued to party.

Finally came the night of the full moon. Sure enough, a giant wave rose up and flooded the island. The wise man set sail with his faithful friends while the foolish man and his people died.

We could continue to relate flood myths from around the world, but what's important in the context of this book is not that they all should have been included in the Bible. Their importance lies in the fact that they existed, that they were well known to people around the world, and that what is often called Noah's flood is just one of many such tales. In other words, the committees that put the Bible together made choices, and what we read today is the result of *their* choice, not necessarily God's.

Where do these stories come from? There are at least three possibilities.

- They are myths that record a single, universal flood that covered the whole earth. Each individual culture remembered their experience of that flood in a different way, and the stories represent those different memories.

• They are myths that record a series of local floods, each of which must have seemed universal in scope to the isolated communities that experienced them. They happened over many thousands of years in many different locations, but because flooding is, after all, a widespread phenomenon that is devastating in its scope, stories about them are bound to be told and retold.

Why do so many cultures have flood stories in their mythologies? One possibility is that there really was a cataclysmic, worldwide flood that engulfed Earth millenia ago.

• They are archetypes that grew out of what psychoanalyst Carl Jung called the collective unconscious. According to Jungian teaching, the human psyche is filled with symbols common to us all. He described the Great Mother, the Shadow, the Tree of Life, and Water, for instance, among many others. Jung might say that because of our experience living in the water of our mother's womb, we probably have recollections of that environment and our "salvation" from it at birth, when we entered a new world and began a new life.

We will probably never know for sure which of these is correct. Maybe all three enter the picture. We need to be careful before we make a definitive decision and choose which camp to settle down in. The important thing is to remember that the choice of what to accept and what to reject must not be made solely on the basis of an old, anonymous committee who had already decided which ideas were correct before they put together the book that later generations claimed was the "only infallible rule of faith and practice."

# THE JOURNEYS OF ABRAHAM

The LORD said to Abram, "Go from your country, your people and your father's household to the land I will show you. I will make you into a great nation, and I will bless you; I will make your name great, and you will be a blessing. (Genesis 12:2)

By faith Abraham, when he was called, obeyed by going out to a place which he was to receive for an inheritance; and he went out, not knowing where he was going. (Hebrews 11:8)

Who can be better in religion than one who submits his whole self to Allah, does good, and follows the way of *Ibrahim* the true in Faith? For Allah did take *Ibrahim* for a friend. (Quran 4:125)

Abram, Abraham, Ibrahim. By whatever name he is called, he is considered to be the spiritual father, in many cases the actual biological father, of 12 million Jews, two billion Christians, and one billion Muslims. Many claim that he was history's first monotheist. And yet, upon closer inspection, it becomes obvious that few people understand him. They may know some things *about* him, but aside from a few stories here and there, they don't really *know* him. Perhaps if they did, his children wouldn't fight so much.

He was born into a family that shared a long and rich tradition of wandering and moving across the landscape, although never very far from an urban center of trade. They were given various labels—*Aramean, Aramu, Arabu*—that eventually coalesced into the word *Arab*.

Although the Bible does not specify exactly the place of his birth, many Jews and Christians have concentrated on Ur Kasdim, or "Ur of the Chaldeans." That would put him down in Mesopotamia. But the great thirteenth-century rabbinic scholar Moses ben Nahman, also known as Nachmanides, argued that his true place of birth was further north, in the land near Haran. Muslims unequivocally claim that honor for the city of Urfa, modern Şanlıurfa, in southern Turkey.

Wherever the place of his birth is located, there is little doubt that soon after he came into the world, his father moved the family to the ancient city of Harran (spelled Haran in the Bible), where he lived for almost seven decades. Harran is in Şanlıurfa province in present-day Turkey.

An 1857 fresco at Altlerchenfelder Church in Vienna, Austria, depicts Abraham, the patron of the world's three major monotheistic religions: Judaism, Christianity, and Islam.

Abraham's early history is fragmented but colorful. From just a few short Bible verses and a plethora of legends, we can piece together a tapestry of incidents that do more to arouse curiosity than answer questions. The young Abram (the name means "the father is exalted") is said to have been born into a family that earned its daily bread by making and selling pagan idols, a strange beginning for one who is said to be the father of monotheism. At the ripe young age of 75, he heard the voice of God calling him to submit and follow the command of the Almighty.

That's when things really heated up. He gathered up his family and set out for the land of Canaan, some 300 miles (480 kilometers) to the south, whereupon he promptly panicked and continued on to Egypt. There, he almost caused an international incident. He later returned to Canaan, circumcised himself (no easy task!), fathered two sons, abandoned one of them, set out to sacrifice the other before he was stopped at the last minute by divine intervention, fought a great war, and, at its conclusion, along with the mysterious Melchizedek, high priest of Salem (now Jerusalem), instituted the custom of tithing and participated in the first communion service 2,000 years before the birth of Christ. He then bought some land, buried his wife, started another family, and lived to the age of 175. Along the way he managed to unknowingly entertain two angels, who were on their way to destroy Sodom and Gomorrah.

With all this activity to his credit, is it any wonder that his name appears so often in the Hebrew Bible, the Islamic Quran, and the Christian New Testament?

All this took place after Abram submitted to the will of God, in the process earning a new name. With that simple act of faith, he became *Abra-*

*ham*, which means "father of a multitude." For this reason, Muslims (the name means "one who submits") revere him. Through his son Ishmael, with whom he is said to have the built the Kaaba in Mecca, greatest of all holy Islamic sites, he formed the basis of what would later become the faith of Islam. Through Isaac, his second son, were descended the 12 tribes of Israel and their spiritual offspring, Christianity.

Isaac, Abraham's second son, was the ancestor of the 12 tribes of Israel.

Şanlıurfa, along with the nearby ruins of Harran, is often called "the home of the patriarchs." Not merely the birthplace, or at least a dwelling place, of Abraham, it is a city of prophets. Job himself, famous for his patience and his own submission to the will of God, is said to have faced his travails there. Jacob, after his fallout with Esau, fled back to his grandfather's home country of Harran to escape his brother's wrath. There, he married the women who would give birth to the 12 patriarchs of Judaism.

Thus, it is not without reason that Şanlıurfa and Harran are often called "the Jerusalem of Anatolia." Jews, Christians, and Muslims call this place sacred and flock to experience its long-standing sense of holiness, history, and awe. Close by are Göbekli Tepe and Mount Ararat, where Noah's ark is said to have concluded its first and only voyage. As we saw earlier, the Garden of Eden is close by, at the headwaters of the Tigris and Euphrates rivers, if one cares to read the ancient texts literally.

One of the finest museums in all of Turkey is located in Şanlıurfa. It houses the famous Urfa Man, usually considered to be "the oldest naturalistic life-sized sculpture of a human" to be found anywhere in the world. It dates back to the time of Göbekli Tepe, more than 11,000 years ago. Pottery wasn't yet invented when some unknown artist created this masterpiece.

High on a nearby hillside stand two Corinthian columns that rise above the ruined walls of a castle. It is rumored that from here, the evil King Nemrut catapulted Ibrahim (Abraham) down into a valley of flames below, but when Nemrut's daughter, after falling in love with the prophet, leaped into the fire, God turned the flames into water and the burning wood into fish. This

Discovered at a dig in excavations in Balikligöl near Urfa in Turkey, the Urfa Man sculpture stands about 6 feet, 3 inches (1.9 meters) tall and is about 11,000 years old.

marked the creation of Ayn-i Ze-liha Lake, where tourists gather in droves to feed the sacred fish.

Harran is best known today for its beehive houses. Formerly known as Helenopolis, it was burned and destroyed by Mongolian invaders in 1260. When archaeologists excavated the city, they uncovered the walls and a citadel that marked the location of the oldest Islamic university in the world.

Şanlıurfa remained a strategic city long after biblical times. The Greeks called it Orrhoe or Osrhoe. Seleucus Nicator of Antioch made it the capital of his eastern realm during the period of history following Alexander the Great's campaigns that resulted in what is now called Hellenism, or the overlay of Greek culture and language upon that of indigenous, conquered peoples. Macedonian veterans who served here, missing their home country, named it after their native province of Edessa.

During the time of the Romans, it became a center of Christianity, even if the brand practiced here, called Monophysitism, was later declared heretical. The Council of Chalcedon, held in 451 C.E., decided that Jesus Christ had both a divine and a human nature, melded in what was called hypostatic union. Monophysitism declared he had only one divine nature. Of such doctrinal disputes, wars have been fought and thousands killed.

Edessa became a great city of learning. Many ancient scientific works were translated here, along with detailed commentaries. Had the scholars not done so, we might have lost them forever because they made their way in Arabic translations into far-flung capitals, where they escaped the fires of Alexandria that destroyed so many records of ancient wisdom.

When Edessa was sacked by the Kurdish Zengi dynasty in 1146, it disappeared from history for a while. This is typical of Mongolian conquests. But it reappeared as Urfa. And when the local population resisted the French attempts to meld it into Syria during the Ottoman period, it was awarded the right to receive the honorific "Sanl" to its name. Thus, Urfa became Şanlıurfa, and it remains so to this day.

One might think that Şanlıurfa and Harran came into their own during biblical times. After all, the "City of Prophets" and the "Jerusalem of Anatolia" certainly imply ancient greatness. And a walk through the famous bazaars and old ruins, while surrounded by legends and stories of old, spark such thoughts. Even Turkey's Fertile Crescent restaurants, featuring kebabs and Turkish cuisine, recall earlier times.

> THE COUNCIL OF CHALCEDON, HELD IN 451 C.E., DECIDED THAT JESUS CHRIST HAD BOTH A DIVINE AND A HUMAN NATURE, MELDED IN WHAT WAS CALLED HYPOSTATIC UNION. MONOPHYSITISM DECLARED HE HAD ONLY ONE DIVINE NATURE.

But the significance of this area goes back much further in time. This location marks, quite simply, the birth of civilization. It is here that agriculture and animal husbandry came into their own. It took the discovery of Göbekli Tepe to unveil the truth, but civilization did not begin downriver at Sumer or along the Nile in Egypt. The art of agriculture was discovered and developed right here in Anatolia, seven thousand years before the time of Abraham. That discovery led to the biggest change in human development the world has ever seen. It made possible cities, trade, settled occupations, writing, division of labor, disputes over land, wars, traffic, morning commutes, ecological disasters, global corporations, and all the other comforts of civilization we all hold dear.

This is the place where it all began. In one cultural, quantum leap, and in a very short time, we moved from the Stone Age to the path that led to modernity. When building projects first began here, humanity consisted of wandering bands of hunter-gatherers. Shortly after, they launched the most ambitious construction projects the world has yet uncovered.

So, the question hangs high in suspension over the history concerning ancient days in Şanlıurfa province. Did the Neolithic people who once lived here wake up one morning and decide to change their way of living? Did they invent civilization? Or were they taught the necessary skills by a people whom history has forgotten?

Likewise, another question permeates the very air of Şanlıurfa. Is this the place where monotheism began as well? Was there ever a historic figure

Abraham's Pool in Şanlıurfa is one of several sites of interest in the ancient city. Here, according to legend, King Nimrod tried to burn Abraham at the stake, but God turned the fire into water. The fish here are considered sacred, and if you see a white carp, it is a sign you are blessed.

known as Abraham who woke up one morning and heard the voice of God? Or is he a composite mythological figure, representing a number of men whose lives were intertwined into one compelling story? For that matter, did he, or those who may have inspired his story, ever exist at all?

Whatever the answer, he is at the center of three worldwide monotheistic faith traditions. If he never existed in reality, he would probably have to have been invented. That's why Şanlıurfa and its surrounding environs are so important. Maybe they are not infused with the *person* of Abram, or Abraham, or Ibrahim. Maybe what folks hear is his echoing *story*. He is not remembered because he was a god: precisely the opposite. He is remembered because he was *not* a god. He was the prototypical human being who launched out on faith—who left the safe confines of where he felt comfortable to strive for something better just over the horizon. In doing so he submitted his life to a new concept, a new understanding, a new way of experiencing the holy.

In this sense he embodies what Bruce Feiler, in his excellent book with the simple title *Abraham*, calls "the *ur* man, the man who reminds us that even though God may have cut the umbilical cord with humans, humans still need nourishment from God."

Ultimately, that's why people today still make the pilgrimage to Şanlıurfa. They go there, maybe without realizing it, because they need to experience what it is to "go out, not knowing (exactly) where (they are) going."

Abraham was not a Jew. If he lived at all, it was long before the time of Moses. He was not a Christian. He preceded Jesus by some 2,000 years. He was not a Muslim. The prophet Muhammad's vision was still 2,500 years in Ibrahim's future. His story reveals a flawed man rather than a saint. But his is the story in which are captured the hopes and dreams of us all.

So, it is important to remember that the story told in the Bible is not the only one. Numerous versions of the Abraham tale have been told. The one familiar to most monotheistic believers who read the Bible today is a redacted version. Again, we are forced to wonder. If the whole story and all the legends had been known and studied over the last few thousand years, would the lessons gleaned from them have added even more to religious studies?

# CHARIOTS OF FIRE

As Elijah and Elisha were walking along and talking together, suddenly a chariot of fire and horses of fire appeared and separated the two of them, and Elijah went up to heaven in a whirlwind. Elisha saw this and cried out, "My father! My father! The chariots and horsemen of Israel!" And Elisha saw him no more. (2 Kings 2:11, 12)

Yosef ben Matityahu, better known today as Josephus, was a first-century Jewish patriot who fought against the Romans as head of the Jewish forces in Galilee during the first Jewish–Roman war. It wasn't long, however, before he could see which way the winds of history were blowing. In 67 C.E. he surrendered his forces to the army of Vespasian, a Roman general, and earned a reputation in Judea as a traitor. Being a historian even then, he earned the favor of Vespasian by claiming that the Jewish messianic prophecies referred to Vespasian, thus earning the favor of the leader of the forces who had defeated him after a six-week siege at Jotapata. His father was of Jewish priestly descent, and it occurred to Vespasian that it might prove useful to keep Josephus around as a slave.

When Vespasian was anointed emperor in 69 C.E., he granted Josephus a full pardon along with his freedom, and Josephus took on the Vespasian family name, becoming known thereafter as Flavius Josephus.

By 70 C.E. Flavius Josephus had fully defected to the point of becoming a full Roman citizen in time to serve alongside Vespasian's son Titus when he destroyed the city of Jerusalem and led the Jews away in the great Diaspora, their exile among the nations.

Thus it was that a Roman citizen is best known for writing the great historic accounts still studied today, *The Jewish War* (75 C.E.) and *Antiquities of the Jews* (94 C.E.).

*The Jewish War* recounts what Josephus calls a Jewish revolt against Roman occupation, ending in the famous siege at Masada. *Antiquities* interprets the history of the world from a Jewish perspective and was probably written for a Greek and Roman audience. Together, they synthesize some valuable insights for historians who want to study early Christianity in the context of the Jewish/Roman world. Next to the Bible, the works of Josephus represent the chief source used to understand the history of ancient Palestine during the times attributed to early Christianity.

*Elijah Taken Up in a Chariot of Fire* (c. 1740) by Giuseppe Angeli illustrates the passage from 2 Kings in which the prophet is taken up into heaven. Might the "chariot" have been a description of an alien ship?

One of the most fascinating aspects of Josephus's history is found in a passage that describes an event that occurred in 66 C.E., during the first Jewish war:

> A certain prodigious and incredible phenomenon appeared; I suppose the account of it would seem to be a fable were not the events that followed it of so considerable a nature as to deserve such signals. For before sun-setting, chariots and troops of soldiers in their armor were seen running about among the clouds. Moreover, at that feast which we call Pentecost, as the priests were going by night into the inner temple they said that, in the first place, they felt a quaking, and heard a great noise.

If Josephus is describing an actual event, rather than simply employing metaphorical imagery for the benefit of his readers, he seems to be recounting the presence of what today would be called unidentified flying objects and alien beings.

Although Christians would later echo these kinds of images in the book of Revelation, written some years later, descriptions of UFOs and alien beings are found in other ancient Hebrew texts as well. Take, for example, this passage from the book of Ezekiel, written some 600 years before Josephus was born. It's so important that I'll quote the whole first chapter:

In my thirtieth year, in the fourth month on the fifth day, while I was among the exiles by the Kebar River, the heavens were opened and I saw visions of God....

I looked, and I saw a windstorm coming out of the north—an immense cloud with flashing lightning and surrounded by brilliant light. The center of the fire looked like glowing metal, and in the fire was what looked like four living creatures. In appearance their form was human, but each of them had four faces and four wings. Their legs were straight; their feet

First-century Romano-Jewish historian Flavius Josephus wrote authoritative accounts of the First Roman–Jewish War, including the siege at Masada.

were like those of a calf and gleamed like burnished bronze. Under their wings on their four sides they had human hands. All four of them had faces and wings, and the wings of one touched the wings of another. Each one went straight ahead; they did not turn as they moved.

Their faces looked like this: Each of the four had the face of a human being, and on the right side each had the face of a lion, and on the left the face of an ox; each also had the face of an eagle. Such were their faces. They each had two wings spreading out upward, each wing touching that of the creature on either side; and each had two other wings covering its body. Each one went straight ahead. Wherever the spirit would go, they would go, without turning as they went. The appearance of the living creatures was like burning coals of fire or like torches. Fire moved back and forth among the creatures; it was bright, and lightning flashed out of it. The creatures sped back and forth like flashes of lightning.

As I looked at the living creatures, I saw a wheel on the ground beside each creature with its four faces. This was the appearance and structure of the wheels: They sparkled like topaz, and

An illustration of the first chapter of Ezekiel shows the four-faced being and wheel.

all four looked alike. Each appeared to be made like a wheel intersecting a wheel. As they moved, they would go in any one of the four directions the creatures faced; the wheels did not change direction as the creatures went. Their rims were high and awesome, and all four rims were full of eyes all around.

When the living creatures moved, the wheels beside them moved; and when the living creatures rose from the ground, the wheels also rose. Wherever the spirit would go, they would go, and the wheels would rise along with them, because the spirit of the living creatures was in the wheels. When the creatures moved, they also moved; when the creatures stood still, they also stood still; and when the creatures rose from the ground, the wheels rose along with them, because the spirit of the living creatures was in the wheels.

Spread out above the heads of the living creatures was what looked something like a vault, sparkling like crystal, and awesome. Under the vault their wings were stretched out one toward the other, and each had two wings covering its body. When the creatures moved, I heard the sound of their wings, like the roar of rushing waters, like the voice of the Almighty, like the tumult of an army. When they stood still, they lowered their wings.

Then there came a voice from above the vault over their heads as they stood with lowered wings. Above the vault over their heads was what looked like a throne of lapis lazuli, and high above on the throne was a figure like that of a man. I saw that from what appeared to be his waist up he looked like glowing metal, as if full of fire, and that from there down he looked like fire; and brilliant light surrounded him. Like the appearance of a rainbow in the clouds on a rainy day, so was the radiance around him.

This was the appearance of the likeness of the glory of the LORD. When I saw it, I fell facedown, and I heard the voice of one speaking.

He said to me, "Son of Man, stand up on your feet and I will speak to you." (Ezekiel 1:1–2:1)

Were it not for the fact that this text appears in the Bible, it might be read as a straightforward account of an encounter with a UFO. Ezekiel is very specific about giving the event an exact time and place, setting it in a historical context rather than a metaphorical one. And the description of an actual vehicle powered by beings who were definitely not of this earth is breathtaking. To decide that this is anything other than an actual account of an alien encounter speaks more to the pre-held beliefs of the reader than it does to the mindset of Ezekiel.

WERE IT NOT FOR THE FACT THAT THIS TEXT APPEARS IN THE BIBLE, IT MIGHT BE READ AS A STRAIGHTFORWARD ACCOUNT OF AN ENCOUNTER WITH A UFO.

The Bible has quite a repertoire of out-of-body trips as well. Take, for instance, this passage from Isaiah:

> In the year that king Uzziah died I saw the LORD sitting upon a throne, high and lifted up, and his train filled the temple. Above it stood the seraphim: each one had six wings; with two he covered his face, and with two he covered his feet, and with two he did fly. And one cried unto another, and said, "Holy, holy, holy, is the LORD of hosts: the whole earth is full of his glory." And the posts of the door moved at the voice of him that cried, and the house was filled with smoke. Then said I, "Woe is me! for I am undone; because I am a man of unclean lips, and I dwell in the midst of a people of unclean lips: for mine eyes have seen the King, the LORD of hosts." Then flew one of the seraphims unto me, having a live coal in his hand, which he had taken with the tongs from off the altar: And he laid it upon my mouth, and said, "Lo, this hath touched thy lips; and thine iniquity is taken away, and thy sin purged." Also I heard the voice of the Lord, saying, "Whom shall I send, and who will go for us?" Then said I, "Here am I; send me." (Isaiah 6:1–8)

This account has all the trappings of a typical shamanic vision. It features a traditional call, an otherworldly setting, hybrid animal-human figures, and a command to return back to the world with a message of healing. This is the classic formula for a shamanic journey. Once again, an exact date anchors the experience in time: "the year that king Uzziah died."

Evidence thus indicates that Josephus's account falls within a context of historical underpinning in Jewish history. Tacitus, a Roman historian,

An illustration from the 14th-century manuscript *Petites heures de Jean de Berry* shows Seraphim with six wings just as they were described in Isaiah 6.

wrote his *Histories* in 115 C.E., in which he refers to the work of Josephus. As late as 325 C.E., Eusebius, a Christian historian, quotes Josephus in his *Ecclesiastical History*.

The common way most modern scholars interpret all this alien activity is to simply say the writers were employing poetic license. But maybe it's time to cast off twenty-first-century eyeglasses and let the texts speak for themselves. The ancients certainly believed they were reporting history. There is nothing in their writing that suggests these are anything but real events.

This brings us back full circle to the work of Flavius Josephus. The world is full of mysteries. Josephus, an accredited and trusted historian in many respects, claims to have seen an unexplained phenomenon in the skies over Jotapata in 66 C.E. Today, we can choose whether or not to believe his record of the event based on many factors, including historical accuracy and the possibility of his being deceived or simply mistaken. What we must not do, however, is accept the rest of his work as accurate and negate this passage simply because we don't personally believe in UFO phenomena. That approach smacks of patronizing cultural prejudice and should have no part in real research.

But that is precisely what we've seen happen again and again when it comes to the work of those gatekeepers who ultimately put together the Bible. A close examination reveals time and time again that they might very well have succumbed to the common mistake of first believing whether or not something is true and then selecting those texts which fortify their position. That's not scholarship. It's censorship.

# THE "NEW" TESTAMENT:
# THE SHADOW OF THE FOURTH CENTURY

I believe in one God, the Father almighty,

maker of heaven and earth, of all things visible and invisible.

I believe in one Lord Jesus Christ, the Only Begotten Son of God,

born of the Father before all ages.

God from God, Light from Light, true God from true God, begotten, not made,

consubstantial with the Father; through him all things were made.

For us men and for our salvation he came down from heaven,

and by the Holy Spirit was incarnate of the Virgin Mary, and became man.

For our sake he was crucified under Pontius Pilate, he suffered death and was buried,

and rose again on the third day in accordance with the Scriptures.

He ascended into heaven and is seated at the right hand of the Father.

He will come again in glory to judge the living and the dead

and his kingdom will have no end.

I believe in the Holy Spirit, the Lord, the giver of life, who proceeds from the Father and the Son,

who with the Father and the Son is adored and glorified, who has spoken through the prophets.

I believe in one, holy, catholic and apostolic Church.

I confess one Baptism for the forgiveness of sins and I look forward

to the resurrection of the dead and the life of the world to come.

Amen.

—Nicene Creed

Is God one or three beings? This question about the Father, Son, and Holy Spirit (or Holy Ghost) needed to be resolved by the early Church to bring unity to the followers of Christianity.

In 325 C.E., the Christian Church faced a crisis that would determine its future. The problem was a simple and stark division concerning theology related to the nature of Jesus Christ. Followers of the Libyan scholar Arius, then serving as a priest in Alexandria, Egypt, held that since God was one, the supreme being, Jesus, could not have been eternally God. He must, therefore, be the oldest and most beloved of all God's creations. He was created from nothing and is thus a direct offspring of God. This was the official position of the Alexandrian Church in Egypt.

Rome, however, disagreed. They said that Jesus was eternally God and was, in their words, "of one substance with the Father."

Furthermore, there was a third aspect of deity to consider. This was the Holy Spirit, through which God worked his miraculous act of continuous creation.

If you had lived in Constantinople, now known as Istanbul, at this time, where East met West and both sides flourished, it would have been common to hear some people swearing "by the One" and others swearing "by the Three." Soon, they would be swearing at each other. Clearly, something had to be done.

The Emperor Constantine had converted to Christianity in 312 C.E. He needed this problem cleared up so he could unite the entire Roman world under one religion. His solution was to call together the bishops of the Church in a great ecumenical council that would once and for all settle the matter. They met on May 1, 325 C.E., in the city of Nicaea, in present-day Turkey. A month later they reached a controversial decision that was summed up in what became known as the Nicene Creed.

Henceforth, if you wanted to call yourself a Christian, a position that was increasingly favorable to a political career, you had to recite this creed and follow its precepts. To this very day, most Christian churches at least pay lip service to this creed by reciting it, if not every Sunday, at least on special occasions. It declares, in what was then considered to be perfectly clear language, that God is a Trinity consisting of Father, Son, and Holy Spirit. The three are separate and one, both at the same time.

> It [the Church] declares, in what was then considered to be perfectly clear language, that God is a Trinity consisting of Father, Son, and Holy Spirit. The three are separate and one, both at the same time.

"How can that be?" you might ask, finding it a difficult concept to grasp.

If that's what you are thinking, you are in good company. Almost every Christian who ever grew up in the Church has asked the same question at one time or another, usually during a confirmation class or some other kind of religious instruction given to young people.

The answer is usually delivered by a minister or priest with great fervor: "It's a mystery!"

And that's supposed to settle it. The implication is clear. Don't ask questions. Just accept it.

A group of dissenters at Nicaea called the Arians—named for the theologian Arius—couldn't do that, so they were declared heretical and banished. To this day their position—that Jesus Christ is subordinate to God the Father—is referred to as the Arian heresy in Christian history books.

But once the decision was reached, with the Emperor Constantine himself presiding over the meeting, it became the central doctrine of the Church. God is a Trinity, three in one.

In the words of the Creed that summed up the results of the meeting:

I believe in one God, the Father almighty,

maker of heaven and earth, of all things visible and invisible.

I believe in one Lord Jesus Christ, the Only Begotten Son of God,

born of the Father before all ages.

God from God, Light from Light, true God from true God, begotten, not made,

consubstantial with the Father; through him all things were made.

For us men and for our salvation he came down from heaven,

An icon depicts Emperor Constantine and several bishops holding the Nicene Creed, which codified Church doctrine for the next two millenia.

and by the Holy Spirit was incarnate of the Virgin Mary, and became man.

Jesus was considered to be one with God in hypostatic union. What that meant was that he was sometimes God and sometimes human. He was not part God and part human. He was fully God and fully human at the same time.

That doctrine has stood for almost 2,000 years, casting its shadow over everything the Church is and has accomplished, and it took less than a month to decide it and write it down. Never were the words of the Gloria Patri more true: "As it was in the beginning, is now and ever shall be."

But was Constantine interested in pure theology? Or did he have other motives?

Undoubtedly, the latter. If he was to use the Church to unite an empire, he needed structure. Undoubtedly, his motivations were political, not theological, in nature. If Arians had to be sacrificed along the way, so be it. The ends justified the means, as far as he was concerned.

Meanwhile, the orthodoxy expressed in the Nicene Creed conveniently solved another problem that had been around for 100 years, maybe even a lot longer. Since at least the first century, there had been a growing sect within the Church who are now referred to as Gnostics.

Their name comes from the Greek word *gnosis*, or knowledge. In this case it refers specifically to spiritual wisdom. By the second century, it had grown to include a variety of groups, all of whom would have disagreed with the Nicene Creed.

Although many today claim to be able to define Gnosticism, the truth about their varied beliefs has really been lost to history because a monolithic Gnostic structure never existed. We're soon going to study some of the texts that have been labeled Gnostic Gospels, but the best they can do is point out what various local sects believed. Gnostics never developed their version of a defining Nicene Creed, so their beliefs were never set in stone, so to speak.

We have already looked at one aspect of Gnostic teaching in a previous chapter titled "Pseudepigrapha and Other Disguises," but to briefly recap: Many Gnostics believed the world was not ruled by Almighty God. It couldn't be, because God is good, and the fact that evil exists is patently obvious. Therefore, a lesser divinity, sometimes called the demiurge, is actually in charge.

> GNOSTICS BELIEVED THE WORLD WAS NOT RULED BY ALMIGHTY GOD. IT COULDN'T BE, BECAUSE GOD IS GOOD, AND THE FACT THAT EVIL EXISTS IS PATENTLY OBVIOUS.

This belief even leaked its way into the Christian New Testament: "We know that we are children of God, and that the whole world is under the control of the evil one" (1 John 5:19). Jesus, therefore, must have been an emissary of the remote supreme being, sent to save the world from evil.

In the next chapter, we're going to examine some of what are now called Gnostic Gospels—texts that never made the final cut when it came time to put the Bible together. But before we begin, we may now identify why they were rejected. There were aspects of them that didn't agree with the Nicene Creed. They were rejected because the committee had already decided they were to be considered heretical.

In this way, the Council of Nicaea, which met for a month in May early in the fourth century, cast a shadow over human history that is still seen when church members gather together to recite the words:

I believe in one, holy, catholic and apostolic Church.

I confess one Baptism for the forgiveness of sins and I look forward

to the resurrection of the dead and the life of the world to come.

Amen.

# Treasures of Nag Hammadi

B y now the story is almost as well known as that of the discovery of the Dead Sea Scrolls. It has undoubtedly grown with the telling, but it probably happened something like this.

On a day in December 1945, an Arab peasant was digging around a boulder, ostensibly looking for fertilizer he could put on his fields. It happened near the town of Nag Hammadi in Upper Egypt, which is located in the southern part of Egypt. It's called "Upper" because of the Nile River, which rises in the south and flows north to the delta and the Mediterranean. Thus, Upper Egypt refers to the south, above the Aswan Dam, and Lower Egypt refers to the north.

At any rate, this person didn't realize he was about to change the course of New Testament studies forever when he unearthed a very old, large, red, earthenware jar. He first thought he might have discovered a treasure trove, but he was also cautious because finding *jinns*, or genies, in sealed jars has been a vital part of Muslim tradition ever since Aladdin and his famous lamp. Nevertheless, curiosity got the better of him, and he smashed the jar to reveal what was inside.

No genie appeared. But there was, he thought, no treasure to be found, either. At least he didn't recognize it as such. Instead, what he found were more than a dozen texts, called codices, bound in rich brown, leather covers that had been preserved in the dry climate. He didn't know it, but they had been deliberately buried there more than 1,500 years before. Those who had hidden them were probably monks from the ancient nearby monastery of St. Pachomius. They had been ordered to destroy all heretical texts as the Church was furiously going about the business of stamping out what they had declared to be the heresies of Arianism and Gnosticism. The monks feared for their lives if they disobeyed, but the fact that they clearly disagreed with the Church's newfound orthodoxy is obvious because they chose to hide the books rather than burn them.

Just as those who buried the Dead Sea Scrolls probably thought they would one day return, so the early Christian monks of St. Pachomius probably intended one day to retrieve their codices. However, they disappeared into the mists of history, never to reclaim what they considered to be a sacred trust, and their treasure lay buried in the sands of the Egyptian desert until discovered by a Muslim farmer more than 1,500 years later.

Eventually, through a long and complicated process full of twists and turns, lies, fraudulent claims, and even some backstabbing shenanigans, the

A fragment of the Apocalypse of Peter, part of the Nag Hammadi Library, circa 150 C.E.

books made their way into the halls of academic scholarship, and 50 years later, the Nag Hammadi Library was revealed to the public in multiple translations. Thirteen codices, written on parchment, contained 52 ancient texts that illustrated to the world what the early Gnostics had thought about who Jesus really was and the complex diversity that comprised the early Church. That which the victorious Trinitarian sect of the early Church had most feared eventually came to pass, beginning in 1945. The secrets of the fragmented early Church were now revealed. The history of how Christianity came to be was laid bare for the world to see.

As it turns out, things were not nearly so cut and dried as seminary students had been taught for more than a millennium. Christianity had struggled through a complicated birth.

In the previous chapter, we established that Gnosticism had no central theological core that formed a belief system. Nevertheless, there are a few principles that seem to have been prevalent.

First of all, as we have already seen, the word "Gnosticism" comes from the Greek word for knowledge, or the act of knowing. Thus, "agnosticism" literally means "not-knowing." The Greeks differentiated between rational, left-brained knowledge and intuitive knowledge, accumulated through spiritual insight or perception. This second kind of knowledge constitutes *gnosis*. In this case, they were way ahead of Western thought, which separates science from spirituality. They believed both were necessary to complete a person, not one or the other. They never saw a reason for the two to go to war.

The first century saw what might be called the beginnings of that war. This was a time of the emergence of what we now call systematic theology, or the reasoned, thought-based creation of a system of belief. In some ways, an argument could be made that the Apostle Paul himself was the Church's first systematic theologian. His closely reasoned theology is typical of what was to follow, finding its zenith during the Protestant Reformation of the sixteenth and seventeenth centuries and theologians such as Martin Luther and John Calvin.

But before that, soon after the birth of Christianity, there were those who believed they were the possessors of a special wisdom given by God, experienced in the metaphorical heart rather than the physical brain. They claimed to have experienced a spiritual revelation, not just an intellectual conversion. In their view, Jesus had imparted these secret teachings to his inner circle of disciples. It was this experience of *gnosis* that set them apart and made them seem so dangerous to a Church fast on track to become institutionalized and a medium of political power as much as spiritual force.

> IT'S IMPORTANT TO KNOW THAT GNOSTICISM ONCE HELD A STRONG POSITION OF IMPORTANCE IN THE EARLY CHURCH, ESPECIALLY IN THE EGYPTIAN ALEXANDRIAN BRANCH.

Stephan Hoeller is an American scholar who was born in Budapest into a family descended from Austro-Hungarian nobility. Before World War II broke out, he was forced into exile, but he managed to study extensively in Austria, Belgium, and Italy before moving to the United States. Sharing his profound academic knowledge of Gnostics, he says that "these [early] Christians held a conviction that direct, personal, and absolute knowledge of the authentic truths of existence is accessible to human beings, and, moreover, that the attainment of such knowledge must always constitute the supreme achievement of human life."

It's important to know that Gnosticism once held a strong position of importance in the early Church, especially in the Egyptian Alexandrian branch. One of the foremost teachers of this period was a scholar by the name of Valentinus. Historians argue about this, but he may have been in contention at one point to be elected bishop of Rome—the pope! One can only wonder how that would have changed the course of history because Valentinus was unquestionably a highly educated, gifted teacher. He was also a strong proponent of Gnosticism. Mid-career, he moved to Rome and took an active part in developing the Church there.

According to Valentinus, the inherent problem of Gnosticism, at least from a tactical standpoint, was that Gnostics considered themselves to be keepers of a secret, sacred tradition. It took effort to be a Gnostic. You really had to work at it by learning rituals and reading hidden texts. It was not for the faint of heart or the proverbial man on the street.

This was in direct contrast to the brand of Christianity that eventually triumphed—a religion for the common person, designed to unify an entire empire. Valentinus professed to have received what he called apostolic sanction through none other than a disciple and student of the Apostle Paul, a man named Theudas. He declared himself to be a keeper and custodian of doctrines and rituals that were overlooked and ignored by mainstream theologians and the leaders of what was to become the Christianity we know today. With statements such as these, he was soon ostracized by the Roman Church, declared a heretic, and forced from public attention.

The Church rejected the Gnostic Valentinus, and instead, the bishop of Lyon, Irenaeus, rose to prominence. The bishop attacked the Gnostics, and their teachings came to be considered heretical.

If he had triumphed, there is no doubt that Christianity today would be a totally different proposition. But with his ouster, the tide of history turned against Gnosticism during the middle years of the second century. After Valentinus, there was never again a prominent Gnostic in any position to effect change, so the idea of knowing God personally through direct revelation was replaced by the necessity of a layer of intervening priests, the better to control the masses. The Church, in other words, became political as well as spiritual. From then on, Church leaders would decide which texts were allowed and which were to be destroyed. By 180 C.E., the bishop, who is even today considered to be one of the greatest Church founders, a priest by the name of Irenaeus, the bishop of Lyon, began to publish a series of attacks on Gnosticism, declaring it heretical. Similar attacks continued throughout the second and third century. Following the fourth-century Council of Nicaea, it was, for all practical purposes, pronounced dead and buried. Were it not for the codices discovered at Nag Hammadi, we might not even know of its existence today except for the attacks against it that have survived down through the centuries.

Here's the important point for our purposes. The first committees that, as far as anyone knows, actually compiled the 27 books of the New Testament that are recognized today as the Canon of Scripture were probably a group that met at the councils held in North Africa at Hippo in 393 C.E. and Carthage in 397. These men knew about Gnosticism. They had read the texts. But, knowing what side their political bread was buttered on, they rejected them and ordered them destroyed as heretical. Thus, Gnosticism, as a Christian tradition, was eradicated. Its followers were excommunicated, its texts destroyed, and even its memory purged from public consciousness.

That's the way the matter would have stood forever, were it not for the monks of St. Pachomius. They could not bring themselves to destroy their

The Gnostics were not completely wiped out by the early Christian Church leaders. An ethnoreligious group known as the Mandaeans in southern Iraq still practice a form of the belief.

sacred library, so they buried it in the desert sands near Nag Hammadi, praying that someday, their work would be discovered and brought again into the light of day. In 1945, their prayers were answered.

If Gnosticism means "knowing," it's time to ask what it was that these "knowers" knew. What was so dangerous about their teaching that the early Church felt the need to so thoroughly destroy it?

We've already pointed out that Gnosticism was an esoteric system of belief that no one really understands in all its fullness. There is no central text that defines and characterizes it. But by studying the texts that have surfaced, we can at least begin to summarize this early Christian approach to God. Understand that this is by no means a comprehensive analysis, but it is at least a place to start. In summarizing this, I owe a great debt to the Gnostic Society Library. A deeper and richer explanation can be found on the society's website at gnosis.org.

- First, as we have already made clear, the essential characteristic of Gnosticism is the emphasis upon personal and direct communication between the believer and God. There is no need for an intermediary, be it priestly or liturgical in nature. *Gnosis* is not achieved via a logical, rational, left-brained, thought-out approach. Direct revelation can happen anytime, anywhere. The lowest person on the totem pole can

An illustration of the demiurge, known by various names, who is responsible for corrupting the once perfect world created by God.

access God just as easily as those at the top, maybe even more easily because there is no logical, reasoned system of belief for God to have to pass through. In the words of the great psychologist and student of philosophy Carl Jung, "We find in Gnosticism what was lacking in the centuries that followed: a belief in the efficacy of individual revelation and individual knowledge. This belief was rooted in the proud feeling of man's affinity with the gods."

• Second, God resides within the human heart, not off in the clouds. A belief in such intimate presence is often called *immanent* belief, rather than *transcendent* belief. In his book *The American Religion*, Harold Bloom says that Gnosticism is "a knowing, by and of an uncreated self, or self-within-the self, and [this] knowledge leads to freedom." This inner freedom, consisting of an inner light or presence, is the very presence of the immanent God. In the book of Colossians, the Apostle Paul said it was a great secret, fully revealed in Jesus: "For God wanted them to know that the riches and glory of Christ are for you Gentiles, too. And this is the secret: Christ lives in you. This gives you assurance of sharing his glory." To access this presence, Gnostics used different methods. Some practiced extreme asceticism. Others, reasoning that spirit was more important than flesh, indulged their desires. There was no set practice approved by a religious hierarchy. The essence of this belief was extremely paradoxical. Human beings are not God, but they are godly. It was up to the individual to work that out in his or her own way.

• Third, we have already talked in great detail about the god of this age. Gnostics believed that he was not the creator. How could he be? The creation was declared "very good" at the beginning. Obviously, now it is not. What happened? The demiurge, sometimes called Saklas the Fool or Iadebaoth the Blind, wrested control in Eden and now rules.

He is a counterfeit who has deceived the world into believing in and worshipping him, confusing him with the creator god. In other words, the god worshipped by the Roman victors is the devil. Theodotus, a Gnostic teacher who lived in Asia Minor from 140 to 160 C.E., said the *gnosis* reveals "who we were, what we have become, where we have been cast out of, where we are bound for, what we have been purified of, what generation and regeneration are." The Gospel of Thomas, one of the Gnostic Gospels we will look at later in greater depth, has Jesus telling his disciples words that must have seemed anathema to the Roman Church but that were often quoted much later by Joseph Campbell, the great mythologist: "I am not your master.... He who will drink from my mouth will become as I am. I myself shall become he, and the things that are hidden will be revealed to him."

• Fourth, Gnostics revered sacred texts and scriptures. This is why they could not destroy them. The Roman Church, however, was deathly afraid that such texts could fall into the wrong hands and cause damage among the masses. Beginning in the fourth century, continuing right up through the conquests of Central and South America, and even with regard to the works of Isaac Newton, the Church censored and destroyed thousands of texts that could have revealed the nature of a totally different way to think about God. It's almost impossible to imagine the effect the preservation of such texts would have had on the modern world.

• Fifth, in many of the Nag Hammadi texts, God is defined in terms of dualism. What this means is that both male and female aspects of God are discussed. This is probably the most far-reaching aspect of Gnosticism we have discovered about this early Christian sect. There is no question that the Church as it existed after the fourth century was a male-dominated institution. In many ways, it still is. The Nag Hammadi scriptures contained books written ostensibly by and about women. Later, we will look at the traditions surrounding Mary Magdalene, who the Gnostics believed was a consort, if not the wife, of Jesus. The Gospel of Philip, censored from the Bible but discovered at Nag Hammadi, features this now famous quote: "The companion of the Savior is Mary Magdalene. But Christ loved her more than all the disciples, and used to kiss her often on her mouth. The rest of the disciples were offended.... They said to him, 'Why do you love her more than all of us?' The Savior answered and said to them, 'Why do I not love you as I love her?'" Other texts refer to God as Mother/Father. Imagine a world in which a great majority of its conquerors began their most famous prayer, "Our Mother and Father, who art in heaven...." In fact, an early Gnostic text begins, "From

Thee, Father, and through Thee, Mother, the two immortal names, Parents of the divine being, and thou, dweller in heaven, humanity, of the mighty name...."

- Sixth, the Roman Church that eventually emerged from the fourth century recognized seven sacraments: baptism, Eucharist, confirmation, reconciliation, anointing of the sick, marriage, and holy orders. Much of the Protestant Church that broke away in the sixteenth century reduced these to two: baptism and Eucharist. The Gnostics seem to have recognized five: baptism, chrism, Eucharist, redemption, and bridal chamber. It's the last one, bridal chamber, that opens most eyes today. Does it refer to sacred sexual relations, or is it a metaphor for the union of spirit and flesh? No one knows for sure. Even today, at a marriage ceremony, the priest or minister is apt to say, "The two shall be one flesh." What the Gnostics were talking about is a mystery.

This, then, in vastly simplified form, is what fourth-century Gnosticism might have looked like. We'll never know for sure, of course, but it probably comes pretty close. We are left to contemplate the unknowable mystery. What would the world have looked like if Gnosticism had won and Roman Christianity had lost on the battleground of the fourth century? What would have happened if even some form of Gnosticism been allowed to participate and shape the conversation? How would modern life have been influenced? There is no question that things would have been different.

We can speculate, but what those differences would have been will never be known.

# OUT OF EGYPT

> And so was fulfilled what the Lord had said through the pro-
> phet: "Out of Egypt have I called my son." (Matthew 2:17)

On the west bank of the Nile River, south of Luxor, lies the ancient city of Edfu. There stands a great temple dedicated to the god Horus, always pictured with the head of a falcon. The temple was completed in about 57 B.C.E., after a 180-year period of construction. The Gospel according to Matthew claims that the holy family—Joseph, Mary, and young Jesus—fled to Egypt to escape the slaughter of innocents wrought by King Herod in an effort to kill the baby whom the Magi claimed was born "King of the Jews." In Egypt, they might have seen this great edifice, finished only a few decades before the birth of Jesus. Whether Joseph and Mary ever saw the temple or not, those who compiled the New Testament must have known about the texts it contained. They were famous throughout the Roman Empire, which constituted the bulk of the Western world. Every educated person would have at least heard about them.

Archaeology at Edfu reveals that this site was built to be a huge and extensive library, written in the form of hieroglyphs, or sacred scripts, carved on the temple walls. Even more interesting is the fact that when the texts began to be translated, it became apparent that this temple stands on the location of an even older temple that dates back to a forgotten time known as the Zep Tepi, or "First Time," which happened thousands of years before the first Pharaohs.

Seven sages, the texts reveal, appeared in ancient Egypt, sailing from somewhere called the Homeland of the Primeval Ones, which was a sacred island in the middle of the ocean. A great cataclysm had destroyed the island on which "the earliest mansions of the gods" had once stood. Some of the inhabitants survived and, according to the Edfu texts, set forth in their great ships to wander the world and bring about "the resurrection of the former world of the gods." Their mission, in other words, was to re-create their destroyed world.

They established a series of sacred mounds up and down the course of the Nile River. These mounds, according to the Edfu texts, established the foundations of all future temples to be built in Egypt.

The similarity to the flood stories found in Genesis immediately stands out. Even the similarities between this and the Atlantis tradition are apparent.

The story of the Egyptian god Horus (often depicted as a falcon or a man with a falcon's head) has parallels to the Christ story in the Bible.

But what is even more important are the connections to be found concerning the god Horus, to whom the temple is dedicated, and the story of Jesus. Horus, it seems, was born of a virgin, a "son of God." And that's just the beginning of the story. Is the Horus legend the basis of what the Gospels would later present as the Christ story?

Tom Harpur (1929–2017) was an Anglican priest, a seminary professor, and a religion writer for the *Toronto Star* who wrote a number of best-selling books about the Bible and related themes. Perhaps his most controversial one was *The Pagan Christ*, which was published in 2004. In it, he puts forth the theory that the entire Jesus story found in the Bible is a rendering of the story of Osiris, Isis, and Horus, which would have been well known in Israel. The homeland of the Bible, after all, stands at a crossroads. Anyone traveling north from Egypt by land on the way to Europe, Asia, or anywhere along the Fertile Crescent has to go through Israel. Israel thus served as a sort of melting pot of ideas, mixing East with West and North with South. The Apostle Paul would certainly have been familiar with the Egyptian story, being both a Jewish scholar and a Roman citizen.

Harpur sums up his theory in *The Pagan Christ* by quoting the nineteenth-century English Egyptologist Gerald Massey:

> The Christian myths were first related of Horus or Osiris, who was the embodiment of divine goodness, wisdom, truth and purity.... This was the greatest hero that ever lived in the mind of man—not in the flesh—to influence with transforming force; the only hero to whom the miracles were natural because he was not human.

Harpur was drawn to the Egyptian myth after becoming convinced that Egypt, not Israel, was really the "cradle of the Jesus figure of the Gospels." In his own words:

> Here already was the story of how the divine son "left the courts of heaven" and descended to earth as the baby Horus.

Born of a virgin (through whom he "became flesh" or entered into matter), he then became a substitute for humanity, went down into Hades as the quickener of the dead, their justifier and redeemer, "the first fruits" and leader of the resurrection into the life to come.

> THE BIBLICAL GOSPELS ... ARE REALLY A DRAMATIZATION OF THE STORY ABOUT INCARNATION AND RESURRECTION THAT EGYPTIAN PRIESTS HAD BEEN RECOUNTING FOR PERHAPS THOUSANDS OF YEARS.

The biblical Gospels, according to Harpur's theory, are really a dramatization of the story about incarnation and resurrection that Egyptian priests had been recounting for perhaps thousands of years. They were transferred to the pages of the Bible from Egyptian mythology, through Egyptian Gnostic mysticism, then Hellenic philosophy, then Hebrew religion, and finally into the Greek of the New Testament and into the arena of history.

Harpur goes on to say:

> Unaware that the original mythos of messianic mystery, the virgin motherhood, the incarnation and birth, the life and character, the crucifixion and resurrection of the savior Son who was the word of all ages, the alpha and omega, was already part of the Egyptian religion since earliest times, the compilers of the New Testament missed the point entirely that *the whole thing was meant allegorically.*

Harpur is probably being generous when he says the compilers of the New Testament were unaware of the Egyptian texts. It's hard to believe they could not have known what every other educated scholar knew at the time. We can even surmise that the Apostle Paul, himself an educated scholar, might have made use of the story in his quest to shape the Jewish faith into one that was open and welcoming to Gentiles as well. The Roman Church eventually used the same techniques, "baptizing," as it were, other pagan holidays that became known as Christmas and Easter, among others, in order to create a unifying religion and thus cement an empire.

So, it becomes appropriate to ask what the early biblical writers knew about Egyptian mythology, especially when it comes to the Osiris/Isis/Horus story.

A professor with the delightful name of Sir Ernest Alfred Thompson Wallis Budge was an English Egyptologist who worked with the British Museum before his death in 1934. Known not only for his historical work, he was a philologist, meaning he was an expert in languages and their interconnections.

He wrote about Egyptian mythology in these words:

From the hieroglyphic texts of all periods of the dynastic history of Egypt we learn that the god of the dead, par excellence, was the god commonly known to us as "Osiris." The oldest religious texts known to us refer to him as the great god of the dead, and in fact he was in respect of the dead and of the Underworld what Ra (the primary Egyptian Sun god) was to the living and to this world.

In Egyptian mythology, Isis was either the consort or wife of Osiris. She was the great goddess whose love pervaded the heavens, the earth, and even the abode of the dead. She was the personification of that feminine creative power that conceived and brought forth every

An Egyptian statue from the Twenty-second Dynasty (943–716 B.C.E.) showing Horus (left), Osiris (center), and Isis (right). Osiris and Isis were reflective of the masculine and feminine aspects of god, respectively.

living creature. Horus was her son and, thus, "a son of god." Osiris and Isis therefore gave birth to Horus, to whom the temple at Edfu was dedicated.

It was a story known all over the Greco-Roman world. Eventually, what was called the Hellenistic Mysteries of Isis became a universal cult. The "male god, female god, son of god" story was well known. Could this have been the basis of the "God, Mary, Jesus" story, especially considering the Gospel according to Matthew specifically says, "Out of Egypt have I called my son"?

Harpur devotes a whole book to examining the similarities. Here are just a few of them:

1. Horus was baptized in the River Eridanus by a godlike figure known as Anup the Baptizer. Jesus was baptized in the Jordan River by a mysterious figure named John the Baptist.

2. Like Jesus, Horus had no history between the ages of 12 and 30.

3. Like Jesus, Horus walked on water, cast out demons, and healed the sick.

4. Like Jesus, Horus was transfigured on a mountain.

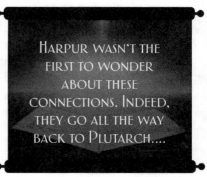

5. Horus delivered his own version of a "Sermon on the Mount," and his followers ever after faithfully recounted the sayings of the one they called Iusa.

6. Horus was crucified between two thieves, buried in a tomb, and resurrected. His personal title was either *Iusa* or *Iusu*, the "ever-becoming son" of *Ptah* or "the Father."

HARPUR WASN'T THE FIRST TO WONDER ABOUT THESE CONNECTIONS. INDEED, THEY GO ALL THE WAY BACK TO PLUTARCH....

7. Significantly, Horus was called the "Anointed One," from a word that was inscribed or painted on the lid of a mummy's coffin millennia before Christianity duplicated the story.

8. Horus was called the Good Shepherd, the Lamb of God, the Bread of Life, the Son of Man, the Word, and the Fisher of Men.

9. Horus was not considered to be simply the path to heaven. Instead, he was thought to be the way by which the dead travel out of the sepulcher. He was the god whose name was written as the "road to salvation." He was thus "the way, the truth, and the life."

Harpur wasn't the first to wonder about these connections. Indeed, they go all the way back to Plutarch, a Greek philosopher who lived sometime between 45 and 119 C.E., which would place him right in the range of years when the Gospels were written. He, too, studied Egyptian mythology in great depth and commented on the universality of its implications. So, Harpur was by no means the first to think along these lines.

Other similarities between various mythologies echo the Jesus story—similarities that were well known to those who wrote the Bible. The Iranian god Mithras, for instance, was called "the soldier's god" because his cult was recognized by many soldiers in the Roman army of the first century. Born of a virgin at Christmastime, he came forth to slay the sacred bull, shedding its holy blood to save humankind. At the conclusion of a final meal of bread and wine with his followers, he ascended to heaven after promising he would one day return.

The stories go on and on. Our purpose in recounting them is so that they may once again serve as a reminder. We do not seek to discredit the Christian story. It has, after all, stood the test of time and comforted many millions of believers. But we need to remind ourselves over and over again that it is not the *only* story that features mythological themes found around the world and down through time. The presence of these themes need not discredit any given story or be considered a way of disproving any or all of them. Instead, they point to the universality of what the themes represent. They all point to the same source. They all reference the human need for aid in a complex life and the certainty of the ancients that we are not alone but rather part of a greater story that is being enacted on the pages of history. Whether they are read literally or allegorically, the truth they point to is real, declare the ancient writers, and not confined by national or religious boundaries.

# THE PROTOEVANGELIUM OF JAMES

More than a century after the time of Jesus, somewhere around the year 150 C.E., a Gospel account of the life of Jesus was written, purportedly by James, later called James the Just, who in the well-known Gospels we have today is referred to as the brother of Jesus. Sometimes called the Gospel of James, the Infancy Gospel of James, or more commonly the Protoevangelium of James, it is the earliest known Gospel that declares that Mary, the mother of Jesus, was a perpetual virgin, calling her "the New Eve." According to this story, Joseph, Jesus's father, was a widower who had other sons and daughters. James was one of them. Mary was, in effect, entrusted to Joseph's care by God.

Were it not for the writings of Origen, a Catholic scholar who wrote about the book 200 years after it was written, we might never have heard about it because Pope Gelasius I, who ruled from 492 to 496, issued his Decretum Gelasianum, or "Gelasian Decree," forbidding Catholics from having anything to do with this book.

The problem, according to religious scholars, involved Jesus's relationship with James. According to Orthodox Roman Catholic belief, Jesus didn't have any brothers or sisters. Those listed in the Bible are thought to be his cousins. The Eastern Orthodox Church and, later, the Protestants disagreed, but that was to be expected. The three groups disagreed about a lot of things. But the Protoevangelium of James considered Mary, Joseph, and their children to be one big, happy family.

How did scholars deduce the fact that the book was written in 150 C.E. if we didn't even hear about it until the third century? Well, that's what puts food on the table for those who study the development of language and many other arcane dating techniques. They claim that the author didn't seem to be aware of customs that a real first-century Jew would have known about, and the language is indicative of that used "sometime in the second century C.E." It is apparently based more on the Greek translation of the Old Testament, called the Septuagint, than the Hebrew Bible, which is based on what is called the Masoretic Text.

Whenever the book was written, and whoever wrote it, it does offer some entertaining details that are not found in the Gospels according to Matthew or Luke, which are the only two accepted Gospels that give any details at all about the young Jesus.

It must have been popular reading back in the first few centuries before it was banned. There are more than 130 surviving manuscripts that quote

Not to be confused with the Apostle James, son of Zebedee, James the Just (also known as James the Lesser and James, son of Alphaeus) has been speculated to be a half brother of Jesus or possibly one of his cousins. He left behind the Gospel of James.

from it, and excerpts have been found that were translated into Syriac, Ethiopic, Coptic, Georgian, Old Slavonic, Armenian, Arabic, Irish, and Latin.

Originally, it was divided into three sections, each containing eight chapters.

*Part 1*—This section tells the story of Mary's unique birth and childhood. She was assigned to the temple because of her holiness and devotion to God.

*Part 2*—This rather intimate section tells of how Mary's virginity was tested after she was discovered to be pregnant and how she was assigned to Joseph, who would serve as her guardian.

*Part 3*—Here we find the story of the nativity, when Mary was visited by midwives to aid her in her delivery. Soon after the birth of Jesus, the child was hidden from Herod the Great, who sought to kill all newborns who might be in consideration to be "the King of the Jews." He is hidden in the hills, where Mary meets up with her cousin, Elizabeth, the mother of John the Baptist.

Throughout the whole book is found the grace of God in Mary's life. She is held up as a paragon of virtue and perpetually a virgin both before and after the birth of her son, a fact which was confirmed by a midwife and a woman named Salome, who might be the Salome mentioned in the Gospel according to Mark who was present at the crucifixion.

According to the Protoevangelium of James, Jesus was not born in a stable but in a cave. Joseph was elderly by this time, which might explain why he disappears after Jesus grows to adulthood.

This book is one of a number of books called a protoevangelium. That means pre-Gospel or infancy narrative. These works appeared rather quickly, hoping to fill in details that people wanted to know about what it was like for Jesus as a young boy. They all show very little familiarity with authentic

Jewish life in the first century, but in their time, they satisfied a certain curiosity about what Jesus might have been like in day-to-day activities. Similar books that have survived include the Infancy Gospel of Thomas, which was probably part of one of the books discovered in the Nag Hammadi Library, the Gospel of Pseudo-Matthew (based on the Protoevangelium of James and on the Infancy Gospel of Thomas), and the so-called Arabic Infancy Gospel. We'll turn to those next.

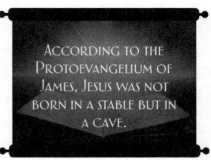

ACCORDING TO THE PROTOEVANGELIUM OF JAMES, JESUS WAS NOT BORN IN A STABLE BUT IN A CAVE.

# THE GOSPEL OF THOMAS

Jesus said, "He who drinks from my mouth will become like me, and I will become like him, and the hidden things will be revealed to him." (Gospel of Thomas, verse 108, Blatz translation)

Of all the books discovered near the desert town of Nag Hammadi, the one that has undoubtedly received the most public attention is the Gospel of Thomas, purportedly written by the disciple known as Doubting Thomas. This name comes from the fact that according to the Gospel according to John, Thomas at first doubted the resurrection of Jesus:

Now Thomas, one of the twelve, was not with the disciples when Jesus first came. So the other disciples told him, "We have seen the Lord!" But he said to them, "Unless I see the nail marks in his hands and put my finger where the nails were, and put my hand into his side, I will not believe."

A week later his disciples were in the house again, and Thomas was with them. Though the doors were locked, Jesus came and stood among them and said, "Peace be with you!" Then he said to Thomas, "Put your finger here; see my hands. Reach out your hand and put it into my side. Stop doubting and believe."

Thomas said to him, "My Lord and my God!"

Then Jesus told him, "Because you have seen me, you have believed; blessed are those who have not seen and yet have believed." (John 20:24–29)

The Gospel of Thomas was probably not written by Thomas at all. Scholars disagree widely over when it was written. Some say as early as 60 C.E., which would make it by far the earliest Gospel account written. Others date it as late as 140 C.E. The fact that it doesn't appear to have been written in Greek, like all the other books of the Bible, didn't help its cause any. The copies discovered at Nag Hammadi are written in Coptic, but they may be translations.

If the early date is correct, it opens up some interesting possibilities. Matthew, Mark, and Luke, the first three Gospels in the New Testament, are called the Synoptic Gospels, "synoptic" meaning "similar." They share so many of the same stories about the life of Jesus that many scholars have come

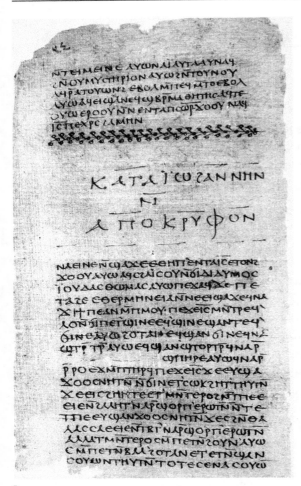

The Gospel of Thomas, unlike other Gospels, is written in Coptic instead of Greek. It might be the earliest Gospel found, with some scholars dating it back to 60 C.E.

to the conclusion that they are all taken from a single source document called the "Q" document. "Q" is short for *quelle*, the German word for "source." In other words, they believe that when the authors of Matthew, Mark, and Luke sat down to write their Gospel accounts, each had before him a copy of the sayings of Jesus. This is called the "Q Document Theory." When Thomas was discovered and given a very early date of composition—one only a few decades after Jesus's death—many scholars wondered if this might be the long-lost "Q" source document that served as a basis for the Synoptic Gospels.

Thomas has also been called the Gnostic Gospel because many see Gnostic beliefs running through it. The fact that it was hidden in the desert shortly after the decree that banned Gnostic teachings might indicate this is the case.

This book is different from the other accounts of Jesus's life and death, however. It doesn't tell stories as much as it recounts sayings, called *logia*. The fact that more than half of them appear in the four traditional Gospels indicates that they were well known at the time the other Gospels were written. In the introduction to the book, the author says, "These are the hidden words that the living Jesus spoke, and Didymus Judas Thomas wrote them down." *Didymus* means "twin." For that matter, so does *Thomas* in Aramaic. Who the other twin is remains a mystery.

The Gospel of Thomas is, itself, a mystery. Nowhere, for instance, does it claim that Jesus was divine. On the other hand, it doesn't deny it, either. When Jesus is asked whether he is God, he pivots with the skill of a politician and ambiguously inquires why they don't see what is right in front of them. Then, he leaves it at that. It doesn't mention his death, except for one rather obscure reference, and it leaves out anything about his crucifixion, resurrection, and final judgment. It doesn't refer in any way to the possibility that he is or is not the Messiah. But there is an outright order that may indicate the importance of James the Just, said to be Jesus's brother.

> THE GOSPEL OF THOMAS IS, ITSELF, A MYSTERY. NOWHERE, FOR INSTANCE, DOES IT CLAIM THAT JESUS WAS DIVINE. ON THE OTHER HAND, IT DOESN'T DENY IT, EITHER.

The disciples say to Jesus, "We are aware that you will depart from us. Who will be our leader?"

Jesus answers, "No matter where you come it is to James the Just that you shall go, for whose sake heaven and earth have come to exist."

That's it. No commentary, just a rather enigmatic statement of fact.

But there is an even more alluring side of this mysterious text. A fragment called the Infancy Gospel of Thomas was discovered that many scholars consider to be part of the Gospel of Thomas. It introduces a story that soon became controversial not only to the early Christian Church but to Muslims as well. Here is the central story that caused all the talk:

> I, Thomas, an Israelite, judged it necessary to make known to our brethren among the Gentiles, the actions and miracles of Christ in his childhood, which our Lord and God Jesus Christ wrought after his birth in Bethlehem in our country, at which I myself was astonished; the beginning of which was as follows. When the child Jesus was five years of age and there had been a shower of rain that was now over, Jesus was playing with other Hebrew boys by a running stream, and the waters ran over the banks and stood in little lakes. But the water instantly became clear and useful again; they readily obeyed him after he touched them only by his word. Then he took from the bank of the stream some soft clay and formed out of it twelve sparrows; and there were other boys playing with him. But a certain Jew seeing the things which he was doing, namely, his forming clay into the figures of sparrows on the Sabbath day, went presently away and told his father Joseph, "Behold, your boy is playing by the river side, and has taken clay and formed it into twelve sparrows, and profanes the Sabbath." Then Joseph came to the place where he was, and when he saw him, called to him, and said, "Why do you that which is not lawful to do on the Sabbath day?" Then Jesus clapping together the palms of his hands, called to the sparrows, and said to them: "Go, fly away; and while you live remember me." So the sparrows fled away, making a noise. The

A 1340 illustration from a German folio shows the boy Jesus (at right) animating the clay sparrows in a story from the Gospel of Thomas.

Jews seeing this, were astonished and went away and told their chief persons what a strange miracle they had seen wrought by Jesus.

Needless to say, this was just the sort of spicy detail that people hunger for when they wonder about the young Jesus growing up and coming to grips with magical—or miraculous, depending on your point of view—powers. Apparently, it even appealed to the prophet Muhammad, for he mentions the incident in the Quran.

In Alfred Guillaume's 1955 translation of Ibn Ishaq's *Life of Muhammad: A Translation of Ishaq's Sirat Rasul Allah*, this comment appears:

They argue that he is God because he used to raise the dead, and heal the sick, and declare the unseen; and make clay birds and then breathe into them so that they flew away; and all this was by the command of God Almighty, "We will make him a sign to men."

Aside from all this, the Gospel of Thomas is considered to be dangerous in that it seems to point to a present reality called the "kingdom" or "realm" of God that is ever present and already here on earth. Heaven is not a hoped-for future reality, waiting for us when we die. It is already here, and we just don't see it. That takes away the reward aspect, a destiny earned when we toe the line and stay on the straight and narrow path.

Thomas has Jesus say it this way:

If those who lead you say to you: See, the kingdom is in heaven, then the birds of the heaven will go before you; if they say to you: It is in the sea, then the fish will go before you. But the kingdom is within you, and it is outside of you. When

you know yourselves, then you will be
known, and you will know that you are
the sons of the living Father. But if you
do not know yourselves, then you are in
poverty, and you are poverty.

> [T]HE GOSPEL OF THOMAS
> IS CONSIDERED TO BE
> DANGEROUS IN THAT IT
> SEEMS TO POINT TO A
> PRESENT REALITY CALLED
> THE "KINGDOM" OR
> "REALM" OF GOD
> THAT IS EVER PRESENT
> AND ALREADY HERE
> ON EARTH.

This puts the responsibility for salvation or
enlightenment squarely on the shoulders of the
individual. It doesn't grant such power to a priest
or intermediary. The Roman emperor Constantine would have been robbed of the political
power he intended to employ through the
Church if this book had been added to the
canon. Is it any wonder the Church ordered it
destroyed?

Once again, we owe a debt of gratitude to the
Alexandrian Church fathers who buried it in the desert, thereby risking the
wrath of an emperor.

# THE MYSTERIOUS MARY OF MAGDALENE

After this, Jesus traveled about from one town and village to another, proclaiming the good news of the kingdom of God. The Twelve were with him, and also some women who had been cured of evil spirits and diseases: Mary (called Magdalene) from whom seven demons had come out; Joanna the wife of Chuza, the manager of Herod's household; Susanna; and many others. These women were helping to support them out of their own means. (Luke 8:1–3)

After the Sabbath, at dawn on the first day of the week, Mary Magdalene and the other Mary went to look at the tomb. There was a violent earthquake, for an angel of the Lord came down from heaven and, going to the tomb, rolled back the stone and sat on it. His appearance was like lightning, and his clothes were white as snow. The guards were so afraid of him that they shook and became like dead men. The angel said to the women, "Do not be afraid, for I know that you are looking for Jesus, who was crucified. He is not here; he has risen, just as he said. Come and see the place where he lay. Then go quickly and tell his disciples: 'He has risen from the dead and is going ahead of you into Galilee. There you will see him.' Now I have told you." So the women hurried away from the tomb, afraid yet filled with joy, and ran to tell his disciples. (Matthew 28: 1–8)

In the year 591 C.E., Pope Gregory I pronounced Mary Magdalene, or Mary of the Town of Magdala, a "sinful woman." Ever since then, until recently, she has been branded a prostitute. Why did the Pope say what he did without any biblical support? No one knows for sure. Perhaps he was afraid that Mary—a woman, obviously—was attracting too much power as one who was favored by Jesus. Such a position could upset the male hierarchy that had arisen in the Church since the early days.

Whatever the Pope's reason, he sure tainted the reputation of someone who seemed very important in the biblical accounts of the life and ministry of Jesus. In the first verse, quoted above, she was a wealthy patron who subsidized his work. In the second, she was the first to attest to the resurrection. In the course of the last 50 years or so, aided by a blockbuster novel by Dan

The idea that Mary Magdalene was a sinful prostitute finds its roots in the words of Pope Gregory I, who possibly wanted to ensure that a woman did not gain too much popularity among Christians.

Brown and the subsequent movie, *The Da Vinci Code*, things began to change. It wasn't long before Mary became "the disciple whom Jesus loved" more than all the rest, the mother of his child, and perhaps his wife.

Magdala was a Galilean fishing village. If Mary, a first-century Jewish woman, had enough money to underwrite an itinerate teacher and his band of traveling disciples, she probably inherited it from a deceased husband. As a rule, women did not inherit from their fathers. They were married off as soon as they were old enough to bear children. But the evidence that she was faithful to the end is seen in the fact that of all the disciples, she and another woman named Mary—"the other Mary"—were the only ones brave enough to visit Jesus's grave and the first to witness the resurrection.

Who is this mysterious figure?

The novelist Dan Brown makes quite a statement when he claims that Renaissance artist Leonardo da Vinci's famous mural *The Last Supper* actually shows Mary sitting at the right hand of Jesus during this pivotal meal. The Bible says this place was occupied by "the beloved disciple," but it doesn't specifically say who this disciple was. Usually, John is said to be that disciple, but although the phrase is used six times in the Bible, all the references appear in one Gospel, the Gospel according to John. If John is indeed talking about himself, then the author is not free from the charge of being a bit prejudiced.

If Mary did sit with the men at the famous supper, it would certainly have been a break with tradition. In the first century, a woman's place was usually in the kitchen. If Mary Magdalene is the "beloved disciple," the "one who Jesus loved," it would be dangerous to early Church authorities. Very early on, the Church was a male-dominated institution. The Apostle Paul himself makes this very clear in 1 Timothy 2:12: "I do not permit a woman to teach or to have authority over a man; she must be silent."

Some say that the figure to the left of Jesus (on Jesus' right) in the famous painting by Leonardo da Vinci at the church of Santa Maria delle Grazie in Milan is not a disciple but, instead, Jesus' beloved Mary. Indeed, the figure *does* look more like a woman than a man.

All this came into focus with the discovery of the Gospel of Mary, fragments of which were discovered near Akhmim, Egypt, in the late nineteenth century and eventually wound up in Berlin in 1986. It was quickly labeled a Gnostic Gospel, and it attracted a lot of attention when it was translated from Coptic because it had Peter asking a woman named Mary—apparently, Mary Magdalene—to tell the disciples some of the things Jesus had said to her but not to the other disciples.

Her reply would have been troubling to the Apostle Paul: "Yes, I will tell you what has been hidden from you." So much for Paul's admonition for women to be quiet.

Along with the discovery of the Gospel of Mary was found a text that has come to be known as the Apocryphon of John and the even more puzzling Sophia of Jesus Christ. "Sophia" is a Greek word meaning "wisdom" and is always used in the feminine sense. In other words, Sophia stands for feminine wisdom. That troubled the early Church fathers. Wisdom was not supposed to be in the possession of women. They were supposed to stay home and learn from their husbands.

To make things worse, a copy of the Sophia of Jesus Christ was later found in the Nag Hammadi Library, discovered in 1945. It was dated to the early second century, before Gnosticism was branded as heretical. It must have been a popular book. So far, three fragments, all from the second century, have been discovered, written in both Greek and Coptic. This is extremely rare. Usually, only one copy of anything this ancient survives. It must have been widely distributed to show up in three separate locations.

The Gospel of Mary, discovered in Akhmim, Egypt, relates some knowledge of Jesus that was told to Mary Magdalene but not the disciples.

Unfortunately, the first six pages of the book have never been found. No one knows what information they might have provided. All we have begins on page 7, right in the middle of a sentence.

The Gospel of Mary has never been recognized as canonical by the Church. Perhaps that is because, according to the text, Mary Magdalene was the only disciple who really understood Jesus's message. She got the fact that the kingdom to which Jesus referred was not going to supernaturally appear at some time in the future. It was here and now, but people didn't see it because it was a spiritual kingdom, not a physical one.

So, who was Mary Magdalene? Was she Jesus's beloved disciple? Was she his wife? Was she a Sybil—a mystic? Did she stand by Jesus when the men all stayed in hiding? Was she a devoted believer? Was she a prostitute? Was she labeled a "sinful woman" by a pope who did what many men do when they are threatened by a powerful woman—attack her character and reputation? Was she the matriarch of a secret dynasty that grew up in France and Europe, as Dan Brown put forth in his fictional account? Did she pass on Jesus's bloodline? In that sense, did she, herself, become the Holy Grail— the vessel that contained the blood of Christ?

From the rather sketchy accounts we find in the traditional four Gospels, we really can't answer those questions. But there is no doubt that she has become a blank page on which is written the changing cultural prejudices of Western civilization. When we wanted a celibate nun, we pointed to Mary Magdalene. When we wanted an erotic feminine presence, there she was. When we wanted a shrewd businesswoman with the means to support Jesus and his disciples, we looked her up. When we needed a courageous feminine witness to a miracle, one who stood strong when men trembled in their homes, she stood astride religious tradition like a colossus of spirituality in the face of persecution. When we needed a scapegoat, she provided a convenient example.

Who *was* Mary Magdalene? We don't know.

Who *is* Mary Magdalene? Simply put, she is whoever we want her to be. Christians worship Mary, the mother of Jesus. But they can identify with Mary of Magdala. And that is a big difference.

# The Censored Gospel in Item 17,202

> Pharaoh gave Joseph the name Zaphenath-Paneah and gave him Aseneth daughter of Potiphera, priest of On, to be his wife.
>
> And Joseph went throughout the land of Egypt. (Genesis 41:45)

If the story is true, 1,450 years ago an ancient, anonymous monk wrote an account that purports to tell the real history of the life and times of Jesus, including never-before-heard details about his social life, his family, and his political life. Written in Syriac, it has only recently been translated into English. It confirms that Jesus was married to Mary Magdalene, gives the names of their two children, and reveals that 13 years prior to the crucifixion, there was a foiled assassination attempt on his life that involved not only Jesus but his whole family. It asserts that Jesus was connected to powerful politicians high in the Roman Empire and that he was part of a religious movement that predates the activities of the Apostle Paul.

The whole story is told in a book published in 2014 called *The Lost Gospel: Decoding the Ancient Text That Reveals Jesus' Marriage to Mary the Magdalene*, written by Simcha Jacobovici, an investigative journalist, and Barrie Wilson, a religious studies historian.

According to their research, Mary Magdalene was not Jewish at all. She was a Phoenician or Egyptian priestess who was thought to be an incarnation of the goddess Artemis. Jesus was a figure modeled after Helios, god of the sun. Their history was written during his lifetime and finally encoded in a sixth-century manuscript called "Joseph and Aseneth." It lay buried among the stacks of the British Library in London until its discovery by the authors of *The Lost Gospel*.

The new book has, of course, been the subject of scathing attacks. Even late-night TV hosts got in on it. In March 2014, Conan O'Brien, the popular host of an evening talk show, when hearing that Jesus was married and had two kids, quipped, "In other words, he suffered even more than we thought."

How did the authors break the coded manuscript that had remained hidden in plain sight all these years?

It was easy. When they translated into English the ancient manuscript that formed a part of a group of texts dubbed Item 17,202, all they did was replace the name "Joseph" with "Jesus" and "Aseneth" with "Mary Magdalene."

The 1656 painting *Jacob Blessing Ephraim and Mannaseh* by Rembrandt illustrates a scene from the popular tale of Joseph and Aseneth.

The original story was embellished from one Bible verse, Genesis 41:45, and told a complex tale about the love affair between the biblical Joseph and Aseneth, his wife, who bore him two sons, Manasseh and Ephraim. Scholars have long debated whether it was an allegory or historical account, but the version titled "Joseph and Aseneth" was probably written somewhere between 200 B.C.E. and 200 C.E.

Aseneth was the daughter of an Egyptian priest who served in Heliopolis. Joseph, of course, was the Jewish patriarch who was sold into slavery by his brothers and, through a long, convoluted process, wound up as an Egyptian political ruler second only to Pharaoh. Aseneth is fed honey by a disguised heavenly entity and soon converts to Judaism, worshipping the god of Joseph. Following a period of romance and eventual marriage, she bears Joseph two sons. The story develops a complicated twist when the son of the Pharaoh, envious of Joseph's standing with the Egyptian hierarchy, recruits Dan and Gad, two of Joseph's brothers, to kill Joseph. The plot is thwarted by two of his other brothers, Benjamin and Levi.

"Joseph and Aseneth" was a popular manuscript. At least 16 sources refer to it, so it was read widely. Written originally in Greek, the oldest existing manuscript is a Syriac manuscript. The names Jesus and Mary Magdalene do not appear anywhere in it. What Jacobovici and Wilson did was simply substitute their names for the heroes of the story. They see in it an encoded allegory that secretly reveals the true story of Jesus. In Jacobovici's words: "It returns Jesus

HE [WILSON] SEES IT AS A DISTORTION OF JESUS'S MESSAGE, INVENTED TO PROMOTE PAUL'S OWN POLITICAL AGENDA.

to history, it returns Mary Magdalene to the story. Not only is he married—but [the manuscript] celebrates his sexuality. She, his wife, is not just Mrs. Jesus. She's actually a goddess. He's the son of God, she's the daughter of God." No wonder Jacobovici refers to himself as "the Jew who found Jesus."

Read this way, the story reveals that Jesus was much more than a lowly carpenter's son from the town of Nazareth. He was a powerful political figure who was the target of a plot engineered at the highest levels of government.

Wilson, the coauthor, has long held the position that Christianity began as a political/religious movement orchestrated by the Apostle Paul. He sees it as a distortion of Jesus's message, invented to promote Paul's own political agenda. Paul was both a Jewish scholar and a Roman citizen. As a Jew he could not have attained the personal power he craved, but as the leader of a movement that eventually rose to become the state religion of Rome, his opportunities would have been limitless had things turned out differently. Jesus's religion, according to Wilson, was much more, shall we say, sensual than the religion that grew to promote asceticism and male hierarchy.

The authors of *The Lost Gospel* claim that "Joseph and Aseneth" was written during Jesus's lifetime and presents the real picture—a form of religion that featured the figure of James, the Lord's brother. If it had flourished, it would have promoted Gnosticism.

The four canonical Gospels, on the other hand, were modeled after the religion later developed by the Apostle Paul. Jacobovici and Wilson find many other clues in the text involving hidden meanings, encoded to protect the lives of the original authors. They refer to examples such as the phrases "Son of God" and "Bride of God," which later made their way into Christian vocabulary. They point out that the text itself seems to refer to hidden meanings.

*The Lost Gospel* has been viciously attacked and called everything from "historical nonsense" to "a Monty Python sketch." Those attacks, in themselves, constitute a good reason to read it. I have noted in other books that when facts are scarce, the usual way to attack a theory is to ridicule the character of its author. Jacobovici and Wilson have certainly drawn more than their fair share of ridicule.

Simcha Jacobovici is an Emmy-winning investigative journalist and film director. Along with religious history scholar Barrie Wilson, he wrote the controversial *The Lost Gospel* in 2014.

On the other hand, no less a biblical scholar than Dr. Rivka Nir, a professor in the Department of History, Philosophy, and Judaic Studies at the Open University of Israel, is on record with quite a different take:

Despite the problematic thesis, this is a serious-minded, thought-provoking and interesting book, giving expression to an excellent knowledge of early Christian sources and the ability to analyze and integrate them into a clear and comprehensible picture. The book abounds with historical surveys and enlightening discussions on its sources, terms, characters and various period-related aspects....

This book will certainly occupy a highly important place in the scholarly quest for the historical Jesus, as it raises the fundamental question: how far can scholars go in this quest?

How far, indeed? As in all quests for new and controversial ways of approaching biblical studies and, for that matter, most other creative endeavors as well, stay tuned!

# THE HIDDEN YEARS

A t the inauguration of U.S. President Barack Obama in January 2009, the invocation was delivered by Rev. Rick Warren, the Christian evangelical pastor of Saddleback Church, a California megachurch associated with the Southern Baptist Convention. In it, he referred to Jesus, Yeshua, and Isa.

Most English-speaking people recognize the name Jesus. Those who speak Hebrew will recognize the name Yeshua, from which the English "Jesus" is derived. And the name Isa is found throughout the Quran; it is the name Muhammad used to refer to Jesus. A variant is also used in India. In 1894, Nicolas Notovitch published a book titled *The Life of Saint Issa, Best of the Sons of Man: The Missing Years of Jesus and His Travels in the East.* It purports to be the story of Jesus and his travels in the East during a period in his life called the "missing years."

The four Gospel accounts in the New Testament—Matthew, Mark, Luke, and John—tell the story of Jesus. Of the four, only two refer to his birth—Matthew, which tells the story of the visit of the Magi, or Eastern kings, and Luke, which tells about the angelic visitation to shepherds, out abiding in their fields. These are the only two references in the Bible to Jesus's birth. Not even the Apostle Paul, whose letters comprise a third of the New Testament and were among the first texts to be included in the canon, bothers to mention anything at all about the birth of Jesus, let alone the fact that he was born of a virgin. One would think that if that fact was considered important in the years following Jesus's death, Paul would have at least mentioned it.

So, what we're left with are two chapters in Matthew and one in Luke that cover Jesus's birth. That's it. Then, except for a few brief paragraphs in Luke, all the Gospels skip to Jesus's baptism, an event that happened when he was roughly 30 years old. The only event from these three decades mentioned in the Bible is covered in a few paragraphs in Luke, wherein Jesus makes a trip to Jerusalem when he was 12. There, he amazes the local priests with his knowledge.

So, what happened during the 18 years in the life of Jesus between the ages of 12 and 30? Those are called the "missing years." We've already studied a few accounts called the Infancy Gospels. But they are by no means the only speculative texts. Whole legends have built up about these years, some of them quite imaginative, others purportedly built on historical facts, albeit circumstantial ones. Here are just a few.

The story of the birth of Jesus—though a huge part of Christian culture today—is only given two chapters in Matthew and one in Luke. Except for a brief passage about Jesus at age 12, nothing of his life is mentioned again until he is roughly 30 years old.

## Jesus in Great Britain

The Roman Church likes to claim they "Christianized" the Britons beginning with the mission of Augustine in 597 C.E., but in actuality, there were Christian missions established as early as the first century. As a matter of fact, although the belief has been discredited by most mainstream historians, there are those who claim Christianity was brought to Britain by none other than Joseph of Arimathea, described in all four biblical Gospels as a righteous and wealthy man who volunteered his own tomb as a burial place for Jesus after the crucifixion. Although he was a member of the Jewish Sanhedrin, he believed Jesus to be the Messiah, and along with Nicodemus, another member of the Jewish ruling council, he made sure there was a proper burial. He also was said to have somehow obtained the cup that was used at the Last Supper, an item that became known as the Holy Grail.

Later authors claimed he amassed his fortune in the tin trade. In order to do that, he must have made journeys to Cornwall, a land of tin mines and the major source of that precious product used throughout the Bronze Age. If so, he certainly would have become familiar with British traders. Some legends link him to Jesus, claiming that Joseph of Arimathea was Mary's uncle and that the boy Jesus might even have journeyed to Cornwall with him.

Thus it was that in 1804, the English poet William Blake would write in his epic poem *Jerusalem*, sometimes referred to as England's second national anthem:

> And did those feet in ancient time
> Walk upon England's mountains green:
> And was the Holy Lamb of God,
> On England's pleasant pastures seen?

Legend goes on to claim that St. Philip, one of the original 12 disciples of Jesus, sent Joseph, along with the Holy Grail, to England following the resurrection. There, Joseph built Britain's first church. Some call it the first Christian church ever built anywhere in the world. He hid the grail in the well at Glastonbury. To this day, it's called the Chalice Well. Glastonbury, surrounded by water in those days, is a longtime candidate for the location of the Isle of Avalon, where Arthur and Guinevere are said to have been buried. Early monks claimed to have discovered their grave remains, but most scholars think such claims were a publicity stunt to increase tourism.

Early Christianity in Britain was quite different from the Roman brand that arrived with St. Augustine. It tended to leave a lot more room for so-called pagan beliefs. It embraced more of what later was declared heretical. In other words, it wasn't nearly so dismissive of magicians such as Merlin the Enchanter who, according to legend, was the power behind King Arthur of Camelot. Even centuries later, during the time that just preceded Merlin, there was intensive theological disagreement between Britain and Rome. Pelagius (360–420)—who lived at the same time as Augustine of Hippo (354–430), a favored source of inspiration for the Protestant reformers of the sixteenth century—was a British theologian who favored free will

William Blake's *Joseph of Arimathea among the Rocks of Albion* (1773) adheres to the idea that Joseph was in England as part of his tin trade business. It has been speculated that Jesus might have accompanied him.

and asceticism. Augustine, who believed in predestination, original sin, and the impossibility of humans earning any measure of their salvation by good works alone, declared Pelagius a heretic. When Pelagianism was ruled a heresy by Rome, many British believers simply ignored the decree.

With all this going on, the common folk tended to embrace all of the above. They went to Mass on Sunday, celebrated saints' days throughout the year, prayed to Saints Mary and Joseph, and put out offerings for the local gods every evening at dusk.

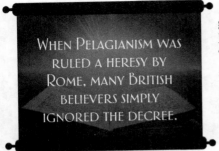

WHEN PELAGIANISM WAS
RULED A HERESY BY
ROME, MANY BRITISH
BELIEVERS SIMPLY
IGNORED THE DECREE.

Somehow, the whole culture was held together by the Roman presence in southern England, and it managed to hang on until 410 C.E. That's when so-called "barbarians" began to nip away at Rome's eastern European borders, making such inroads that the emperor was forced to pull his troops out of Britain and bring them back to protect the homeland.

Almost overnight, Britain was thrown into chaos. The wealthy class, who considered themselves to be Roman citizens, were left with a lot of money and no protection. Many buried their precious jewels and golden tableware and departed for safer lands, hoping to someday return and reclaim their wealth. Perhaps their clandestine endeavors were quietly observed by the native Celts who remained behind, who then looted the treasure troves, burying them again in undisclosed locations. Ever since that time, there have been stories about finding a pot of gold at the end of the rainbow.

Such unprotected wealth attracted other folks as well. Angles and Saxons from western Europe began to dream of easy pickings across the channel and launched exploratory raids. British kings from Cornwall, Wales, and the northern provinces, as well as those who now commanded those areas formerly guarded by Roman troops in the south, began to rise up against one another, hoping to be the central figure that could dominate all of Britain and be the one king who could rule them all in the name of Jesus—who, according to legend, "walked upon England's mountains green" during the missing years of his early life.

## Jesus in India

One of the most prevalent theories about Jesus's missing years has him going to India, where he studied with mystics and rishis, the holy men of Hinduism, and Buddhist adepts. Buddhism was, by the time of Jesus's birth, already 500 years old. Hinduism was already ancient, tracing its roots back as far as 6,000 years or more.

This is the theory put forth in the study we previously mentioned, Nicolas Notovitch's 1894 book *The Life of Saint Issa, Best of the Sons of Man: The Missing Years of Jesus and His Travels in the East.* In that book, Notovitch, a Russian aristocrat and Cossack officer, perhaps even a spy, but certainly a journalist, claimed to have seen what he said was a third-century manuscript purporting that Jesus trained with Buddhist mystics in a monastery high in the Himalayas. To prepare himself for that episode, Jesus studied for six years in Puri and Rajgirh, near Nalanda, an ancient seat of

Hindu teaching. Then, after a journey through Persia, he returned to his homeland at the age of 29, where he was baptized by John in the Jordan River and began his public ministry.

A variant on this theory says that rather than making the journey during his missing years, Jesus survived the crucifixion and secretly traveled there after his supposed death. That, of course, would add fuel to the fires of the empty tomb story. This tale even says Jesus was eventually buried in India.

If any of this is true, those who compiled the New Testament either didn't know about it or neglected to include it when it came time to put the canon of Scripture together.

Those who insist on at least considering these stories have some interesting points to make. The famous trade route

Russian journalist Nicolas Notovitch claimed that Jesus journeyed to India as a boy, where he studied with Hindu and Buddhist teachers.

known today as the Silk Road was heavily used in the first century. It would have been standard practice to travel east with a caravan. Indeed, this is probably the journey in reverse that was made by the Magi, the "Three Kings." ("Three" is the number used, even though the Bible never says how many made the trip. The tradition of assuming there were three of them probably stems from the fact that three gifts were presented at the manger—gold, frankincense, and myrrh.) The Magi are usually identified as Persian, or Zoroastrian, scholars, who were famous for their knowledge of astronomy and astrology. Indeed, the great Indian sage Paramahansa Yogananda—who, during the 32 years he lived in America, introduced millions of people to Kriva Yoga and his Self-Realization Fellowship—claimed he could detect in the life and teaching of Jesus an Eastern overlay.

Tradition has it that St. Thomas was the first Christian apostle to travel to India following the crucifixion. India claims that the one called "Doubting" Thomas lived and taught Christianity there for 20 years until his death.

SMITHSONIAN MAGAZINE PUBLISHED AN ARTICLE IN JANUARY 2013 THAT REPORTED THE INTERESTING STORY OF THE SHINGO SAVIOR.

## Jesus in Japan

One of the most entertaining "missing years" theories is that during that time, Jesus became a disciple of a Buddhist master who taught in the vicinity of Mount Fuji. There, he became fluent in the Japanese language.

It gets stranger. *Smithsonian* magazine published an article in January 2013 that reported the interesting story of the Shingo Savior.

In northern Japan, in the town of Shingo some 480 miles (780 kilometers) from Mount Fuji, lies a tomb of a shepherd who, some 2,000 years ago, settled down to grow garlic. He fell in love with a farmer's daughter whose name was Miyuko, married her, and had three children. After a long life, he died at the age of 106. The people who lived there call him Daitenku Taro Jurai. The rest of the world knows him as Jesus Christ.

Thus it is that the native inhabitants of Shingo refer to their village as *Kirisuto no Sato*, which roughly translates to "Christ's Hometown." Every year thousands of pilgrims visit the site, supplementing the town's income, which otherwise comes from a local yogurt factory. The visitors view the tomb and visit the Legend of Christ Museum, whose gift shop sells them religious relics and the staple of all museums, Jesus coffee mugs. Every spring visitors flock to attend the annual Christ Festival. As the *Smithsonian* article describes it, it is "a mashup of multidenominational rites in which kimono-clad women dance around the twin graves and chant a three-line litany in an unknown language. The ceremony, designed to console the spirit of Jesus, has been staged by the local tourism bureau since 1964."

How did this all come about? It's a fascinating story.

Apparently, Jesus first came to Japan during his missing years when he was 21 years old to study theology. His ship landed at the coastal port of Amanohashidate in Miyazu Bay, and from there, he traveled nearly 300 miles (480 kilometers) to study with a master teacher in the shadow of Mount Fuji.

At the age of 33, he returned home to Judea, traveling through Morocco on the way.

Then follows the well-known story as it is told in the biblical Gospels but with a twist. Jesus, it seems, didn't die on the cross. Instead, he traded places with his brother, Isukiri. He secretly got out of town and traveled back to Japan, carrying one of Isukiri's severed ears and a lock of hair from the Virgin Mary as keepsakes. This time he made a four-year journey through Siberia to Alaska and thence another journey home to Japan, landing in Hachinohe, where he rode overland in an oxcart to the village of Shingo.

Legend among some Christians in Japan is that Jesus did not die on the cross but, instead, returned to Japan after his initial visit. There, he died peacefully in Shingo Village, where visitors can visit the tomb pictured here.

There, he lived in obscurity, took on a new identity, and raised a family. For the rest of his life, he ministered to the sick and needy.

According to local legend, he was mostly bald, with a few gray hairs, and had a distinctive nose, which the museum brochure says earned him the reputation of being a "long-nosed goblin."

When Jesus died of very old age, according to custom, his body was left exposed on a hill for four years. Then his bones were gathered and buried in a grave. That grave now sports a timber cross and is kept safe from gawkers by a picket fence. Isukiri's severed ear is buried in the adjacent burial plot.

Although only about 1 percent of Japanese today are Christian, the stories go that in ancient times, the people who lived in this section of Japan wore clothes that resembled the togalike robes of biblical Palestine. Women wore veils, and babies were carried in baskets like those in the Holy Land. Newborn children were swaddled in clothes embroidered with a design that resembled a Star of David, and their foreheads were marked with charcoal crosses.

Is any of this true? You'll have to decide for yourself, but the folks who run the museum sure seem to think it is.

The Inca god Viracocha (also known by the variants Wiracocha, Apu Gun Tiqsi Wiraqutra, Con-Tici, and Kon-Tiki) was said to be a white man of tall stature who could walk on water and brought peace to the land.

## Jesus in America

Throughout the Americas, from Canada down to Peru and further, there are ancient stories of a "white prophet" who appeared mysteriously among the people. In Peru and Bolivia lived a civilization with a rich legacy and a vivid memory of the past. Their mythology, later transcribed by Spanish priests whose predecessors had burned all the original documents, spoke of a "white man of large stature and authoritative demeanor." He was old and gray-haired, and, in their words, "he spoke to them with love." They recounted that he brought them the blessings of civilization.

Before he appeared, they said, the land was full of chaos. But when he left them to travel across the Pacific—some say he walked on the water, others say he used rafts—he left order and a better life behind. His name, they said, was Viracocha, the "Foam of the Sea." In other versions of the tale, he was called Kon Tiki.

A similar story is found in Mexico and Central America. The one who brought civilization to these places was called Quetzalcoatl. He is remembered as an *hombre blanco*, a large, white man, and he had a flowing beard. Like Viracocha to the west and south, he wore a long, white robe; condemned the sacrifices that spiritually polluted the people; taught them how to use proper cooking fires; and showed them how to "live together as husband and wife." He arrived from the sea "in a boat that moved without paddles" and "taught the people how to live in peace." When he was eventually rebuffed by a local group who felt threatened by his message, he departed, sailing away "toward the rising sun."

Further north, and later in time, a Mound Building culture arose, but no one really knows why. For the next 5,000 years or so, the culture would go through at least three separate phases, called the Adena, Hopewell, and Mississippian periods. The mounds certainly caught on. The practice spread up the Mississippi River to the Great Lakes and all the way to the East Coast.

Ever since the 1800s, most scholars have assumed the mounds were built by the indigenous people who lived there, but some have made other guesses. Some people, including many who are members of the Church of Jesus Christ of Latter-day Saints, believe they were built by members of the Ten Lost Tribes of Israel, including the Nephites, the Laminites, and the Mulekites.

According to LDS (Latter-day Saints) doctrine, Joseph Smith discovered the original LDS Scriptures in Palmyra, New York, at Hill Cumorah, a drumlin (long hill) left by the last glacier that slowly receded from upper New York State 10,000 years ago. The texts were purported to have been written on gold tablets or plates in ancient

The Church of Jesus Christ of Latter-day Saints (Mormons) was founded by Joseph Smith, a man who claimed he found tablets in New York about how a group of Jews fled to the New World and that Jesus later visited them there.

times by a 24-year-old man named Mormon, who, before his death, passed them on to his son Moroni. Moroni was a general of a tribe called the Nephites and was the last survivor of a battle with the Lamanites. Before his death he buried the plates on Hill Cumorah. About 1,400 years later, Joseph Smith is said to have found and translated them.

According to Church history, when he was 14 years old, Joseph Smith became caught up in one of the many religious revivals that swept through the area. He prayed to God to let him know which church to join.

God's answer to Smith's prayer was that he shouldn't join any church but should instead wait for guidance. In Smith's words, "I saw a pillar of light exactly over my head, above the brightness of the sun, which descended gradually until it fell upon me."

Seven years later, Moroni, now a resurrected angel, visited Smith and told him about the buried plates. He led Joseph to Hill Cumorah and revealed the hiding place. The tablets were written in a language Smith called Re-

JOSEPH SMITH WAS CONVINCED THAT THE "OTHER SHEEP" WERE THE DESCENDANTS OF LEHI, IN FAR-OFF AMERICA.

formed Egyptian Hieroglyphics, a language totally unknown to the young man. But he was given a pair of special spectacles that allowed him to read and translate the text. The result is called the Book of Mormon.

The story of the book begins with a Jewish prophet named Lehi who lived in Jerusalem before the time of Christ. In true Jewish prophetic fashion, Lehi warned the sinners around him that they would be punished and destroyed if they didn't repent, but they rejected his message.

Lehi escaped into the wilderness with his wife, Sariah, and his sons, Laman, Lemuel, Sam, and Nephi, taking with them the history of his people that had been written on brass plates. Lehi's response was simple obedience: "I will go and do the things which the Lord hath commanded."

Guided by a gift from God called a *liahona*, a kind of compass, Lehi eventually came to the sea, where he was told to build a boat and sail to the Promised Land.

Nephi was obedient to his father. Laman and Lemuel were not. Their descendants came to be known as Lamanites. The descendants of Nephi became the Nephites. The Nephites were charged with continuing to keep the records originally begun on the plates they carried with them.

After many adventures in a new land, now called the Americas, the wicked Lamanites eventually fought an epic battle with the righteous Nephites. Before the end, however, a Lamanite prophet named Samuel prophesied that Jesus Christ would soon be born.

The Bible records that this birth took place in a little town called Bethlehem, in Judea. There, Jesus grew to manhood, healed and blessed the people, was crucified, and, three days later, rose from the dead.

But he had left a message behind. "Other sheep I have, which are not of this fold: them also I must bring, and they shall hear my voice; and there shall be one fold, and one shepherd" (John 10:16).

Joseph Smith was convinced that the "other sheep" were the descendants of Lehi, in far-off America.

Sure enough, LDS doctrine teaches that after his resurrection in Jerusalem, Jesus indeed appeared in the New World, carrying on the ministry he had begun in Jerusalem.

The story ties in the visit to Mesoamerica of Quetzalcoatl, a bearded stranger from across the sea, found in Olmec, Maya, and Inca oral history, with the legends of a fierce battle way up north on the plain below Hill Cumorah in New York

An 1841 illustration shows Joseph Smith preaching to Indians. Some Indians today, such as a few Cherokees, still believe they are descendants of the Lamanites.

State. Some project these legends onto the Mound Building cultures of the Ohio Valley. To this day, although recent DNA evidence casts doubts, many Cherokees believe they are descended from the Lost Tribes of Israel.

The lost New World civilizations called the Nephites and the Lamanites even lend their names to American history. The theory that American Indian tribes are descended from ancient Israelites used to be called the "Lamanite theory," and it was popular well into the early twentieth century.

The legend reaches out and embraces more connections between ancient Israel and the Americas. A parallel theme in the Book of Mormon theorizes that the Americas became the home of the Jaredite civilization after the events related in the biblical stories about the breakup of humankind following the confounding of languages at the Tower of Babel.

Traditional archaeologists are quick to point out discrepancies in these stories. Especially popular are arguments thought to be anachronistic. Certain domesticated animals such as horses, cattle, sheep, and swine are all mentioned in the Book of Mormon, but archaeological evidence seems to indicate that these animals were not yet raised during the time frames given in the texts.

Likewise, certain technologies, such as chariots, seem out of place, given the fact that Mesoamerican civilizations had not yet invented the wheel. The

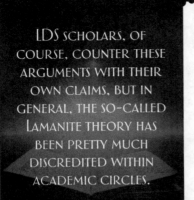

LDS SCHOLARS, OF COURSE, COUNTER THESE ARGUMENTS WITH THEIR OWN CLAIMS, BUT IN GENERAL, THE SO-CALLED LAMANITE THEORY HAS BEEN PRETTY MUCH DISCREDITED WITHIN ACADEMIC CIRCLES.

swords used by the armies of Lamanites and Nephites were said to have rusted with age, but iron wasn't known in the Americas until much later. Barley and wheat appear in the Book of Mormon, but they weren't introduced to the Americas until after 1492.

LDS scholars, of course, counter these arguments with their own claims, but in general, the so-called Lamanite theory has been pretty much discredited within academic circles. Typically, anyone who even brings it up is ostracized in any academic discussion. Academics bring up the "magic glasses" Joseph Smith used to translate the Golden Plates and wonder about his reluctance to show them to the public. They ask about their disappearance; the lack of witnesses except for a few carefully chosen, trusted elders; and the reluctance on the part of the LDS church to allow any excavations on Hill Cumorah to look for artifacts left from the last great war that was said to have taken place there, let alone bones from the thousands of warriors said to have died in that battle.

Generally speaking, then, there is a lot of oral history concerning Jesus in the Americas. But acceptance of those stories seems to break down into two camps: those who choose to believe them, and those who don't.

There you have it. What happened to Jesus during his missing years between the ages of 12 and 30? Exotic stories about England, India, Japan, and the Americas are certainly interesting. They're even intriguing. But what evidence backs them up?

The traditional understanding is fairly concrete. We find it in the Gospels of Matthew and Mark—one verse in each, and they are almost identical. Here, for instance, is the verse from Matthew 13:55. When confronted with Jesus and his miracles, this is the reaction from his neighbors:

> Isn't this the carpenter's son? Isn't his mother's name Mary, and aren't his brothers James, Joseph, Simon and Judas?

The Gospel according to Mark adds a further tidbit:

> And they took offense at him.

For centuries, the understanding was that Joseph was a carpenter and that Jesus followed in his footsteps until the age of 30, when he hit the road as a traveling prophet and evangelist.

The most outlandish interpretation orthodox scholarship would risk is typical of that proposed by Robby Gallaty, pastor of the Long Hollow Baptist

Church in Nashville, Tennessee. In his book *The Forgotten Jesus*, he points out that both Matthew and Mark use the Greek word *tekton*, which doesn't necessarily refer to a worker in wood, as is implied with the word "carpenter." The term could also refer to a stonemason or craftsman. He points out that most houses in Nazareth were constructed of stone in those days, trees being in short supply. Also, Nazareth was located only three miles from Sepphoris, which at that time was undergoing urban renewal and was located only a few miles from a massive rock quarry.

Armed with this information, he asks, "Was Jesus really a carpenter?" To add to his breakthrough, he quotes Bible verses such as Psalm 118:22 and Luke 20:17–18:

> The stone which the builders rejected has become the chief cornerstone.

> Jesus looked directly at them and asked, "Then what is the meaning of that which is written: 'The stone the builders rejected has become the cornerstone'? Everyone who falls on that stone will be broken to pieces; anyone on whom it falls will be crushed."

This is interesting stuff, to be sure. But really—stonemason, carpenter—does it make a lot of difference? The basic idea is the same. Jesus spent his time during the mysterious missing years working at his father's trade. Does the exact description of that trade really matter?

Even Gallaty recognizes his inconsequential argument: "Whether Jesus was a carpenter working with wood or a stonemason has no bearing on his work as Savior of the world, but it does help us when we read the Bible, bringing a fresh sense of his words and their meaning."

Perhaps it does. Either way, the missing years are still mysterious, and the intrigue they generate still resounds throughout history. Assuming Jesus was a historical figure and not an invention springing forth from the mind of the Apostle Paul or some other power-hungry personage with a political agenda, what happened during those years? How did Jesus the youth transform into Jesus the visionary, perhaps even the savior of the world?

The truth is, we may never know.

# SHROUDED IN MYSTERY:
# THE ENIGMATIC SHROUD OF TURIN

For 2,000 years, Christians have insisted that Jesus died on the cross, was buried, and rose from the dead on Easter morning. It is perhaps the central, bedrock belief of the faith. The Apostle Paul summed it up in two famous verses:

> For I delivered to you as of first importance what I also received: that Christ died for our sins in accordance with the Scriptures, that he was buried, that he was raised on the third day in accordance with the Scriptures. (1 Corinthians 15:3–4)

The proof of these events was to be found in the testimony of three men who claimed to be eyewitnesses—Matthew, Luke, and John—who were believed to have written the Gospel accounts. We can't really include Mark in this company because the earliest copies of his Gospel don't include the resurrection. Mark's final chapter, chapter 16, which now appears in most versions of the Bible, speaks of the resurrection, but it was a later addition.

For those who didn't accept as valid the supernatural miracle behind these accounts, a pattern of reasoning eventually grew up that ran something like this. If Jesus didn't miraculously rise from the dead, what happened to the body? Only three scenarios could have brought about the empty tomb on resurrection morning:

- His enemies, presumably the Romans, but maybe conservative Jews who considered him to be a charlatan Messiah, snuck in and removed it during the night. The counter to this argument is one of motive. If that's what happened, it would have started the very rumors they wanted to quell. Why would they do such a thing?

- His friends could have quietly removed it. But to do so they would have had to overcome a Roman guard put there to prevent that very thing and then remove a great stone placed over the grave opening to keep anybody from getting in. Besides, even if they had managed to pull it off, news of the plot would assuredly have leaked out. Someone would have found out about it.

- If his enemies didn't do it, and his friends didn't do it, the only logical conclusion is that God did it, and the resurrection happened as Matthew, Luke, and John said it did.

A replica of the Tomb of Jesus in Nazareth Village in Israel reproduces the general belief of a round stone that covered the entrance and that Jesus arose and slid the stone aside in a miraculous resurrection.

This pattern of thought is based on a fallacy, however. It assumes that the Gospel accounts are accurate, written by those who were eyewitnesses and reliable in terms of the historical story they tell. But as textual criticism began to suggest that the Gospel accounts were written, in some cases, almost a hundred years after the events they record, by which time the authors whose names are affixed to the titles were long dead, a different, more scientific kind of evidence was sought. Does any forensic evidence exist that could stand up in a court of law?

Enter the famous Shroud of Turin. It purports to be the blood-stained burial cloth in which the body of Jesus was wrapped and reveals his negative image, complete with nail-scarred hands and feet, "recorded" on the very cloth itself, similar to a photographic plate. The recording process is said to have happened during the miraculous physical and spiritual transformation that brought Jesus back to life.

According to the Gospel of John, it happened like this:

> Joseph of Arimathea asked Pilate for the body of Jesus. Now Joseph was a disciple of Jesus, but secretly, because he feared the Jewish leaders. With Pilate's permission, he came and took the body away. He was accompanied by Nicodemus, the man who earlier had visited Jesus at night. Nicodemus brought a

mixture of myrrh and aloes, about seventy-five pounds. Taking Jesus' body, the two of them wrapped it, with the spices, in strips of linen. This was in accordance with Jewish burial customs. At the place where Jesus was crucified, there was a garden, and in the garden a new tomb, in which no one had ever been laid. Because it was the Jewish day of Preparation, and since the tomb was nearby, they laid Jesus there.

Notice the key words, "the two of them wrapped it … in strips of linen." This was the famous burial shroud that many believe is the Shroud of Turin. Those who support this thesis insist it contains actual forensic evidence that Jesus rose from the dead "in accordance with the Scriptures."

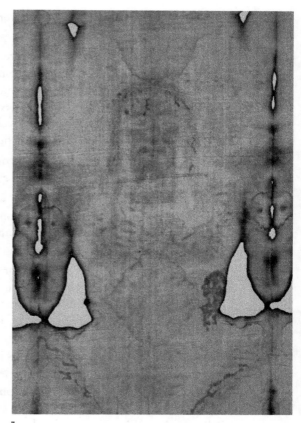

The famous Shroud of Turin shows a negative image of a man resembling Jesus. Some call it a fake, but a spectroscopy test in 2013 dated it back to between 280 B.C.E. and 220 C.E.

But is it authentic? Certainly, it contains bloodstains and an actual image and conforms to the typical burial customs of the times. But is it real, or is it a forgery? If it is a forgery, who did it? How old is the cloth? Can it be traced by physical evidence to first-century Palestine? That remains a mystery.

An extrabiblical text called the Gospel of the Hebrews is a second-century account that consists of only about 20 lines of surviving text. In it can be found one of the first references to what might be the Shroud of Turin: "After He had given the linen cloth to the servant of the priest he appeared to James."

It seems to talk about a burial shroud, certainly. But is it the shroud that can be seen today on display at the cathedral of Saint John the Baptist in Turin, Italy? Is this evidence that the shroud was actually handled and perhaps even venerated by the early followers of Jesus?

Let's take a quick walk through history to see if we can follow the 2,000-year journey of the Shroud of Turin.

According to the Bible, somewhere between the years 27 and 36 C.E., the apostles Peter and John and two women named Mary visited the tomb early in the morning of the "first day of the week." Jesus's body was gone, but the burial shroud in which it was wrapped remained, along with something that called John calls a *sudarium*, or facecloth, which was neatly folded and placed on the shelf where the body had been laid.

Here's how John describes the discovery:

> And so Simon Peter also came, following him, and entered the tomb; and he saw the linen wrappings lying there, and the face-cloth which had been on His head, not lying with the linen wrappings, but rolled up in a place by itself. (John 20:6–7)

This mysterious "facecloth" is sometimes called the Second Shroud of Turin. Jewish customs call for washing and covering the face of the deceased. Such a facecloth, or "napkin," was used to show respect to the family. Separate from the shroud that covered the body, John claims that this covering was neatly folded and set off to one side.

Such a facecloth exists today in the town of Oviedo in northern Spain. It has been housed there since 840 C.E. in a special chapel erected to house it, and it is shown three times a year: on Good Friday; on September 14, which is called the Feast of the Triumph of the Cross; and on September 21. Believers claim this is the actual sudarium that John describes in his Gospel.

The shroud, however, got separated from the sudarium a long time ago and now resides in Turin. It is, of course, much larger than the smaller face-cloth, measuring 14 feet, 3 inches (4.34 meters) in length and 3 feet, 7 inches (1.09 meters) in width. It is a single piece of cloth, woven in a herringbone fashion, and bears what appears to be the image of a crucified man—both front and back since the body was supposedly fully wrapped in it. It appears to have been stained with blood in a fashion that would be anatomically correct to crucifixion. The image of the figure retained on the cloth appears to be that of a man who was somewhere between 5 feet, 7 inches (1.7 meters) and 6 feet, 2 inches (1.8 meters) in height, wore a beard and moustache, and parted his hair in the middle. There also seem to be the impressions of coins placed over his eyes.

In 1898, when the cloth was investigated extensively for the first time, the image on the cloth appeared to be a photographic negative. In 1978, when the shroud was again released for extensive investigation, it was determined that the image was not caused by dyes, chemicals of any kind, or scorching. In addition, there was no evidence of any brushstrokes. The bloodstains were confirmed as well, and the blood type was AB positive—the same, incidentally, as that found on the Oviedo sudarium.

How did the relic wind up in Italy? It's quite a story.

Shortly after the crucifixion, when the disciples began to spread out and evangelize the world, a disciple named Thaddeus is reported to have traveled from Jerusalem to the city of Edessa, some 400 miles (643 kilometers) to the north. Edessa later became known as Urfa. Today, it is known as Şanlıurfa, Turkey, and is a place of pilgrimage because it is associated with the biblical prophets Job and Abraham.

The story goes that Thaddeus visited the city's ruler, Abgar V, who had been somehow corresponding with Jesus. Abgar had a disease and hoped Thaddeus might be able to heal him.

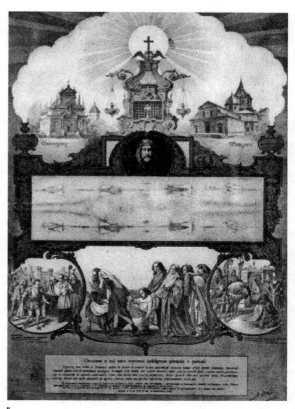

In 1898, the Shroud of Turin was put on exhibit (this is a poster advertising the exhibit). The cloth was examined and judged to be a photographic negative.

When Thaddeus arrived, he reportedly had a mysterious cloth imprinted with the image of Jesus. It became known as the Cloth of Edessa. More than a decade later, Abgar died and was succeeded by his son, who converted back to paganism. The cloth was hidden away to assure its protection.

Nothing more is known until the sixth century. The Persians had invaded and done damage to the walls of Edessa. During subsequent repair work, the cloth was rediscovered, and a church was built in which to safely house it. A manuscript was also discovered that told the story of how Joseph of Arimathea had collected the blood of Jesus on a linen cloth. In a text titled the Acts of Thaddeus, it was recorded that Jesus had wiped his face on the cloth, folded the shroud into four sections, and then left the tomb.

Now, the story jumps forward to 944 C.E., when the Roman emperor Romanus sent an army to transport the cloth from Edessa to Constantinople, now known as Istanbul. There, the cloth was unfurled during special ceremonies, somewhat like a banner to rally the citizenry. But when the Crusaders

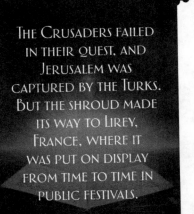

THE CRUSADERS FAILED
IN THEIR QUEST, AND
JERUSALEM WAS
CAPTURED BY THE TURKS.
BUT THE SHROUD MADE
ITS WAY TO LIREY,
FRANCE, WHERE IT
WAS PUT ON DISPLAY
FROM TIME TO TIME IN
PUBLIC FESTIVALS.

looted the treasures of Constantinople on their way to free the Holy Land, the cloth disappeared again, eventually surfacing in Athens, Greece.

The Crusaders failed in their quest, and Jerusalem was captured by the Turks. But the shroud made its way to Lirey, France, where it was put on display from time to time in public festivals. By then, however, its authenticity was questioned, so the festivals were cancelled, and the shroud was put away for another 34 years. This was the time period when the shroud was rumored to be under the protection of the Knights Templar.

Probably through the Templar connection, it somehow became the property of the Dukes of Savoy in Austria. They moved it to Chambery, England, until a fire almost destroyed it in 1578. For reasons of safety, it was moved to Turin, Italy, where, ironically, it survived another fire in 1997. Rumors of arson quickly spread. By then, the Cloth of Edessa was universally known as the Shroud of Turin.

As of this writing, the last time the shroud was exhibited was in August 2018.

At virtually every stage of this journey, some claimed the shroud was a forgery, but it is terribly difficult to figure out how it was created given the technology of the time. In 1988, for instance, a team of scientists from Switzerland, England, and the United States claimed that carbon dating concluded that the shroud originated in the Middle Ages between 1260 and 1390. But in 2013, infrared light and spectroscopy tests dated it back to between 280 B.C.E. and 220 C.E., which would place it within Jesus's lifetime.

It is because of these kinds of conflicting results and claims that the Church calls the shroud an "icon" rather than a "relic." What that means is that the Roman Catholic Church considers it a symbolic, rather than a historic, item. But that, too, is disputed in Church ranks.

How people view the shroud probably depends as much as anything on what they want to believe. But there is no denying the fact that magic and mystery are often associated with tombs, caves, and underground caverns. Ever since our first ancestors crawled back into the great caves of western Europe and began to paint vivid images on the walls of underground caverns, there has been something about deep spaces that has prompted transformative visions.

Jesus was born, supposedly, in a cave, at least according to some accounts. He was buried in a tomb and sealed in with a great stone. Elijah, a prophet of Israel, hid in a cave until he heard God speaking in a "still, small voice." Muhammad regularly retreated to a cave to meditate until he heard the voice of God telling him to write the Quran.

There is something about mysterious caves that still speaks to us. Is the Shroud of Turin the actual burial cloth of Jesus, imprinted by a miraculous or even magical process that transformed death to life in a way that was sheltered by the embrace of Mother Earth?

In the end, we each have to approach the mystery in our own way.

# CONCLUSIONS: A PERSONAL CONFESSION

> Of making many books there is no end, and much study wearies the body. (Ecclesiastes 12:12)

This book is divided into three main sections. The first, Part I, which we have just concluded, is a look at texts that didn't make the final cut when the Bible was assembled into the form we are familiar with today.

Part II examines conflicting texts from distinct cultures that were destroyed by the Church long after it had settled on the 66 (for Protestants), 73 (for Roman Catholics), or 78 (for Eastern Orthodox adherents) canonical books of the Bible. These texts, primarily from civilizations that were considered pagan and therefore heretical, seemed contradictory to accepted tradition.

Finally, in Part III, we look at texts that carry implications about the linear direction of history that most Bible believers accept.

At the end of each section, we'll try to draw some conclusions about the material we've studied. These insights, by their very nature, will need to be personal rather than objective. A historian cannot help but be influenced by the episodes of his or her own life, and I am no exception to the rule. I can't claim to be purely objective when it comes to biblical studies. I can try, but my personal conclusions will no doubt be shaped by the events of my own life.

If I can't be purely objective, then, I can at least warn you when I suspect my own prejudices are about to surface. Consider yourself duly forewarned.

What is the Bible, really? Why does it consist of some books and not others? Why is our version of Genesis or Matthew considered to be correct, maybe even divinely inspired, while the Genesis Apocryphon or the book of Enoch is not?

In short, the Bible, like it or not, is a special book, if not because it claims divine inspiration then because it holds a special place in the hearts of millions of believers, whether or not they have ever read it. Let me show you how this process works and, by doing so, try to make you understand why this subject has practical value in the life of everyone who takes it seriously. Bible study is not just an academic exercise. It can influence a life beyond measure.

When I first began to study the Bible in depth, I had undergone a recent, rather powerful, life-changing conversion experience. I soon became a

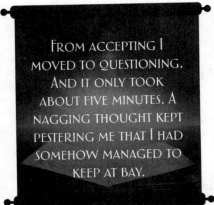

FROM ACCEPTING I MOVED TO QUESTIONING. AND IT ONLY TOOK ABOUT FIVE MINUTES. A NAGGING THOUGHT KEPT PESTERING ME THAT I HAD SOMEHOW MANAGED TO KEEP AT BAY.

Christian fundamentalist. Typical of most fundamentalists, be they religious, political, academic, or social, I was convinced of my beliefs. Foremost among them was that the Bible, as I understood it, was the word of God. Please understand that I meant only good. I thought that what I had come to believe was so powerful that it could change the world for the better. Chalk it up to the naiveté and idealism of youth.

Although I am no longer a fundamentalist, I still consider myself a Christian, but for a while, I walked a pretty tight line and eventually came within a hair's breadth of falling off. The more I studied the Bible and built my intellectual systematic theology on what I considered to be its inerrant texts, the more I came to believe that I was preaching a truth that could change people's lives for the better.

One day the whole structure fell apart. It was long in coming, and I'm sure I knew it on some level for years before I admitted it to myself, but there it was. From accepting I moved to questioning. And it only took about five minutes. A nagging thought kept pestering me that I had somehow managed to keep at bay. By this time, I had been studying the Bible in much more depth than most people ever bother to do. But the very fact of my familiarity became the problem. You see, when it came to content, the Bible held no secrets from me. We were like an old married couple who knew each other's strengths and weaknesses, so I was very much aware that there were troubling texts that seemed contradictory, inaccurate, or wrong. I had learned how to skirt around those portions, pretending they didn't exist. I had become similar to a lawyer, arguing in defense of a client I secretly knew was guilty. When I finally opened myself up to admitting it, there in the privacy of my lonely office one dark night, it led to my downfall.

Here's what happened. Over the years I had come to base my entire theology on biblical proof texts. This is a process by which you select texts from here and there, grant them all equal importance, and then assemble them to prove a point you have already decided is true.

But what if it could be demonstrated that the Bible is not without error? What if it isn't free from contradictions? What if it even contained some discrepancies or historical inaccuracies? Worse yet, what if the original authors never intended their work to be considered inerrant? In other words, what if the modern doctrine of inerrancy is something that is superimposed over a document that was meant to be understood in quite a different way?

If an argument about the existence of God hinges on proof texts selected from a Bible that is said to be without error, then all you have to do is show that the Bible contains some discrepancies. The argument is then over. God ceases to exist.

IS IT A SINGLE, COHERENT DOCUMENT THAT COMES STRAIGHT FROM THE MOUTH OF GOD? OR IS IT SOMETHING QUITE A BIT DIFFERENT?

Following this train of thought, I wasn't preaching about God anymore. I was preaching about an inerrant, infallible Bible. In my theology, the Bible had taken the place of God.

Put simply, this is the ghost that I have come to believe haunts almost every discussion about what the Bible means today. Is it a single, coherent document that comes straight from the mouth of God? Or is it something quite a bit different? As we have studied the work of various committees and redactors, I hope I have presented the historical fact that more went into writing the Bible than is often believed.

Some will argue that God had complete control over the whole process, from the original writing through the work of the selection committees and the final assembly. Perhaps the Apostle Paul best sums up this belief in 2 Timothy 3:

> All Scripture is God-breathed and is useful for teaching, rebuking, correcting and training in righteousness, so that the servant of God may be thoroughly equipped for every good work.

This argument falls victim to a number of fallacies, however.

First, it represents a faith statement, not evidence.

Second, it uses a proof text to justify the use of proof texting.

Third, it's not entirely clear that Paul even wrote 2 Timothy. Many biblical scholars consider it to be a later addition, written, at best, by a disciple of Paul or perhaps even someone who just wanted to capitalize on his name.

All this is to say that many folks do accept that the Bible is somehow different from other books because of its claim of divine inspiration. I once held that belief and still have many friends who do.

But I have moved on. Does that mean I am no longer a Christian and have rejected the Bible outright? Absolutely not! I still read the Bible almost daily, finding in it a great deal of comfort, wisdom, and inspiration. By pointing out that it might not have been written in the way many believe it was, I am not attempting to denigrate it all. Please don't take that meaning from my argument; it is not at all what I intend. I do not mean to throw out or in any way disparage the ancient texts of the Bible. Just the opposite, in fact. I want to open up and include much of what was known and understood by those who compiled the Bible but was rejected, possibly because of the same kind of predetermined, prejudicial attitudes that once held me firmly in their grasp.

Having made that clear, it's time to move on to a practical demonstration of how important it is to keep those prejudices in check.

Other ancient cultures wrote texts that were unknown to those who compiled the Bible. They were full of wisdom and insight. But they threatened the belief systems of those who came upon them after the Bible had been thoroughly accepted and adopted as "the only infallible rule of faith and practice." The damage inflicted on the cultures of these wisdom keepers was exhaustive. The knowledge lost to the world is incalculable. And most of the damage was perpetrated by those who claimed to be doing the work of God. There is no doubt that those who believed that divine wisdom could only be found within the pages of their own particular holy book influenced the course of world history, and we have all suffered from their actions.

It's time to move on and study a few examples.

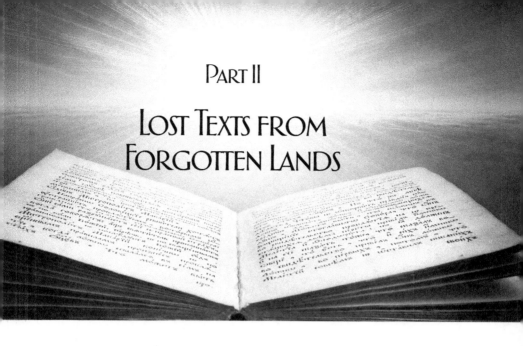

# Part II

# Lost Texts from Forgotten Lands

When the Bible was compiled, the Americas were virtually unknown to those from Europe and Asia.

Does that mean the Americas were uninhabited?

Absolutely not! Rich, full civilizations existed there and had for thousands of years.

Does that mean the people of the Americas were too primitive to discern wisdom from a universal consciousness some people call "God," which managed to produce stellar religious texts?

Again—no! The spirituality of many indigenous American people rivaled, and in many cases surpassed, that of anyone else in the world. And many of them produced texts equally as good as the Bible.

Does that mean there was no intercontinental contact during the time the Bible was being written and assembled?

No, it doesn't. But the average folks who lived in Europe, Africa, Asia, and the Middle East had little knowledge of continents across the sea. They may have known about far-off lands through rumor and gossip, but the idea of communing with them was, for the most part, unheard of.

When Christianity finally did come to the Americas, carried there by the conquistadores of Spain, the results were, for the most part, tragic. Here are a few case studies.

# THE MYSTERIOUS MAYA

When the Spanish conquistadores discovered the spirituality of the Maya people, there were a few among them who believed they had discovered a forgotten branch of the family of God. They found similar stories and ancient texts that were, in many ways, similar to the Bible stories with which they were familiar.

Take, for instance, the Quiché Maya creation text, the Popol Vuh. Because the ruling hierarchy of the Church considered the document to be pagan and "of the devil," they ordered it burned. But portions of some texts survived, thanks to the few farsighted priests who translated them and thought them important enough to be copied and secretly preserved.

The Popol Vuh we know today is undated, but it seems to have been copied down in its final form between 1554 and 1558 C.E. The legends it records, of course, are ancient.

The process was similar to how the Bible was written. Most of the Old Testament, for instance, was written down after 1000 B.C.E. But the stories it contains go back much further in time. Some hear in the Popol Vuh a faint echo of the familiar words of the book of Genesis that describe the creation of the world.

Here is an English translation by Allen J. Christenson interspersed with some familiar verses from Genesis. Read them both, and see if they harmonize. First the words from Genesis, then the Popol Vuh:

In the beginning ...

> This is the beginning of the ancient people of this place called Quiché. Here we shall write. We shall begin to tell the ancient stories of the beginning, the origin of all that was done in the citadel of Quiché, among the people of the Quiché nation.

God created the heavens and the earth ...

> First the earth was created, the mountains and the valleys.

And God said, "Let the waters under the sky be gathered to one place ..."

> The waterways were divided, their branches coursing among the mountains. Thus the waters were divided, revealing the great mountains.

God called the expanse, sky ...

A page from the Popol Vuh transcribed by Father Ximénez, who was in what is now Guatamala in 1701. It is written in both Spanish and the Quiché language of the Maya people.

For thus was the creation of the earth, created then by *Heart of Sky* and *Heart of Earth*, as they are called. They were the first to conceive it. The sky was set apart. The earth also was set apart within the waters.

And God said, "Let the earth team with living creatures ..."

Thus was conceived the successful completion of the work when they thought and when they pondered. Then were conceived the animals of the mountains, the guardians of the forest, and all that populate the mountains—the deer and the birds, the puma and the jaguar, the serpent and the rattlesnake, the pit viper and the guardian of the bushes. *She Who Has Borne Children* and *He Who Has Begotten Sons* then asked: "Shall it be merely solitary, merely silent beneath the trees and the bushes? It is well that there shall be guardians for them," they said. Thus they considered and spoke together, and immediately were created the deer and the birds. Having done this, they then provided homes for the deer and the birds.

Those who have read the first two chapters of the Bible will immediately find themselves on familiar ground. But the Popol Vuh isn't finished. The similarities continue. Here is an account of the creation of the first humans:

And God said, "Let us make humans in our own image ..."

These are the names of the first people who were framed and shaped: the first person was *Balam Quitze*, the second was *Balam Acab*, the third was *Mahucutah* and the fourth was *Iqui Balam*. These, then, were the names of our first mothers and fathers.

Like the Bible assures us, these "first people" seem to be endowed with some rather miraculous powers.

> Their frame and shape were merely brought about by the miraculous power and the spirit essence of the Framer and the Shaper, of *She Who Has Borne Children* and *He Who Has Begotten Sons*, of Sovereign and Quetzal Serpent.... They were able to speak and converse. They were able to look and listen.... Perfect was their sight, and perfect was their knowledge of everything beneath the sky. If they gazed about them, looking intently, they beheld (everything) that was in the sky and that which was upon the earth. Instantly they were able to behold everything. They did not have to walk to see all that existed beneath the sky. They merely saw it from wherever they were. Thus, their knowledge became full. Their vision passed beyond the trees and the rocks, beyond the lakes and the seas, beyond the mountains and the valleys.

Like their biblical counterparts, these "first people" had ambitions of being like God. And just like Adam and Eve, they got into trouble because of it when they said: "We have learned everything, great and small." Here, we see shades of "eating of the tree of the knowledge of good and evil." It seems that gods don't like it when humans try to emulate them too much. "Power to the people" brought about their demise:

> Thus their knowledge was taken back by *She Who Has Borne Children* and *He Who Has Begotten Sons*: "What now can be done to them so that their vision reaches only nearby, so that only a little of the face of the earth can be seen by them? For it is not good what they say.... It is a mistake that they have become like gods. Thus their eyes were blinded. They could (now) see only nearby; things were clear to them only where they were. Thus their knowledge was lost.

Apparently, by the time these stories were written down, the civilization to which they refer had already become lost to history. The writers refer to an ancient time that preceded their own. This is similar to the experience of the original authors of the Old Testament. The culture to which they refer had already made the leap from history to legend and from legend to myth.

We are left with questions the Maya might have been able to answer. They tell us these ancient people possessed a technology "that allowed them to see the whole world without moving from where they were." Given that we all have televisions and smartphones today, remote viewing like this is commonplace. But to what were the Maya referring?

Alas, we will probably never know, thanks to the fact that when confronted with a spiritual wisdom different from their own, the Spanish Christians reacted with force rather than curiosity. The world today is poorer because of it.

# The Aztec Story as Told by the Victors

In 1485, Hernán Cortés de Monroy y Pizarro Altamirano was born in Medellin, Spain. He would grow up to be a don, the marquis of the Valley of Oaxaca. But history remembers him for what he accomplished, ostensibly for the King of Castile, during his work as a Spanish conquistador. In short, he brought about the fall of the Aztec Empire in what is now Mexico. Only a handful of men can claim they almost singlehandedly changed the course of history, but Cortés was one of them, even though it was, to be charitable, not his finest hour.

He stepped ashore what was then called the New World at the age of 19, the first of a number of voyages, one of them to Cuba. In the year 1518, he set his sights upon Mexico and accumulating fame, riches, and glory for God and the Spanish crown there. He was good at his job. Arriving—against orders, by the way—in Mexico with 500 men and 11 ships, he was able to play the political game of aligning one local faction against another. Although back home he was accused of mutiny, eventually, his tactics abroad paid off. He overthrew the Aztecs and was appointed governor of New Spain in 1522 by King Charles I.

By 1529, the Church considered Mexico ready for conversion. Already destroyed were Aztec written records that, had they survived, would certainly have illuminated a large part of American history that is now lost forever. The Spanish Inquisition was still in effect, and everything that was considered to be pagan was condemned and destroyed in the name of God.

A Catholic priest named Fray Bernardino de Sahagún was sent to Mexico to covert the indigenous population that remained, but he had another, secret, mission as well.

Rumors had begun to swirl within the Catholic Church that some Aztec legends were very similar to Christian Bible stories. Could it be that the Church had committed a mistake? Were the Aztecs some of God's lost sheep? If so, the Church would be guilty of murdering real people instead of godless heathens who didn't have souls. That would make for bad publicity. Then as now, image is everything.

After arriving in Mexico, de Sahagún began to do the unthinkable: He talked to old-timers who remembered some of the stories and legends that had been destroyed in the fires of ethnic cleansing only a decade or so earlier.

Surprisingly, he wrote a book about his findings. He called it *Historia general de las cosas de nueva España* (General History of the Things of New Spain). Today, we know it as the *Florentine Codex.*

A page from the *Florentine Codex* by Fray Bernardino de Sahagún. The manuscript records the ancient history and origin stories of the Nahua-speaking people. A copy is maintained at the Laurentian Library of Florence, Italy.

The *Florentine Codex* records the history of the Nahua-speaking people. They were a pre-conquest population from central Mexico, of which the Aztecs were a part. The text was written in the Nahua common tongue but also contained a commentary written in Spanish.

Part of the *Florentine Codex* is devoted to a mysterious and ancient migration story. It speaks of a mysterious place called Tamoanchan, which the old ones described as similar to the biblical Eden of which the Spanish were familiar. Tamoanchan was the birthplace of all Mesoamerican cultures, a paradise they were forced to leave because of a great flood.

The ancients, according to the legends:

> ... came to this land to rule over it. They came from the sea on ships, a multitude of them, and landed on the shore of the sea, to the North. From there they went on, seeking the white mountains, the smoky mountains, led by their priests and by the voice of their gods. Finally, they came to the place that they called Tamoanchan ... and there they settled.

Why wasn't the *Florentine Codex* widely disseminated? This was information that sounded eerily similar to Christian legends. It might have been the proof the Church was searching for, and perhaps, it could have been used as justification for invading the lands in the first place. They could have claimed they were out to free God's chosen people from bondage and poverty.

Well, the problem was that de Sahagún was too good a writer. He had lavishly illustrated his book with pictures, some of which showed the Spanish conquistadores in compromising positions that were not, shall we say, prime examples of Christian virtues.

Needless to say, the censors took over immediately to suppress political embarrassment. The book was not widely distributed.

The *Florentine Codex* goes against the grain of modern academic thought, which maintains that about 1,800 years ago, a Nahua-speaking cul-

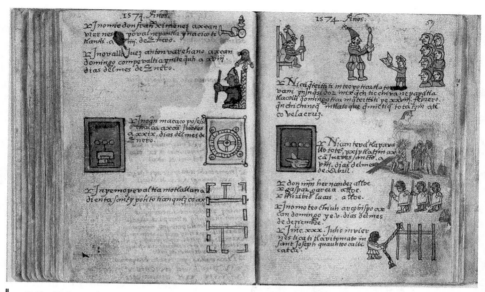

Folio 59 from the 16th-century *Aubin Codex*, a written record of the Aztec tradition relating their history from the time they departed the ancestral home called Aztlá to the time of the Spanish conquests.

ture from the north began to settle in the Valley of Mexico. They are now called Aztec because they came from Aztlán, which means "White Land."

Building an extensive system of canals and dikes, they soon were able to control water levels needed for agriculture. The population began to flourish, and in 1428 an Aztec ruler named Itzcoatl allied his people with Tlacopan and Texcoco. This political treaty formed what is called the Triple Alliance, which controlled Mexico until the Spanish invasion of 1519.

The Aztecs themselves, however, tell a different story. Their version is told in a text called the *Tonalamatl of the Aubin Collection*. We now refer to it as the *Aubin Codex*. It's a compilation of text and illustrations written in 1608. Because it utilizes European paper, it is thought to be the work of sympathetic Spanish translators who wanted to retain whatever they could of Aztec tradition after their church had burned everything else of value.

This version of the story is written in a language called Alphabetic Nahuatl, which is a transliterated Aztec text. The use of indigenous language implies the authors must have made the effort to learn Nahua. Presumably, then, they got their information directly from Aztec elders, who said their ancestors indeed came from the north, but not northern Mexico. The *Aubin Codex* places the Eden of the Aztecs possibly as far away as today's Four Corners region of the southwestern United States, where Utah, Colorado, Arizona, and New Mexico meet.

Quetzalcoatl—which can be translated as both the feathered serpent and the wisest man—was a god of air, wind, and learning. The Aztecs tragically mistook the conquistador Cortés as the second coming of their god.

Just as the biblical Eden marked the beginnings of four rivers, two of them being the Tigris and Euphrates, the *Aubin Codex* claims that four rivers marked the location of Tamoanchan. Some scholars believe these rivers to be the Green, the upper Colorado, and the San Juan, which merge to become the lower Colorado River.

Rock art abounds in this area, some of it dating back some 500 years before the Common Era or longer. According to the elders, a people they call the Mexica, the ancestors of the Aztecs, were forced from their homeland by a "rain of fire." The people moved ever south, following a vision reminiscent of the Hebrew children and their escape from Egypt. Their spirit guides told them to continue their exodus until they found an eagle fighting with a serpent on a "barbed tree," or cactus. This they eventually found, and they settled down to build their capital city, Tenochtitlan.

The modern flag of Mexico, with its motif of eagle and serpent, is based on this legend. Tenochtitlan, built on the place where the eagle fought the serpent, is now called Mexico City.

Once again, we run into a legend that sounds suspiciously similar to the events that occurred at the end of the Younger Dryas Ice Age some 11,500 to 11,800 years ago. If a comet brought about such a cataclysm, it would certainly fit the description of a "rain of fire." If so, this text suddenly deposits the ancestors of the Aztecs a lot further back in history than traditional scholarship is willing to go.

Another train of circumstantial evidence supports the early date. We know that following the Younger Dryas cataclysm, a number of civilizations arose that included extremely sophisticated astronomers. Egypt, Göbekli Tepe, and Sumer are only a few examples. The Aztecs seem to be in the same club. Could all these ancient, star-gazing civilizations have arisen by accident, scattered around the globe as they are? Or was there a previous parent civilization that gave birth to them all? Was Quetzalcoatl—the "feathered serpent" or "plumed serpent," the civilization-bearing god of Central America—a member of this ancient civilization?

Quetzalcoatl was so important to these people that they believed Cortés was the second coming of their ancestral god. This helps explain why the Spanish, outnumbered as they were, could defeat the local people with relative ease.

ONCE AGAIN, WE RUN INTO A LEGEND THAT SOUNDS SUSPICIOUSLY SIMILAR TO THE EVENTS THAT OCCURRED AT THE END OF THE YOUNGER DRYAS ICE AGE SOME 11,500 TO 11,800 YEARS AGO.

Stories such as these remind us that in many respects the Aztecs were no different from the early Jews or the Sumerians, who have similar exodus stories. It makes us wonder if something cosmic is in play that is much bigger than we usually think about. Their story, as is often the case, was told by the victors. Maybe it's time to listen more closely to the ancient texts of the oppressed.

# Hopi Renaissance

It's a mistake to think that other cultures don't have scriptures or mythological texts equally as influential or spiritually important as those in the Bible. Perhaps they remember their scriptures in the form of oral legends and tribal mythology, but the Middle East is not the only place in the world where people contemplated God and their place in the universe.

One of the most important examples of scripture is found in the well-documented accounts recorded in Frank Waters's *Book of the Hopi*. He doesn't call it scripture. Neither do the Hopi. They simply refer to these accounts as oral history. But if the definition of scripture includes the simple annotation of sacred writings, these texts fit the bill.

The Hopi believe we live in what they call the fourth world. During three previous ages, their people grew great civilizations, only to fall victim to the age-old problem of human hubris. But the importance of the Hopi goes far deeper than a simple recitation of history. The Hopi didn't just write about history. They lived it.

The Hopi are descendants of the Ancestral Puebloan people. Until recently, they were known as the Anasazi. Before that, they were known as Cliff Dwellers. They lived primarily in what is known today as the Four Corners region of the U.S. Southwest. In my book *Lost Civilizations,* I examined their roots and eventual mysterious demise. To learn more about them, I refer you to that book.

Theirs was a rich culture. It was from the Ancestral Puebloans that the Spanish first heard the stories of the mythical god/traveler Kokopelli, whose hump-backed, flute-playing image can be found pecked into rock art all over the Southwest even to this day. By examining these images, we can determine that his legend goes back some 3,000 years. According to oral tradition, he was a storyteller, a trader, a fertility god, and a healer.

No one knows where the Ancestral Puebloans came from. Their ancestry is as mysterious as their demise. Many believe they stem from tribes further south, in Mexico and Central America. Very probably, their historical roots go back to the very first people to inhabit the Americas. So, when they tell stories about the history of the world, we need to listen.

Let's follow their progress from the beginning.

Mesa Verde in modern-day southern Colorado is one of the impressive sites left behind by the Pueblo Indians, whose culture can be dated back some 3,000 years.

## The First World: Tokpela

According to Frank Waters in his 1963 *Book of the Hopi*:

> When the first people awakened to life they were instructed by Sotuknang and Spider Woman to respect both Taiowa, the Creator, and the land they were given for their home. Spider Woman had formed it for them, and they were nurtured by its bounty. They discovered vibration centers spread throughout the earth that echoed in similar centers within their own bodies and sang in resonance with the music of the stars in the heavens. The purpose of these centers was to help keep the people in tune with the Creator as they followed his ways.
>
> The people forgot to listen. Ignoring the music of the stars that rang in their hearts, they no longer followed the Way and began to quarrel amongst themselves. It got to be so bad that Sotuknang decided he must destroy the people before they ruined everything they had been given.
>
> But some of the old ones still remembered how to act correctly and show proper respect, so Sotuknang appeared to them with the sound of a mighty wind and said he would lead them to safety if they followed him and obeyed his instruc-

tions. And so it was that a few of the ancient ones took refuge among the Ant
People as the First World was destroyed
by fire. Sotuknang caused the earth to
bellow forth smoke and flame. Volca-
noes erupted from deep below the surface of the land. A Second World was
then prepared for the people.

> THE PEOPLE BECAME
> AWARE OF "VIBRATION
> CENTERS" SPREAD
> THROUGHOUT THE EARTH
> THAT RESONATED WITH
> THE CHAKRA CENTERS
> LOCATED WITHIN THE
> HUMAN BODY.

This is a fascinating account. Notice the
progress.

Soon after their creation, the people were
in touch with the gods who gave them birth. As
Adam and Eve walked in familiar relationship with their god in the cool of
the evening, the first people lived in harmony with their gods, Sotuknang
and Spider Woman, who taught them to respect both Taiowa, the creator,
and Mother Earth, from whence they sprang.

The people became aware of "vibration centers" spread throughout the
earth that resonated with the chakra centers located within the human body.
This speaks of unity, of wholeness and connection to the music of the earth
itself. The Hopi ancestors were, to put it mildly, "in tune" with the harmony
of the music of the spheres. This is similar to Adam and Eve in the Genesis
account. They walked in beauty with the earth. They were one with each other,
one with their environment, and one with God. It was an Eden-like existence.

But, as happened as well according to the Genesis texts, "The people
forgot to listen. Ignoring the music of the stars that rang in their hearts, they
no longer followed the Way and began to quarrel amongst themselves. It got
to be so bad that Sotuknang decided he must destroy the people before they
ruined everything they had been given."

This is almost exactly the same story we read in Genesis. Ignoring the
message of God, the people rebelled. In the biblical story, God then sought
to destroy them with a great flood. But in the Hopi myth, the destruction
came not from flood but from ice.

## The Second World: Tokpa

Waters continues in *The Book of the Hopi*:

> The Second World was almost as beautiful as the first, but in
> this world the animals no longer trusted humans. They kept
> themselves separate and ran away whenever the people came
> upon them. Still, it was a good place to live. It was so good, in
> fact, that the people once again began to think they knew more
> than the Creator and ignored his plan for them. Life was too

Taiowa, the sun spirit, is the creator in Hopi legend and is similar to the god of the Christian Bible.

easy. They had everything they needed, but they wanted more. They thought they could live any way they chose, even if it was disrespectful and selfish, and it soon became apparent that Sotuknang would have to destroy them again.

Once again, Sotuknang called on the Ant People to open their kivas to those who remembered, to those who still sang the songs of Taiowa. He led them again to safety in the underground world.

This time, Poqanghoya and Palongawhoya, the Twins who guarded the poles of the earth, left their posts and the world spun off its axis and went out of control, whirling through space. It soon became covered with ice and was frozen until the Twins once again took up their stations and restored life to the earth. The ice melted and the people could once again return to their new home. This was the home the wise ones called Kuskurza, the Third World.

In this case, the Hopi account is probably closer to the truth of geologic history than Genesis. Ice did cover the world. The Bible is ignorant of ice ages. The Hopi recognized the truth carved into their cultural landscape. Ice froze the world, but the people were protected.

Unfortunately, they didn't learn their lesson. Once again, the people grew victim to their own wants and desires. Once again, they were destroyed. But this time it was by floodwaters.

## The Third World: Kuskurza

Waters continues:

In this third world the people quickly multiplied. They created cities and countries—a whole new civilization. Sotuknang and Spider Woman despaired. The people could not sing the praises of Taiowa, the Creator, when they were too busy being occupied by their earthly plans and selfish dreams.

Some, of course, remembered the old ways. They knew that the further people traveled on the Road of Life, the harder it was to remain faithful and true. They tried to teach the young people the old ways, but the young people refused to listen. Instead, they found new ways to destroy and conquer. They sought to enhance their personal power at the expense of others. Some even invented flying shields, capable of carrying them to villages far away, where they could attack, pillage, and return so quickly that no one knew where they had gone.

> THE POINT HERE, THOUGH, IS TO INDICATE THAT, IN MANY CASES, THE HOPI ACCOUNTS SEEM MORE GEOLOGICALLY AND HISTORICALLY ACCURATE THAN THE BIBLICAL ACCOUNTS.

Sotuknang knew he could not allow this way of life to continue. So he warned Spider Woman that he would again destroy the people, this time with a great flood.

Spider Woman knew of the few people who still listened—who still tried to teach the people the ways of the Creator. But this time she didn't know how to save them. In a great flood, even the home of the Ant People would be destroyed. The people searched long and hard for a solution, for a way of salvation. Finally they hid themselves inside the hollow stems of bamboo trees while their world was drowned.

It seems perfectly reasonable that when the ice melted, floods would come. In other books I've talked about the strange fact that "some even invented flying shields, capable of carrying them to villages far away, where they could attack, pillage, and return so quickly that no one knew where they had gone." This seems to me to indicate that whole civilizations, capable of great technology, arose between the epochs of ice and flood. The point here, though, is to indicate that, in many cases, the Hopi accounts seem more geologically and historically accurate than the biblical accounts.

At any rate, finally came the fourth world, the world we now occupy.

## The Fourth World: Tuwaqachi

Observes Waters:

When the flood waters calmed, the people came out and began again. They made what seemed an endless journey by boat, paddling uphill all the way. But the earth was covered with water. From time to time they would send out birds to scout for a place of safety, but the birds always returned. Finally they began to find land. Islands appeared, like stepping stones, and they offered good places to live. But each time Spider Woman told them they must move on. The places they stopped were too easy, she said. They would soon fall again into their evil ways.

Finally the people were too exhausted to continue on their own. All they could do was open the doors of their hearts and allow Spider Woman to guide them. They were forced to submit to her wisdom.

At long last they came to a sandy shore where they were greeted by Sotuknang, who gave them instructions. They were to separate into different groups, each group following its own star by night and pillar of cloud by day, until they came to a place where the earth met the sea. Each group would keep track of their migration on a tablet of stone, and record in symbol the representation of their journeys. At long last they would be brought together again, but only after much travail. In this way they would finally come to remember what they had forgotten—to obey Taiowa, the Creator, and live according to his plan for them.

Hear the words of Sotuknang, spoken at the beginning of the fourth world:

"I have washed away even the footprints of your Emergence; the stepping-stones which I left for you. Down on the bottom of the seas lie all the proud cities, the flying shields and the worldly treasures corrupted with evil, and those people who found no time to sing praises to the Creator from the tops of their hills. But the day will come, if you preserve the memory and the meaning of your Emergence, when these stepping-stones will emerge again to prove the truth you speak."

The people's freedom was won by the grace of their gods. Even the memories of their previous life were washed away. But the warning was still in effect. If they forgot who they were and what their place in the universe required of them, destruction would come again. This time it would be complete.

Notice the importance of a written record. "Each group would keep track of their migration on a tablet of stone, and record in symbol the representation of their journeys. At long last they would be brought together again, but only after much travail. In this way they would finally come to remember what they had forgotten—to obey Taiowa, the Creator, and live according to his plan for them."

Who is to say that these scriptural texts—for that's exactly what they are—are not just as accurate, and in many ways *more* accurate, than the ones found in Genesis? Is it any wonder that the conquerors would want them destroyed? And that is the ultimate form of censorship.

# PERU IN THE MISTS OF TIME

Hidden in plain sight, high in the Andes mountains of Peru, lie some of the most eloquent examples of forgotten scripture to be found in the entire world. They are not written on parchment. They are carved into the soil of the earth, the dust of the ground. They were there long before Europeans discovered them. Indeed, ever since their mysterious authors created them, they were completely unknown until humans invented the airplane. Who wrote these messages? What was their purpose? It is one of the greatest mysteries of history.

In the March 2010 *National Geographic* magazine, Stephen S. Hall wrote an article about the Nazca Lines of Peru titled "Spirits in the Sand." In it he attempted to respond to that question. He begins by describing the mysterious lines:

> Since they became widely known in the late 1920s, when commercial air travel was introduced between Lima and the southern Peruvian city of Arequipa, the mysterious desert drawings known as the Nazca lines have puzzled archaeologists, anthropologists, and anyone fascinated by ancient cultures in the Americas. For just as long, waves of scientists—and amateurs—have inflicted various interpretations on the lines, as if they were the world's largest set of Rorschach inkblots. At one time or another, they have been explained as Inca roads, irrigation plans, images to be appreciated from primitive hot-air balloons, and, most laughably, landing strips for alien spacecraft.

Notice a few things right off the bat.

First, the lines depicting various animals, birds, human beings, and various other figures were really not noticed by anyone until the advent of air transportation. In other words, they were meant to be seen from the air. Indeed, it is only from the air that they can really be made out at all. There are no towers you can climb or nearby mountaintops where a person can stand and take in the whole panorama. You have to fly over it, as Erich von Däniken did before he introduced the Nazca Lines to the general public with the publication of his now famous—or infamous, depending on your point of view—book *Chariots of the Gods?*

Second, Hall notes that the lines are "puzzling," even to the professionals.

The Nazca Lines are immense drawings, like this spider, that can only be clearly perceived by someone high up, such as in an airplane, yet they were created long before such technology existed.

Third, he disparages such puzzlement by introducing the idea of Rorschach inkblots. Those are always good for a laugh.

Fourth, although he admits they were built by an earth-bound people to be seen from the sky, he dismisses any thought of ancient air transport, especially of the alien variety, as "laughable."

As he continues, he does appreciate a possible spiritual component to the product:

The parched desert and hillsides made an inviting canvas: By simply removing a layer of dark stones cluttering the ground, exposing the lighter sand beneath, the Nazca created markings that have endured for centuries in the dry climate. Archaeologists believe both the construction and maintenance of the lines were communal activities—"like building a cathedral."

He then proceeds to offer his own conclusions. They are practical, of course. He sees the whole Nazca project as an elaborate way to provide water to a parched desert land and the effigies as a way to placate various animistic deities who might be called on for assistance.

At the very end of the article, however, he returns to the mystical component:

As my footsteps continued around the curves of the spiral, it occurred to me that one of the most important functions of the "mysterious" Nazca lines is no mystery at all. The geoglyphs surely provided a kinetic, ritualistic reminder to the Nazca people that their fate was tied to their environment—its natural beauty, its ephemeral abundance, and its life-threatening austerity. You can read their reverence for nature, in times of plenty and in times of desperate want, in every line and curve they scratched onto the desert floor. When your feet inhabit their sacred space, even for a brief and humbling moment, you can feel it.

It is precisely here that I find myself most drawn to Hall's beautiful prose. He felt the wonder. That is obvious. As should we all. The Nazca Lines are a captivating mystery. They imply a lost history and hidden truths from a mysterious people whose motivation is now, and perhaps forever, lost in the mists of a forgotten time.

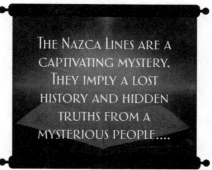

THE NAZCA LINES ARE A CAPTIVATING MYSTERY. THEY IMPLY A LOST HISTORY AND HIDDEN TRUTHS FROM A MYSTERIOUS PEOPLE....

Why did they do it? We just don't know.

Near the Nazca Lines, on the very same plateau, some 6,900 holes have been carved into rock. They form a band about eight to ten holes wide and about a mile long across some of the most rugged terrain you would ever want to cross on foot. Each hole is about 3 feet wide and 3 to 6 feet deep. Sometimes they line up very precisely, but they often appear staggered, with seemingly no pattern at all.

It was obviously a long, backbreaking job that, in some instances, seems to be unfinished. When asked why these holes were carved and who carved them, the current inhabitants of the area say they don't have the faintest idea.

Once again, we are stymied by an ancient mystery and a lack of information. There is little doubt that, had the conquistadores not gone to such lengths to censor the work of those they considered to be pagan, the world would understand a lot more about not just ancient art but human history. In the end, is there any difference between redacting previously written texts and destroying those that do not agree with ones you already have?

# NATURE RECLAIMS THE AMAZON

The Amazon rain forest is a profoundly vast and extensive weather machine. Its vegetation takes in pollutants and breathes out life-supporting oxygen. In this way, it forms the lungs of planet Earth, providing more than 20 percent of our oxygen and 25 percent of our pharmaceuticals. Seventy percent of plants identified as being effective against cancer are native to the region. It is home to at least 50 indigenous tribes, many living independently from the outside world. Hundreds of endangered animal species call the Amazon home as well as more than 137 species of endangered plants.

But even as I write these words, the Amazon is being ruthlessly destroyed to produce agricultural land and cattle grazing at the rate of 1.5 acres every single second of the day. This is done to provide the world with fast-food hamburgers.

The only good thing to come of this tragedy is that the newly open land has revealed the remains of villages and ceremonial earthworks called geoglyphs. We are beginning to realize, only in the last few decades, that the Amazon is not the pristine wilderness outsiders once thought it was. It has been home to a vast civilization that invaders never suspected existed. New discoveries have yielded a wealth of ceramic pottery and clues that indicate how people lived and thrived before European diseases killed them. Their surviving descendants now live a nomadic existence. We assumed they had done this for untold thousands of years. We were wrong.

Models discovered from cameras in space and explorers on the ground now indicate that there are more than 1,300 geoglyphs and villages scattered over an area of some 154,000 square miles (400,000 square kilometers) in the southern Amazon alone. Two-thirds of them haven't been found yet. But indications of a connecting infrastructure of roads and paths offer tantalizing clues that point to a once flourishing civilization.

José Iriarte, an archaeologist at the University of Exeter, writing for the *National Geographic*, said it very succinctly: "We need to re-evaluate the history of the Amazon."

In the history we are about to explore, there was no committee around to deliberately censor or destroy indigenous texts. The censorship came about in a more deliberate manner. The texts were there for all to read. The problem came because no one believed them. It happened in this way.

In 1541, Francisco de Orellana became the first European explorer to successfully travel the length of the Amazon River. He had just come off a

This geoglyph was once concealed by the Amazonian rain forest. Turned into farmland, we can now see a picture that was created around 1283 C.E.

busy period in his life during which he helped his close friend (and possibly cousin), the conquistador Francisco Pizarro, conquer Peru. Many people of his age and time were obsessed with the legend of the mysterious city El Dorado. Its streets, it was said, were paved with gold.

De Orellana didn't find El Dorado, but he did report seeing large villages, farms, and even cities sprawled along the mysterious river he was forced to navigate because he started traveling with the current and went too far before he realized the river was too strong to navigate back upstream. So, he made the best of it and turned his voyage into one of discovery. He carefully charted his journey, documented locations, and delivered his diaries to the proper authorities upon his return to civilization. He died before he was able to return.

Centuries later, explorers and missionaries who had read his carefully stored texts finally got around to following up on his information. What they found was nothing but wild tangles of jungle that, according to the scientists of his day, could never have supported the kind of civilization de Orellana claimed to have seen. His material was declared, at the very least, mistaken. Privately, most scholars considered the journals an outright fraud.

Until the end of the twentieth century, most experts thought that although the Amazon rain forest was dense and thick with vegetation, the soil itself could never support the kind of vigorous population he described. It was too poor in nutrients to grow sustainable crops.

Then came the discovery of *terra preta de Índio*, "the dark earth of the Indian" or, as it's sometimes called, "superdirt." It's a mixture of charcoal and organic material that is extremely good fertilizer, created by the slash-and-burn method of cultivation used to clear vast acres of natural vegetation. The technique produces organic waste, composed of smoldering plant growth, animal bones, and feces. Wherever these conditions are found in the Amazon, archaeologists find potsherds and signs of human habitation.

Recently, Michael Palace, of the University of New Hampshire, decided to use satellite imagery to better understand the extent of superdirt accumulations in the Amazon region. What he found shocked everybody. It soon became apparent that the region was once home to an immense civilization that no one had suspected existed. Francisco de Orellana's journals had been accurate after all. He is now known to be the very first, and the very last, European to visit this civilization.

What had happened? Why had it vanished?

A bust of Francisco de Orellana, the Spanish explorer who traveled down the Amazon River and reported seeing large towns and even cities there. However, explorers who followed found no such cities.

The best guess is that when de Orellana and his crew put ashore for supplies, they infected the local populations with a whole host of European diseases to which the indigenous people had absolutely no natural immunity. An epidemic consisting of everything from smallpox to syphilis was unleashed on the doomed people. Computer models indicate that between 500,000 and 1,000,000 people once lived in an area that covers less than 7 percent of the Amazon basin.

It is hard to imagine how terrifying it must have been for the people already living there. First, they must have been struck dumb by the completely unexpected appearance of foreign-looking Spanish explorers. Then, in a matter of weeks after the visitors departed downriver, villagers began to die by the thousands. Even the pandemic of 2020 could not have compared to the horror. In a very short time, there was probably no one left who was healthy enough to aid the survivors. Finally, in a misery of silence, the last one died alone. The rain forest grew back, reclaiming its own. The land returned to what it had been before humans arrived on the scene. Two hundred years later, when explorers finally came back, they saw no sign of human habitation whatsoever.

In the March 27, 2018, edition of *National Geographic*, Erin Blakemore reported on an even greater population, scattered over a larger area. This time

> IN A VERY SHORT TIME,
> THERE WAS PROBABLY NO
> ONE LEFT WHO WAS
> HEALTHY ENOUGH TO
> AID THE SURVIVORS.
> FINALLY, IN A MISERY OF
> SILENCE, THE LAST ONE
> DIED ALONE.

the discovery came not from satellites orbiting the earth but from renewed, deliberate deforestation brought about by human greed and development. For the first time, workers penetrated areas of the rain forest that few had visited for hundreds of years. There, they found structures that had been overgrown, building foundations, evidence of roads, and other infrastructure. The once "virgin" forest turned out to be not so old after all. All because no one believed the texts— the journals of Francisco de Orellana. Because they were not believed, they were ignored and thereby censored. And the wealth of pharmaceutical wisdom, and perhaps even spiritual insight, that once was the possession of Amazonian shamans was lost to the world, perhaps forever.

# Conclusions

In Part I we learned how extensively teams of censors allowed their preconceived religious biases to influence which texts were allowed to form the official canon of the Bible we know today. The fact that they didn't simply ignore but actively sought to destroy the rest is sufficient to conclude that they didn't want their work reviewed or even questioned. They were ruthless, and it was only because communities such as those of Qumran and Nag Hammadi risked life and limb to hide, rather than destroy, their copies of banned books do we even know about the existence of these suppressed scriptures.

In Part II, we discovered another form of censorship. By the time of the European discovery and invasion of the Americas, the Bible had long since been completed and accepted as authoritative. It was so authoritative, as a matter of fact, that the sacred texts of any other cultures were judged to be pagan superstition and the work of the devil. The conquerors were ruthless. They didn't just outlaw the texts they discovered; they ordered them burned and destroyed. They attempted to prevent anyone from even reading them, much less studying them.

But a few brave souls managed to copy portions of some texts and spirit them away. Were it not for them, we wouldn't know there even was a Popol Vuh, let alone what it said. The Hopi creation story, memorized and transferred down through the generations by highly trained wise men and women, has finally been brought into the light of day, where the masses can learn from it and catch glimpses into our past.

Now it's time to explore literary masterpieces of quite a different form. Some will be new and others very familiar and hiding in plain sight. I call them songs of distant voices. In many cases, these texts were not censored by outsiders. Quite the contrary: they were accepted and well known. They had many adherents who read them and believed their message. But for the most part, they have been ignored. It's a strange story and illustrates the ultimate way sacred texts are censored. We read them, believe them, and then ignore their message because they speak of a future time that right now doesn't concern us. Sadly, it's an all-too-common practice called hypocrisy. In this case, the gatekeepers are us.

# PART III

# THE SONG OF DISTANT VOICES

C an you sing about "gentle Jesus, meek and mild" and then persecute others because their skin color is closer to that of a first-century Jew than your own? Can you believe strongly that "thou shalt not kill" and then go to war with your neighbor? Can you preach sermons about the dignity of all people and then hold some of them in virtual or actual slavery? Can you "turn the other cheek" while, in daily life, refusing to forgive?

Of course you can. People do it all the time. One of the tragedies of human history is the prevalence of religious hypocrisy. During the Albigensian Crusade at Béziers, France—home to a Christian sect called the Albigensians or Cathars that was deemed heretical—on July 22, 1209, the Crusaders questioned their leaders as to how to separate the heretical Christians from the rest. The command went forth: "*Caedite eos. Novit enim Dominus qui sunt eius.*" Roughly translated, it means, "Kill them all, and let God sort them out!" So much for following the dictates of the Prince of Peace, whom the Crusaders claimed to follow.

War leaders from Joshua to Muhammad fought battles in the name of their god. They claimed they received instructions from God to kill everyone, in some cases even the livestock, after defeating a city.

Evangelical Christians who preach family values have often been guilty of supporting religious leaders and politicians who illustrated the exact opposite traits from those espoused by Jesus in their public lives.

The great tragedy of religious history is not that the core message of the great faiths is wrong. It is that it is too often ignored.

THE GREAT TRAGEDY OF
RELIGIOUS HISTORY IS
NOT THAT THE CORE
MESSAGE OF THE GREAT
FAITHS IS WRONG. IT IS
THAT IT IS TOO OFTEN
IGNORED.

We're now about to look at four well-known religious texts that are similar to one another. One comes from Egypt, one from Babylon, one from Rome, and one from Greece. They all claim to foresee the future and issue warnings that, in every case, have already begun to come to pass. They are examples of apocalyptic literature. People are fascinated by them, and the texts are quite clear about what the future holds. But their message is seldom observed by any kind of practical public policy.

The word "apocalypse" comes from a Greek word (*apokálypsis*) that means "revelation." It describes a genre of literature that claims to reveal the future. Specifically, it tries to unveil what the world will look like just before civilization collapses. Usually, it purports to be a warning from an angel or otherworldly visitor.

One would think that if God sent a message to reveal the future, believers would examine it, weigh the evidence, and, if it stood up to scrutiny, mend their ways. To ignore a message from God is the ultimate act of rejection. It is blasphemous. After all, if the Creator of All That Is goes to the trouble of warning you what is about to happen, how could you, as a believer, *not* listen and heed? Even if you don't believe in a god, prophecy can be measured and scrutinized. There are nontheists who nonetheless believe in the work of psychics, seers, and mystics such as Nostradamus and Edgar Cayce. The evidence is in the fulfillment of what they predict, independent of their theology or religious position.

The examples we are about to examine have been, in effect, hiding in plain sight for thousands of years. They are well known to their adherents. They are even revered and studied. But by virtue of the fact that they have been ignored, they are, in effect, censored. One can only wonder how differently history would have progressed had people opened their eyes and ears and, more importantly, their hearts and heeded the warnings.

We do not have to have a traditional concept of God to heed their messages. New discoveries in physics teach us that time can work backward. It is entirely possible that somehow, the unknown authors of these texts could have been tapping into psychic channels that enabled them to foresee the future. We don't know exactly how the messages came through. But the course of history since they were written reveals the truth of what they warned us about. We might dispute the method by which they were conveyed, but we cannot dispute the accuracy of their predictions.

When the U.S. Declaration of Independence and Constitution were written, the country's founders claimed they held certain truths to be self-evident. They firmly believed that "all men are created equal." But they contradicted their own words by restricting equality, at least in terms of voting rights, to white men who owned property.

Were they hypocritical? Of course they were. They said one thing, firmly convinced that they believed what they were saying, and then acted in a totally different manner. The same principle applies to religious believers who read with conviction their own texts and then ignore them.

What would happen if we claimed to believe in gravity yet paid no attention to its power? We could walk off a cliff to our death. And it would be our own fault.

These next texts are similar to the laws of gravity. They might be divinely inspired. They might just be educated guesses. They might have been written by far-seeing visionaries. They might have been written as coded political treatises for contemporaries. Whatever the source of their inspiration, they warn us what will happen if we do not change our ways and pay attention.

If history is any sort of guide, we might be heading for our own metaphorical cliff. Wisdom is a force as powerful as gravity. We would do well to heed its voice before we fall off the edge.

# Corpus Hermeticum—The Lament of Hermes the Egyptian

Do you not know, Asclepius, that Egypt is an image of heaven, or, to speak more exactly, in Egypt all the operations of the powers which rule and work in heaven have been transferred to earth below?

Nay, it should rather be said that the whole Cosmos dwells in this our land as in its sanctuary. And yet, since it is fitting that wise men should have knowledge of all events before they come to pass, you must not be left in ignorance of this: there will come a time when it will be seen that in vain have the Egyptians honored the deity with heartfelt piety and assiduous service; and all our holy worship will be found bootless and ineffectual. For the gods will return from earth to heaven.

Egypt will be forsaken, and the land which was once the home of religion will be left desolate, bereft of the presence of its deities.

This land and region will be filled with foreigners. Not only will men neglect the service of the gods, but Egypt will be occupied ... by some such race from the barbarian countries thereabout. In that day will our most holy land, this land of shrines and temples, be filled with funerals and corpses....

Do you weep at this, Asclepius? There is worse to come. Egypt herself will have yet more to suffer. She will fall into a far more piteous plight, and will be infected with yet more, grievous plagues. And this land, which once was holy, a land which loved the gods, and wherein alone, in reward for her devotion, the gods deigned to sojourn upon earth, a land which was the teacher of mankind in holiness and piety, this land will go beyond all in cruel deeds. The dead will far outnumber the living; and the survivors will be known for Egyptians by their tongue alone, but in their actions they will seem to be men of another race.

O Egypt, Egypt, of thy religion nothing will remain but an empty tale, which thine own children in time to come will not believe. Nothing will be left but graven words, and only the stones will tell of thy piety. And in that day men will be weary of life, and they will cease to think the universe worthy of reverent wonder and of worship. And so religion, the greatest of all blessings, for there is nothing, nor has been, nor ever shall be, that can be deemed a greater boon, will be threatened with destruction; men will think it a burden, and will come to scorn it. They will no longer love this world around us, this incomparable work of God, this glorious structure which he has built, this sum of good made up of things of many diverse forms, this instrument whereby the will of God operates in that which he has made, ungrudgingly favoring man's welfare, this combination and accumulation of all the manifold things that can call forth the veneration, praise, and love of the beholder....

And so the gods will depart from mankind, a grievous thing!, and only evil angels will remain, who will mingle with men, and drive the poor wretches by main force into all manner of reckless crime, into wars, and robberies, and frauds, and all things hostile to the nature of the soul....

But when all this has befallen, Asclepius, then the Master and Father, God, the first before all, the maker of that god who first came into being, will look on that which has come to pass, and will stay the disorder by the counterworking of his will, which is the good.... He will cleanse the world from evil, now washing it away with water-floods, now burning it out with fiercest fire, or again expelling it by war and pestilence.... Such is the new birth of the Cosmos; it is a making again of all things good, a holy and awe-striking restoration of all nature; and it is wrought in the process of time by the eternal will of God.

I quote *The Lament of Hermes the Egyptian*, adapted here from a translation by Philip Coppens, in such detail because I'm quite sure it is unfamiliar to the great majority of folks who will read this book, even though it is entirely within the public domain. In many ways it is similar to the biblical book of Revelation. The *Lament* predicts the end of the Egyptian world. In most cases, it has proven to be an extremely accurate prediction of what has befallen the land in which it was conceived.

First, some background.

The text titled the *Corpus Hermeticum* was written somewhere between the first and third centuries C.E. It was probably written in Greek and later translated into Latin. Only the Latin is now known to scholars. The original Greek version has long been lost.

The author is said to be the mythical god *Hermes Trismegistus*, which means, accurately even if it is a bit cumbersome, "Hermes the three-times big." For many years it was thought that this book was written during the Middle Ages, but then came the discovery of a copy contained in the Nag Hammadi Library in Egypt. As we saw earlier, that discovery happened in 1945 and consisted of a lot of Gnostic literature. The *Lament* is a part of the *Corpus Hermeticum*, so the

A 1471 Latin edition of the *Corpus Hermeticum* was translated by Marsilio Ficino. The original version was in Greek but has been lost to time.

discovery indicates that this text was known to the early Gnostic Christian movement.

The *Lament* is very moving. It predicts an end to true religion in Egypt:

> There will come a time when it will be seen that in vain have the Egyptians honored the deity with heartfelt piety and assiduous service; and all our holy worship will be found bootless and ineffectual. For the gods will return from earth to heaven.

> Egypt will be forsaken, and the land which was once the home of religion will be left desolate, bereft of the presence of its deities.

In many of my books, I have quoted the famous ancient dictum, "As above, so below." It is found in the familiar Lord's Prayer: "Thy kingdom come on earth as it is in heaven."

As mentioned more fully above, here is how Hermes puts it:

> Do you not know, Asclepius, that Egypt is an image of heaven, or, to speak more exactly, in Egypt all the operations of the powers which rule and work in heaven have been transferred to earth below? Nay, it should rather be said that the whole Cosmos dwells in this our land as in its sanctuary.

Many archaeologists have suggested that, contrary to traditionally accepted wisdom, the Egyptian pyramids and megaliths were built not as tombs—or at least not only as tombs—but as earthly representations of the heavens. In other words, if we were able to fly high above the land and look down, we would be seeing, in effect, a mirror image of the principal constellations of the heavens.

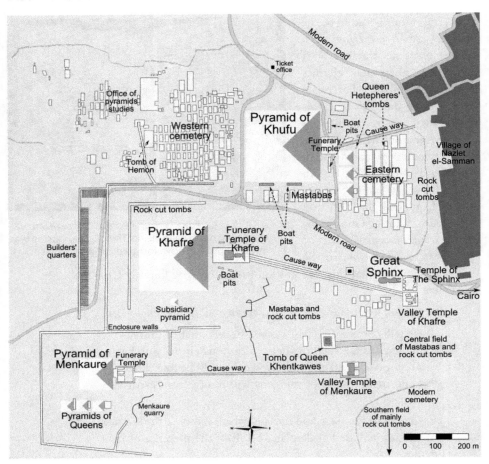

One theory about the Pyramids of Egypt is that they were not tombs but rather maps of the cosmos. For example, one could consider the positioning of the pyramids as Giza as forming the constellation of Orion.

The theory goes even further than this. The psalmist said, "Know ye not that ye are gods?" (Psalm 82). What this means is that if we want to find God, we need to look deep into the human heart. God is not just "up there" in the heavens. God is also "down here" in the human heart. What we do here on earth, we do because we are manifestations of God.

This idea, of course, was not popular in the first-century Roman branch of the Church. Indeed, it was considered heretical to think in these terms. The fact that the ruling elite in the Church wanted such texts destroyed is obvious in that the *Lament* was buried with other so-called heretical works lest it be destroyed.

But it is not *just* an early Gnostic text. That's why I've placed it here rather than in the chapters that deal with that kind of literature.

Egypt was once a land of magic. The Pharaoh was seen not just as a king; he was a god, the very presence on earth of the divine in human form. Ritual dominated the Egyptian landscape. It was important to do things "decently and in order," as the old Scottish rite phrased it. It was the duty of a magician to be a bridge between the material world and the spiritual world.

When Moses stood before Pharaoh and called for freedom, he confronted court magicians. In the great contest of plagues that led to the Exodus, the magicians fought against him, mimicking his miracles until they fell by the wayside and eventually lost.

They did not fulfill a shamanic role. Shamans travel between two worlds as well, but their role is usually not to lead ritualistic ceremonies. That is the job of the priest.

It was in this priestly role that Gnosticism found its way into early Christianity, and it is why it was considered so dangerous. The early Alexandrian Gnostics, influenced as they were by the culture of Egyptian magicians who surrounded them, must have realized their end was near. The world was about to change. It was about to become much more rooted in practical politics than revelatory religion. Thus, they wrote:

> This land, which once was holy, a land which loved the gods, and wherein alone, in reward for her devotion, the gods deigned to sojourn upon earth, a land which was the teacher of mankind in holiness and piety, this land will go beyond all in cruel deeds … the survivors will be known for Egyptians by their tongue alone, but in their actions they will seem to be men of another race. O Egypt, Egypt, of thy religion nothing will remain but an empty tale, which thine own children in time to come will not believe. Nothing will be left but graven words, and only the stones will tell of thy piety.

There are those who will say this has all but come to pass. The ancient Egyptian religion of magic and mystery is, for the most part, gone, buried in the shifting sands of the desert. What is left are the "stones," the enigmatic pyramids and monuments that tell a story written in a language people have forgotten how to read.

We stand in front of Horus and see only a statue. We gaze at the temple of Edfu, which once told a story full of wonder, and see only hieroglyphic carvings. We gaze at the pyramids, and our principal question is not "What do they mean?" but "How did they do it?" The bond that was once so strong, that connected earth to the heavens, is broken:

> And so the gods will depart from mankind, a grievous thing!, and only evil angels will remain, who will mingle with men, and drive the poor wretches by main force into all manner of

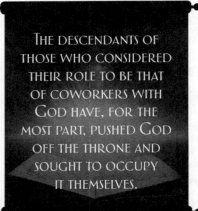

THE DESCENDANTS OF THOSE WHO CONSIDERED THEIR ROLE TO BE THAT OF COWORKERS WITH GOD HAVE, FOR THE MOST PART, PUSHED GOD OFF THE THRONE AND SOUGHT TO OCCUPY IT THEMSELVES.

reckless crime, into wars, and robberies, and frauds, and all things hostile to the nature of the soul.

The gods have departed, and all we see today are the scars of war and materialistic, economic pride and ego.

But all is not necessarily lost. The *Lament* offers hope:

> But when all this has befallen, … God, the first before all, the maker of that god who first came into being, will look on that which has come to pass, and will stay the disorder by the counterworking of his will, which is the good. He will call back to the right path those who have gone astray; he will cleanse the world from evil, now washing it away with water-floods, now burning it out with fiercest fire, or again expelling it by war and pestilence. And thus he will bring back his world to its former aspect, so that the Cosmos will once more be deemed worthy of worship and wondering reverence, and God, the maker and restorer of the mighty fabric, will be adored by the men of that day with unceasing hymns of praise and blessing. Such is the new birth of the Cosmos.

The descendants of those who considered their role to be that of co-workers with God have, for the most part, pushed God off the throne and sought to occupy it themselves. They now live in an era fraught with wars and rumors of wars.

There is something else important to consider about the one who called himself Hermes Trismegistus. We have earlier pointed out that twice in the Bible, once in the Old Testament and once in the New Testament, we find the words "Know ye not that ye are gods?" This sentiment is echoed by the author of the *Lament*:

> If then you do not make yourself equal to God, you cannot apprehend God; for like is known by like. Leap clear of all that is corporeal, and make yourself grown to a like expanse with that greatness which is beyond all measure; rise above all time and become eternal; then you will apprehend God.

Apparently, the idea that human beings are a manifestation of the divine was once prevalent. Then, at some point, the idea became so frightening to religious authorities that they tried to stamp it out.

Ever since it was shaped by the letters of the Apostle Paul, the Church has been comfortable singing songs such as "Amazing grace ... that saved a wretch like me." It's easier to control "wretches" than divine manifestations of God, especially if the only way out of wretchedness is to be granted absolution by those who control the keys to God's kingdom.

Sadly, our modern world, filled with pandemics and plagues, pollution and politicians, priests and potentates, has too often censored the wisdom of elders. Texts that suggested a divine presence within have too often been sought out and burned, destroyed, and forgotten. We have emphasized original sin at the expense of original blessing.

"God saw all that he had made, and behold it was very good." Harmony and balance, long the catchwords of the ancients, were broken in favor of human hubris. The ancients tried to teach us. But we would not listen.

In 1972, Don McLean wrote a popular song titled "Vincent (Starry, Starry Night)." It was a tribute to the artist Vincent van Gogh. In it, McLean captured, perhaps as well as anyone ever has, the plight of those who listen to distant voices that are drowned out by human hubris:

> Now I think I know what you tried to say to me,
> How you suffered for your sanity,
> How you tried to set them free.
> They would not listen, they're not listening still.
> Perhaps they never will.

No doubt the author of the *Lament* would have identified with McLean's song. Hermes Trismegistus saw the end not only of a way of life but of a way of thinking and a way of seeing purpose and meaning behind life's vicissitudes. Real religion, he said, consisted of living in harmony with our surroundings while we listen for unspoken words and unsung songs. It is a tragedy that the force that censored this lament, with all of its wisdom and melancholy, was the Church, aided by its political arm, the state. The world has never quite recovered.

# DANIEL'S DREAM

> But Daniel, keep this prophecy a secret; seal it up so that it will not be understood until the end times, when travel and education shall be vastly increased! (Daniel 12:4)

The traditional date of the Babylonian Captivity, the era in which the army of Nebuchadnezzar captured Jerusalem, is usually thought to be 586 B.C.E. Historians now argue that other dates are more accurate, but that will do as well as any other. The story told in the Jewish Scriptures, known by Christians as the Old Testament, is that a great deportation took place. The cream of the Jewish nation were enslaved and marched back to Babylon. Among them was a young man named Daniel. He was to figure prominently in Babylonian, Persian, and Hebrew history, and his story is told in the book of Daniel, an important book in the Hebrew Bible.

The book of Daniel is sometimes called the "Little Book of Revelation." In many ways it is the Old Testament equivalent of the New Testament apocalypse. It represents an important plank in the platform of most prophetic interpretive systems.

Those who believe that it tells the future of the human race are in good company with scholars of long ago. Flavius Josephus, a Hebrew historian who lived circa 40–100 C.E., wrote in his monumental *Antiquities of the Jews* that when Alexander the Great was shown the book of Daniel, wherein Daniel declared that one of the Greeks would destroy the empire of the Persians, Alexander supposed that he himself was the person intended.

Whether or not Daniel actually wrote the book that bears his name, the text purports to outline a progression of nations beginning with Babylon; continuing through Persia, Greece, and Rome; and ending with, according to some interpretations, a revived European empire at the end of time, during which the Messiah will come. But there are problems with this book that are not always apparent when one simply picks up a Bible and begins to read.

First, different versions of the Bible contain different versions of Daniel. Roman Catholic and Eastern Orthodox Bibles have different versions from the one found in Protestant Bibles. Protestant Bibles omit sections called "Daniel and Susanna" and "Bel and the Dragon" as well as an addition to chapter 3 called the "Prayer of Azariah."

Also, one of the requirements for including books in the Hebrew Bible, purportedly established by the rabbis at Jamnia in the late first century C.E.,

THE BOOK OF DANIEL IS SOMETIMES CALLED THE "LITTLE BOOK OF REVELATION." IN MANY WAYS, IT IS THE OLD TESTAMENT EQUIVALENT OF THE NEW TESTAMENT APOCALYPSE.

when the canon was said to have been settled and fixed in its present form, was ostensibly that books had to be written in Hebrew. But only parts of Daniel were written in that language. Chapter 2, verse 4, through chapter 7 was written in Aramaic.

The interpretive difficulties don't end with questions of what belongs or doesn't belong in the text. The oldest, and therefore supposedly most reliable and complete, version of Daniel known today is a Greek translation copied by Origen in the third century C.E. Many scholars accuse him of both editing and allegorizing Scripture.

Besides all this, Daniel 9 is probably the most difficult chapter to interpret in the whole Bible. There are hundreds of fragments for scholars to pore over, and very few of them are exactly alike. According to conservative Christian theologians, that chapter contains the principal prophecy concerning a period called the Church Age and the final seven years of history leading up to the battle of Armageddon.

Many scholars, probably a majority of those teaching in mainline seminaries, believe that Daniel was written by at least two authors, one writing in the sixth century B.C.E. and the other in the second century B.C.E. The first writer lived during the Babylonian Captivity, the second during the time of Antiochus IV Epiphanes and the Maccabean revolt that gave rise to the celebration of Hanukkah. If that is the case, the authors were probably not writing about a time in the future, even though they appear to say that they are. More likely, they were writing about times in which they were living, presenting coded references of experiences familiar to their contemporaries.

That said, Daniel tells a compelling story of a young, Jewish boy carried away into captivity in Babylon. There, he grows to be a confidant of the king, Nebuchadnezzar. He remains true to his heritage by refusing the king's orders to consume nonkosher royal food and wine, but Nebuchadnezzar comes to respect him because Daniel, like Joseph of old, could interpret dreams.

In chapter 2, Daniel seems to prophesy that four kingdoms will arise. Nebuchadnezzar recounts his dream of a great, manlike statue with a head of gold. Daniel interprets this to represent the Babylonian kingdom. The chest and arms were of silver. To Daniel, this represents the combined kingdom of Media and Persia. The trunk of the statue was made of bronze. This, says Daniel, represents Greece. The legs and feet were made of iron. According to Daniel, this stands for Rome. (It is important to note here that Daniel does not specifically name any of these kingdoms except Babylon. But his descriptions leave little room for doubt.) The value of the metals decreased, from gold to iron, but their strength increased, meaning that each succeeding nation will be greater in might but of less value ethically and morally than its predecessors.

The feet of the statue were part iron and part clay. Presumably, each foot had five toes. According to conservative Christian scholars, that means that the final form of the Roman, or European, empire will consist of ten nations. In Nebuchadnezzar's dream, a "rock was cut out, but not by human hands. It struck the statue on its feet of iron and clay, and smashed them." This is how Daniel explains it:

> In the time of those [ten] kings, the God of Heaven will set up a kingdom that will never be destroyed, nor will it be left to another people. It will crush all those kingdoms and bring them to an

Nebuchadnezzar dreams about a statue of a man with a golden head, chest, and arms of silver; trunk of bronze; and legs and feet of iron. The differing metals represent differing strengths and moral characters of kingdoms through history, as Daniel interpreted it.

end, but it will itself endure forever. This is the meaning of the vision of the rock cut out of a mountain, but not by human hands—a rock that broke the iron, the bronze, the clay, the silver and the gold to pieces. The great God has shown the king what will take place in the future. The dream is true and the interpretation is trustworthy. (Daniel 2:44–46)

King Nebuchadnezzar is so impressed that he promotes Daniel to great heights within the kingdom.

If this dream and its interpretation took place between 570 and 536 B.C.E., it would certainly be a wonder, seemingly predicting the rise of Rome centuries in advance. This is the position taken by conservative scholars who follow what is called the futurist method of interpreting apocalyptic literature. What that means is that they believe prophets are foreseeing future events.

On the other hand, if the book was written during the early days of the Roman Empire, it could simply be recalling history. This is the position of the past-historic school of interpretation.

The futurists insist that the "rock" cut out of the mountain at the end of time, destroying that which represents human history, is Jesus Christ. The ten toes of the statue represent a revived Roman Empire existing in Europe at the end of time. It will be smashed by Jesus Christ at his Second Coming. According to this system of interpretation, the words "in the time of those kings" refers to a yet future day.

On top of all this, conservative scholars point to the possibility of further symbolism that springs from this vision. Right after Daniel's dream interpretation of chapter 2, a series of events unfolds that seem to symbolize the events described in the New Testament book of Revelation. Daniel is "placed in a high position" and made a ruler. According to some conservative scholars, this represents the Rapture of the Church, that time near the end of days when Christ will "snatch up" his believers prior to his return.

But in chapter 3, after Daniel's symbolic "rapture," Nebuchadnezzar sets up an image, a statue, and tells all the people to worship it. This idol supposedly represents the "beast" of Revelation 13:15. Some refuse to worship the image. Daniel's friends, Shadrach, Meshach, and Abednego, are thrown into a fiery furnace for their insubordination, an event interpreted as prefiguring the Tribulation, which is that time at the end of days when the earth is subjected to the rule of Satan.

Like the faithful remnants who are kept safe through the Tribulation, the three pass through the flames unscathed. All others, just like those of Revelation 20:7–15, are destroyed in the furnace. This is the schematic format followed by most modern evangelical students of prophecy.

If that alone were all the prophecy found in the book of Daniel, there would be ample material to keep scholars debating. But there is much, much more.

In chapter 7 the motif of the four kingdoms returns, this time in the guise of four different beasts. Babylon is now a roaring lion. Persia becomes a lumbering bear. The bear holds three ribs in his teeth, representing the Medes, Persians, and Babylonians. Greece is pictured as a swift and darting lion with four heads. Conservative scholars most often identify this image with the fact that Greece was divided into four spheres of influence following the death of Alexander the Great.

Rome, according to this scheme, is vividly portrayed:

After that, in my vision at night I looked and there before me was a fourth beast—terrifying and frightening and very powerful. It had large iron teeth; it crushed and devoured its victims and trampled underfoot whatever was left. It was different from all the former beasts, and it had ten horns.

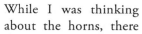

Daniel's dream of the four beasts in chapter 7 of the book represents various historic empires, including the Greeks, Persians, Babylonians, and Medes.

While I was thinking about the horns, there before me was another horn, a little one, which had come up among them; and three of the first horns were uprooted before it. This horn had eyes like the eyes of a man and a mouth that spoke boastfully.

As I looked, thrones were set in place, and the Ancient of Days took his seat....

In my vision at night I looked, and there before me was one like a son of man, coming with the clouds of heaven. He approached the Ancient of Days and was led into his presence. He was given authority, glory, and sovereign power; all people, nations, and men of every language worshiped him. His dominion is an everlasting dominion that will not pass away, and his kingdom is one that will never be destroyed. (Daniel 7:7–14)

Daniel's method of prophecy often revolves around his claim that he does not understand what he sees. He likes to portray himself as an innocent bystander, continually needing help interpreting what he is seeing. He uses this technique again here:

Troubled in spirit, ... I approached one of those standing there and asked him the true meaning of all this. (Daniel 7:15–16)

It is explained to him that:

The fourth beast is a fourth kingdom that will appear on earth. It will be different from all the other kingdoms and will devour the whole earth, trampling it down and crushing it.

THOSE WHO BELIEVE THAT DANIEL WAS FORETELLING THE FUTURE ASSERT THAT THE TEN NATIONS ARISING FROM ROME WILL CONSIST OF A FUTURE TEN-NATION EUROPEAN CONFEDERACY.

The ten horns are ten kings who will arise from this kingdom. After them another king will arise, different from the earlier ones; he will subdue three kings. He will speak against the Most High and oppress his saints and try to change the set times and the laws. The saints will be handed over to him for a time, times and half a time.

But the court will sit, and his power will be taken away and completely destroyed forever. Then the sovereignty, power and greatness of the kingdoms under the whole of heaven will be handed over to the saints, the people of the Most High. His kingdom will be an everlasting kingdom, and all the rulers will worship and obey him. (Daniel 7:23–28)

Those who believe that Daniel was writing about his own time, disguising a political diatribe against Rome in the form of a prophetic vision, offer various claims that this chapter fits with what is known about the political realities of Rome's rule in the second century B.C.E.

Those who believe that Daniel was foretelling the future assert that the ten nations arising from Rome will consist of a future ten-nation European confederacy. One nation will take supremacy by defeating three who rebel.

The "time [one], times [two] and half a time [one-half]" represent the final three and a half years of the Great Tribulation, which precedes the battle of Armageddon. They point out the similarity of this passage to Revelation 17 and John's vision of the woman seated on the "great beast":

> The ten horns you saw are ten kings who have not yet received a kingdom, but who will receive authority as kings along with the beast. They have one purpose and will give their power and authority to the beast. They will make war against the Lamb, but the Lamb will overcome them because he is Lord of lords and King of kings—and with him will be his called, chosen and faithful followers. (Revelation 17:12–14)

Those who don't subscribe to this argument counter that Revelation was probably written by an author who had a close working knowledge of the book of Daniel. Daniel was, after all, part of the Scriptures of first-century Judaism. Jesus quoted it in Matthew 24. John would have been very familiar with the imagery and possibly, consciously or not, incorporated it into his own prophetic scheme.

The debate will not be resolved through academic scholarship. Futurists, as a matter of faith, operate under the presupposition that Daniel was God's prophet and could see the future. Past-historicists do not.

Even these arguments, however, pale in the face of the problems encountered when interpreting Daniel's ninth chapter. It is probably the most difficult passage of the Old Testament to translate, let alone interpret, but it forms the basis for much of the current conservative understanding of end-time chronology.

A summary of the conservative argument is that in this chapter, Daniel supposedly prophesies that there will be a Church Age inserted into a gap between the time of Jesus and a future seven-year time of Tribulation. It's called the Parenthesis Theory. In other words, Daniel, writing as a Jewish prophet before the birth of Christ, predicts that before the Jewish Age comes to its conclusion, the Church Age, a historical parenthesis, will intervene. Then, at the time of the Rapture, when the Church is removed from the earth, the final seven years of Jewish history will take place.

Daniel's final vision is a culmination of all that has gone before. In chapter 10 he claims to see a "great war." The vision was a long time in coming. Daniel prayed and fasted for three weeks before the angel Gabriel appeared to him on the banks of the Tigris River. The reason it took Gabriel so long was that "the prince of the Persian kingdom resisted" him. Michael, the leader of God's heavenly host and a kind of patron guardian of the nation Israel, had to come with reinforcements to clear a path through the enemy so Daniel's prayer could be answered.

Chapter 11 offers a past, present, and future vision. The characters from the past center on Egypt and Syria, and there is a recapitulation of Greece's part in Israel's future. The chapter is full of references to a "king of the South" and a "king of the North" who "march against each other."

Beginning in verse 36, Daniel seems to move into a future time. According to conservative scholarship, it is here that he begins to envision the battle of Armageddon. It's a shorter version than that given by Ezekiel or John, but it contains familiar scenes. The "king of the North" (Russia, according to this interpretive scheme) attacks the "mightiest fortresses" and even "invades the Beautiful Land" (Israel):

> "The king will do as he pleases. He will exalt and magnify himself above every god.... He will show no regard to the god of his fathers, or for the one desired by women, nor will he regard any god.... Instead of them he will honor a god of fortresses; a god unknown to his fathers.... He will attack the mightiest fortresses with the help of a foreign god and will greatly acknowledge him....

"Many countries will fall, but Edom, Moab and the leaders of Ammon will be delivered from his hand. He will extend his power over many countries; Egypt will not escape. He will gain control of the treasures of gold and silver and all the riches of Egypt, with the Libyans and Nubians in submission. But reports from the east and north will alarm him, and he will set out in a great rage to destroy and annihilate many. He will pitch his royal tents between the seas at the beautiful holy mountain. Yet he will come to his end, and no one will help him.

In chapter 10 of the book of Daniel, the angel Gabriel comes to him on the banks of the Tigris River to answer Daniel's prayer.

"At that time Michael, the great prince who protects your people, will arise. There will come a time of distress such has not happened from the beginning of nations until then. But at that time your people—everyone whose name is found written in the book—will be delivered. Multitudes who sleep in the dust of the earth will awake: some to everlasting life, others to shame and everlasting contempt. Those who are wise will shine like the brightness of the heavens, and those who lead many to righteousness, like the stars forever and ever. But you, Daniel, close up and seal the words of the scroll until the time of the end. Many will go here and there to increase knowledge." (Daniel 11:36–12:4)

Once again, Daniel confesses that he doesn't understand what he has just seen. This time, however, he has company. Two men, one standing on Daniel's side of the Tigris River and the other on the opposite bank, have similar questions.

"How long will it be before these astonishing things are fulfilled?" asks one of the men.

Then a ... man clothed in linen, who was above the waters of the river, lifted his hand toward heaven, and I heard him swear by him who lives forever, saying, "It will be for a time, times and half a time. When the power of the holy people has been finally broken, all these things will be completed."

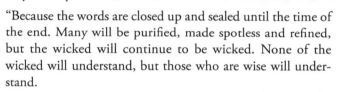

FINDING NO PREVIOUS HISTORY THAT FITS WITH THE IMAGES PRESENTED, THEY ASSUME THAT DANIEL MUST BE SEEING THE FUTURE TIME OF TRIBULATION.

Again, Daniel is confused: "I heard, but I did not understand."

"Go your way, Daniel," he is told:

"Because the words are closed up and sealed until the time of the end. Many will be purified, made spotless and refined, but the wicked will continue to be wicked. None of the wicked will understand, but those who are wise will understand.

"From the time that the daily sacrifice is abolished and the abomination that causes desolation is set up, there will be 1,290 days [almost three and a half years according to the Jewish calendar]. Blessed is the one who waits for and reaches the end of the 1,335 days.

"As for you, go your way till the end. You will rest, and then at the end of the days you will rise to receive your allotted inheritance." (Daniel 12:7–13)

To futurist scholars, these passages form a backdrop to their eschatological scheme of the end times. Finding no previous history that fits with the images presented, they assume that Daniel must be seeing the future time of Tribulation. No one has offered an adequate explanation of these verses before our time because the words have been sealed up until the time of the end:

"But you, Daniel, close up and seal the words of the scroll until the time of the end. Many will go here and there to increase knowledge." (Daniel 12:4)

Some translators, no doubt showing a little futurist bias, translate the passage this way:

"But Daniel, keep this prophecy a secret; seal it up so that it shall not be understood until the end times, when travel and education shall be vastly increased." (*Life Application Bible*)

This verse, according to many conservative scholars, describes the times in which we now live. The computer age, "when travel and education shall be greatly increased," is a sign of the end. Although we might not understand all the nuances of biblical prophecy, for the first time in history, we have the technology to both understand and reproduce many of the visions Daniel claims to have seen. The countries are in place. To the futurists, we must be living in the time of the end.

Most liberal scholars disagree. God does not play head games with the world, they say. The references are obscure and entirely compatible with the rules of classic apocalyptic literature down through the ages. The way to discover what Daniel was writing about is to study the history of his times, not wait for the future.

What all this means is, of course, subject to great debate. How do we deal with so many versions of one book of the Bible? Why can't various Christian denominations agree on which Daniel texts should be included in the canon and which thrown out? How do we handle all the dense symbolism?

The book is an enigma, to put it mildly. Those who attempt an interpretation usually have a bias toward one method of interpretation or another. The problem is not that we can't agree on who is right and who is wrong. The problem is that each group insists theirs is the correct understanding. It's enough to drive a redactor crazy.

# 2 Timothy: Saint Paul's Final Warning

> For the time will come when people will not put up with sound doctrine. Instead, to suit their own desires, they will gather around them a great number of teachers to say what their itching ears want to hear. They will turn their ears away from the truth and turn aside to myths. (2 Timothy 4:2–4)

Paul's second letter to Timothy, his disciple, is generally said to have been the last epistle Paul ever wrote. It is thought that he wrote it from a jail cell in Rome, where he was spending time waiting for his trial, accused of speaking against Roman authority. Because Paul was a Roman citizen as well as a Jewish scholar, he was able to make an appeal directly to Caesar. This was a right afforded all Roman citizens.

Many scholars, however, do not believe this is an authentic Pauline letter. In some cases, they argue, the theology sounds different from that which Paul espoused in some of his earlier authentic letters, such as those addressed to the Romans or the Corinthians.

Whoever wrote it, the excerpt quoted above has often been used to warn about coming apostasy, although there has probably never been a time in history when people didn't "gather around them a great number of teachers to say what their itching ears want to hear." That, after all, is a politician's stock in trade. It's a very human tendency to want our religious leaders, our political representatives, our professors, and other authority figures to confirm what we already believe.

Do we live in that kind of an intellectual environment right now? Sure, we do. And we probably always have.

In any case, Paul had a lot to say about what he called "the last days," whether or not we are currently in them:

> But mark this: There will be terrible times in the last days. People will be lovers of themselves, lovers of money, boastful, proud, abusive, disobedient to their parents, ungrateful, unholy, without love, unforgiving, slanderous, without self-control, brutal, not lovers of the good, treacherous, rash, conceited, lovers of pleasure rather than lovers of God—having a form of godliness but denying its power. Have nothing to do with such people. (2 Timothy 3:1–5)

It is the writings and teachings of Paul that greatly influenced what became the Christian Church, including making the sense of unity, its prevalent doctrine. (*Apostle Paul* by Rembrandt, c. 1633)

With these words he specifically set up a field of duality—good and bad, us against them. This is an old technique used by religions, cults, mystical fraternities and brotherhoods, and many secret societies. From Masons to Grangers, from Greek fraternities and sororities to black magic and voodoo cults, it is common practice to keep secrets and rituals from the general public in order to set off this duality—"We are different from everybody else."

There are secret handshakes, codes, and passwords known only to the initiated and bits of insider information, often protected with vows of secrecy, even to death. The idea is to wall off the club from others. It is the ultimate practice of duality.

Paul gloried in this duality, even though he is the one who was the greatest early proponent of opening up Christianity to everybody when it was, at the very beginning, a closed, Jewish Jesus cult. He saw himself as the one who was divinely appointed to reveal the secrets of God:

> This grace was given us in Christ Jesus before the beginning
> of time, but it has now been revealed through the appearing
> of our Savior, Christ Jesus ... I was appointed a herald and
> an apostle and a teacher. That is why I am suffering as I am.
> (2 Timothy 1:9, 11–12)

To understand the implications of his theology, a theology that went on to become that of the Christian Church, and to understand how duality, and thus divinely imposed separation, rose to such heights, we need to explore the unity/duality paradox.

Try this thought experiment. Picture perfect unity, wherein all is one in perfect harmony. Most people call this heaven. There is no shadow of separation there. It is perfect peace, love, and light.

But something is missing. What is it?

The experience of individuality! There can be no "I" in perfect unity. Call it the Source. It is where we all come from and where we all will return. But there is no individual ego in the Source, for all is one.

Now we can understand the problem. How can the Source, perfect unity, come to know individual experience? To experience that, an individual must make the courageous decision to break off and go it alone.

But what happens when individuality appears? For the first time, it enters the world of duality—separation from the Source—separation from God. This is the first experience of "I" and "Thou"—of "Me" and "You."

> ANOTHER WORD FOR SOURCE, IN MY VIEW, IS CONSCIOUSNESS. IT IS WHAT BOTH ALBERT EINSTEIN AND STEPHEN HAWKING CALLED "THE MIND OF GOD."

Now picture yourself as this individual. Your journey begins, even though you long for what you once had and continue to feel lonely and alone throughout your entire experience of individuality. You move out from the Source. Where do you find yourself? What environment do you now inhabit?

Another word for Source, in my view, is consciousness. It is what both Albert Einstein and Stephen Hawking called "the Mind of God." In consciousness, we still have no mass, either physical or metaphysical, but we are on the way to experiencing it. We haven't yet visualized where we are going or what we will look like, but we are aware that eventually we will.

I find the "Mind of God" an interesting place, hypothetical though it may be. There is still complete unity, but there is also an awareness that something we can only call uniqueness and individuality exist. What's it like to be different from every other individual, perhaps best called, at this point, "waves of energy"? What does it feel like to be alone, for instance? How will we react to an experience no other such energy wave has ever known in the exact way we feel it?

There's only one way to find out. You have to travel onward, and, in doing so, you have to forget where you came from.

Your journey toward that which we call conception and birth now takes you through the first defining field. It's a place wherein we begin to take on shape. Not mass. Not yet. But we grow a little heavier as we begin to transform ourselves into something truly unique and separate.

Taking a cue from ancient Hinduism, in previous books, I have called this place of transformation the Akashic field. Everything that we know and experience around us, every rock, every tree, every flower, every person, every animal, every bird, and every fish was first conceived in Akasha.

Plato once differentiated "horse" from "horseness." "Horseness" is an eternal reality. The "horse" quietly grazing on clover in the pasture by the side of the road is just its physical manifestation.

A "horse" doesn't exist in the Akashic field. But this is where "horseness" is born. Here, we find the field in which uniqueness is first given birth—not in fact but in principle. There are no "horses" here. But there is an idea about what a horse might be as differentiated from a dog or cat. In the same way, "you" don't exist yet. But the "you" you will become, the one you will someday call "I," is now a possibility.

Once again, you have slowed down a little. You have gathered metaphysical mass. You now understand the concept of individuality expressed both in final form and in idea. You understand that unique individuality leads to unique experience. You pass through the Akashic field and become something different. You now have some direction. What's next?

Mathematician, physicist, and astronomer James Hopwood Jeans speculated that the universe was a manifestation of thought.

When you emerge from the Akashic field, you find yourself in a totally different realm. You have now entered quantum reality. This world was discovered by our scientists only about a hundred years ago, but mystics have talked about it for thousands of years. We are just now beginning to explore it.

Sir James Hopwood Jeans (1877–1946) was a brilliant English physicist, astronomer, and mathematician. He once observed that "humanity is at the very beginning of its existence—a new-born babe, with all the unexplored potentialities of babyhood; and until the last few moments its interest has been centered absolutely and exclusively on its cradle and feeding bottle."

By far his most famous quote, which appears in almost every physics textbook and is quoted in hundreds of lectures throughout the world of quantum physics, was this: "The universe begins to look more like a great *thought* than a great *machine*."

For this reason I call the world of quantum reality the place of "thoughts and intentions."

There, you're not human yet. You still have a way to go. But you are beginning to form what might be called a concept of what "human" is. You begin to form an intention that you're going to be one.

Quantum reality is a place of potential. Humans don't really live there. But what Plato might have called "humanness" now exists. The potential for any one human is here. That potential will be soon be realized when you take one more step. In order for "humanness" to become "a human," it must first "collapse" into the environment humans experience. To do that it must pass through the newly discovered Higgs field.

Physicists tell us that the Higgs field is proved by experiment and can best be understood as the field through which energy passes as it begins to take on mass.

It's a reality, but no one quite knows how to describe it. Science writer Andrew Zimmerman Jones put it this way:

> The Higgs field is the theoretical field of energy that permeates the universe, according to the theory put forth in 1964 by Scottish theoretical physicist Peter Higgs. Higgs suggested the field as a possible explanation for how the fundamental particles of the universe came to have mass, because in the 1960s the Standard Model of quantum physics actually couldn't explain the reason for mass itself. He proposed that this field existed throughout all of space and that particles gained their mass by interacting with it.

There are other definitions, but they all involve some pretty complex mathematics. The best we can do is to say that when energy passes through the Higgs field, it emerges on the other side with, for the first time in its journey from the Source, mass. In other words, it becomes material. It is now conceived within our perception realm and begins the birth process.

You've now entered the world of our five senses. You're in the material realm, the realm in which we can experience duality.

But even this world has its hidden realms. When I say "perception realm," I'm referring to the cosmos in all its many manifestations. Here lies the multiverse in its infinite capacity for creativity. Here dwell all possible manifestations of every single possibility. Here lie an infinite number of "yous," each living their own life in woeful ignorance of their doppelgangers in parallel universes.

This particular universe seems to be supported by a mysterious substance called dark matter, which pushes it out toward infinity. Here, we find the mysteries inherent in the mathematics of modern physics. This is the home of string theory, membrane theory, and all the other fantastic ideas cir-

> THIS PARTICULAR
> UNIVERSE SEEMS TO BE
> SUPPORTED BY A
> MYSTERIOUS SUBSTANCE
> CALLED DARK MATTER,
> WHICH PUSHES IT OUT
> TOWARD INFINITY.

culating around the great universities of the world, eventually percolating out to television's Discovery Channel. Here, we find everything that intrigues and mystifies us.

But we still remember the miracle of unity, or perfect peace, and we hope to reestablish that feeling within us. That's why we form small examples of it. Within the "us" of "us against them," we try to recreate that sense of perfect unity.

The Apostle Paul, or whoever wrote this book of the New Testament, was the first to put Christianity on the path toward making this sense of unity the prevalent doctrine it occupies today. To be a Christian, you have to leave the "them" and join with the "us." You have to believe certain things in a certain way. You have to be baptized to partake of the sacraments. Through a process of confirming that baptism, you have to learn mysteries about partaking of the body and blood of the founder. In some Christian sects, you can't even rejoin the Source without the permission and blessing of an earthly representative in a process called the "last" rites, or the sacraments of penance, anointing of the sick, and viaticum.

Although this seems to be in direct contrast to the "Y'all come!" of Jesus, it is, in fact, what the bulk of churches teach today. They believe that as we approach the end times, the close of history as we know it, the differences between "us" and "them" will become more and more apparent.

That, in a nutshell, is the essential meaning of the passage that began this chapter.

Was this what the founder, Jesus Christ, actually believed? We don't know for sure because whatever he said comes to us filtered through the words of others. Paul was the first to write about him in letters that are believed to have come from soon after Jesus lived and walked in Galilee. All the rest came later—in many cases, many decades after Christ was crucified.

So, here we encounter another form of divine censorship. What did the first-century preacher from Nazareth say and mean? We don't know because the earliest evidence of his message comes to us through the filters of one who became a convert after he died.

Who attests to Paul's interpretation? None other than the apostle himself.

The Church as we know it was not shaped by the words of Jesus. It was formed in the mind of one who called himself "an apostle born out of time." According to his own words, "I was appointed a herald and an apostle and a teacher."

Make no mistake here. Paul might have gotten it right. He could very well be the chosen vessel who would interpret the words of Jesus to a waiting world. But we don't know for sure because no one at the time stood by Jesus's side with a pen and paper, much less a recording device.

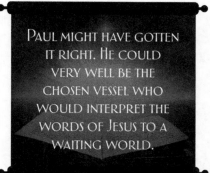

PAUL MIGHT HAVE GOTTEN IT RIGHT. HE COULD VERY WELL BE THE CHOSEN VESSEL WHO WOULD INTERPRET THE WORDS OF JESUS TO A WAITING WORLD.

I'm not suggesting for a minute that we throw out the whole New Testament because of the way it came to us. But I am saying that we need to remember how we got it in the first place. It was not, by any stretch of the imagination, divinely dictated word for word. Paul would later tell Timothy it was "God-breathed." But, again, we have to take Paul's word for it.

So, once again, we find that a committee—or, if Paul did indeed write all the books attributed to him, a single person, once removed, so to speak—stands between us and the voice of God. That is why the early Gnostics insisted that we need to personally experience the presence of God within us all. But since they were cast out of the Church in favor of a theology that put God "out there" somewhere, the prevalent teaching of the Church has been that human beings need an intermediary.

Is that intermediary guilty of censoring God? We need to decide that for ourselves.

# THE APOCALYPSE OF SAINT JOHN

The Revelation of Jesus Christ, which God gave Him to show His servants—things which must shortly take place. And He sent and signified it by His angel to His servant John, who bore witness to the word of God, and to the testimony of Jesus Christ, to all things that he saw. Blessed is he who reads and those who hear the words of this prophecy, and keep those things which are written in it; for the time is near. (Revelation 1:1–3)

The last book of the Bible gets its name from its opening words: "The revelation of Jesus Christ, which God gave him to show his servants what must soon take place." It is an example of apocalyptic writing that has intrigued, mystified, and baffled readers right from the start. More than 19 centuries after its creation, it remains the most famous single source of popular speculation concerning the end of the world.

The author of the book of Revelation introduced terms such as *Armageddon, Antichrist, Millennium,* and *Four Horsemen of the Apocalypse* into modern vocabulary. He was the first to link the serpent of the Garden of Eden in Genesis 3 with "that ancient serpent called the devil, or Satan, who leads the whole world astray" (Revelation 12:9). He is the biblical writer who most fully describes events that are today called the battle of Armageddon and the Second Coming of Christ.

When the committee that put the Bible together in 200 C.E. gathered to decide which books would pass muster, they were divided over whether Revelation should be included. Not until 393 at the Council of Hippo did the book finally get a majority vote. Still, not everyone was persuaded. A fourth-century Church father known as Cyril of Jerusalem decreed that Revelation was not to be read in public or studied in private, and he completely left it out of his version of the Bible. The book was also at the center of a debate between the Roman Catholic Church and the Eastern Orthodox Church. The Eastern branch didn't accept it into the Bible until 810 C.E. and, even then, only reluctantly.

As late as the sixteenth century, German theologian Martin Luther, the man at the forefront of the Protestant Reformation, wondered whether Revelation should be considered inspired Scripture. In a story from his time that may or may not be factual, he is supposed to have emerged from his study

St. John receives the Revelation in this illuminated page from the eleventh-century *Eluminure Apocalypse de Saint Sever. fol. 26v.* Including the book was a matter of great debate in the early Church.

after a lengthy session with the book and complained in exasperation to a student, "A revelation is supposed to *reveal* something!" He finally consented to include it in his own German translation of Scripture but only after remarking that he would rather have seen it tossed into the Elbe River.

His contemporaries in the new Protestant movement had similar views. Swiss theologian Ulrich Zwingli threw it out, and French reformer John Calvin simply ignored it, although he wrote commentaries on every other New Testament book.

So, from the very beginning, the final book of the Bible has caused controversy. It still does. Today, it is at the heart of a disagreement dividing the Christian Church. Christians no longer argue about whether it should be included in the Bible. That issue has been long settled. The central problem today is one of interpretation. Should Revelation be read as yet unfulfilled prophecy? Does it tell the future? Or should it be read as the coded words of people concerned with talking about their own time in language the authorities wouldn't be able to use against them?

The modern controversy, which had been simmering in the Christian Church for centuries, caught the public's attention in 1970 with the publication of American evangelist Hal Lindsey's *Late Great Planet Earth*. He took the view that Revelation was written by a first-century fisherman, the Apostle John, who also wrote the Gospel according to John and three letters called 1, 2, and 3 John. John. In 1997, Lindsey's book *Apocalypse Code* expanded his thesis. In this account John the Apostle was transported from his time into the future. According to Lindsey, that future was the early twenty-first century, and John saw things that he didn't have the vocabulary to describe. Lindsey reads Revelation and envisions supersonic jet aircraft with missiles, hyper-speed cannons, guided bombs, advanced attack helicopters, modern battle tanks, intercontinental ballistic missiles with thermonuclear warheads, battlefield artillery and missiles with neutron-nuclear warheads, biological and chemical weapons, aircraft carriers, missile cruisers, nuclear submarines, laser weapons, space stations and satellites, and a weapon system that can change weather patterns over whole continents, jam global communications systems, disrupt mental processes, and manipulate the earth's upper atmosphere.

> IN SHORT, ACCORDING TO LINDSEY, REVELATION IS DIFFICULT TO UNDERSTAND BECAUSE ITS FIRST-CENTURY AUTHOR SIMPLY HAD NO WORDS TO DESCRIBE TWENTY-FIRST-CENTURY TECHNOLOGY.

In short, according to Lindsey, Revelation is difficult to understand because its first-century author simply had no words to describe twenty-first-century technology. This explanation has been dubbed the millennialist view because it places the events of Revelation before the final thousand-year (or millennial) reign of Jesus Christ.

Most scholars prefer to call this school of interpretation the futurist view because of its belief that the events described in the book will happen in the future. This position has been so popularized by Lindsey, novelists Tim LaHaye and Jerry Jenkins, and others of the religious right that people can be forgiven if they think that it is the primary Christian position concerning Revelation.

There is, however, another view accepted by probably a majority of mainline Christian scholars. It is the view that Revelation was written for those Christians who were contemporaries of its author. When Revelation talks about Rome, for instance, or, more properly, the "woman" who sits "on seven hills" (17:9), followers of this interpretation say that it is not talking about present-day Rome or a future Rome that will arise at the end of time. It is talking about the very real Rome that was, in those first-century days, persecuting Christians. When the author talks about the Messiah coming back to earth on a white horse (19:11), he doesn't mean that Jesus will some-day arrive like a modern-day Wyatt Earp riding in to clean up Dodge City. He is using metaphorical language to give hope to a suffering community.

Similarly, at the time Revelation was written, it was a rather common practice to use gematria, a kind of code based on assigning a number to each letter of the alphabet. Using rules current at the time of the writing and sticking to the Greek language in which Revelation was written, the number 666 decodes into "Caesar Nero." Nero was the first Caesar to persecute Christians. So, there is no reason to search around today for Antichrists with associations to this supposedly mystical number. The author was simply referring to Nero.

American biblical scholar Raymond Brown, writing in his *Introduction to the New Testament*, comments:

Some interpreters of Revelation believe it is simply another version of the ancient "myth of cosmic combat" that exists in the myths of many other cultures.

Revelation is widely popular for the wrong reasons.... A great number of people read it as a guide to how the world will end, assuming that the author was given by Christ detailed knowledge of the future that he communicated in coded symbolism.

American theologian Marcus Borg, author of *Reading the Bible Again for the First Time: Taking the Bible Seriously but Not Literally*, would agree with Brown's dismissal of futurist assumptions. Borg summarizes the past-historic alternative:

The past-historical reading, which grows out of the belief that we understand the message of Revelation only by setting the text in the historical context in which it was written, emphasizes what Revelation would have meant in the past. In this reading, Revelation tells us what the author believed would happen in his time. This approach takes seriously that the visions of Revelation are found in a letter addressed to specific Christian communities in Asia Minor late in the first century. As such, the text was meant to be a message to them, not a message to people thousands of years later.

The past-historic position held by Borg and many other scholars makes a significant point. If the futurist position were correct, then, again in Borg's words:

Though John wrote the Apocalypse to a specific audience, its message could not have been intended for them. To write a letter that has no hope of being understood by its recipients seems a strange thing for God to do.

Followers of the past-historic school believe that Revelation is retelling the ancient "myth of cosmic combat" told by every culture from the Egyptians and Hebrews to the Zoroastrians and Hopi. It's good against evil, God and the devil, Ahura Mazda versus Ahriman. It's the myth reenacted in modern "good guy, bad guy" made-for-television wrestling matches. It tells a story meant to answer the eternal human question of why bad things happen to good people so that good people, while experiencing bad things, can have hope that good will triumph in the end. The rider on the white horse (or Clint Eastwood on a pale horse), the tenth avatar of Vishnu, or the *Return of the King* will eventually set things straight.

Keeping these two interpretations in mind, we can proceed to a summary of what Revelation actually says.

The first chapter of Revelation is a prologue. John, the author, claims to have been "in the Spirit" on "the Lord's Day" (1:10) when he heard a voice telling him, "Write on a scroll what you see and send it to the seven churches" (1:11). He claims that he saw a vision "which God gave him to show his servants what must soon take place" (1:1).

The chapter is a study in significant numbers. It talks about "the seven spirits before [God's] throne" in verse 4. It describes Jesus Christ with a threefold description in verse 5, and "someone 'like a son of man'" with a sevenfold description in verses 14–16. The message of the book is summarized in another threefold phrase. John is told to write "what you have seen, what is now, and what will take place later" (verse 19).

This pattern of threes and sevens is repeated throughout the book.

The second and third chapters contain the text of letters written to seven churches, situated roughly in a circle. Each letter consists of an introduction, an evaluation of the particular church, either a condemnation or an encouragement, and a promise. Some see in these letters a sevenfold description of the history of the Christian Church.

In chapters 4 and 5, John claims to have been taken to heaven and placed in a position where he could look down upon the earth to see the events that next transpire there. This material forms the bulk of the modern interpretive controversy and is found in chapters 6 through 22.

Three visions, or judgments, each containing seven sections, are described in typical apocalyptic language. The first vision is of seven seals fastened upon a scroll that seems to contain judgments about to be released upon the earth. As each seal is opened in heaven, something happens on earth. The second vision concerns the blowing of seven trumpets. Again, at the sound of each trumpet, events happen on earth. The final vision is of seven "bowls of God's wrath" emptied unto the earth. In each series, after the sixth seal, the sixth trumpet, and the sixth bowl, a "meanwhile, back at the ranch" segment returns the reader to heaven to see what is happening there while judgments are being unleashed on the earth.

An overview of these chapters looks like this:

### The Seven Seals (6:1–8:5)

1. A white horse appears whose rider carries a bow (but with no mention of an arrow). He wears a crown and rides as "a conqueror bent on conquest."

2. A red horse appears whose rider has "power to take peace from the earth."

3. A black rider appears whose rider holds "a pair of scales in his hand." A voice cries out, "A quart of wheat for a day's wages, and three quarts of barley for a day's wages, and do not damage the oil and the wine!"

4. A pale horse appears whose rider is named "Death, and Hades was following close behind him." (These are the famous Four Horsemen of the Apocalypse.)

5. At the opening of this seal, those who have died as a result of the "testimony they had maintained" are heard to call out, "How long, Sovereign Lord ... until you judge the inhabitants of the earth and avenge our blood?" They are given "white robes" and "told to wait a little longer."

6. A "great earthquake" takes place, the sun turns black, and the moon turns blood red. The sky rolls up "like a scroll," and mountains and islands are "removed from [their] place."

Meanwhile, in heaven, 144,000 Jews are "sealed," 12,000 from each of the 12 tribes of Israel. A "great multitude that no one could count, from every nation, tribe, people and language" appear in heaven, "holding palm branches in their hands." They sing a great hymn of praise to God and are joined by "all the angels standing around the throne."

As the seventh seal is opened, there is "a great silence in heaven."

### The Seven Trumpets (8:6–11:9)

1. Hail and fire rain down upon the earth.

2. "Something like a great mountain, all ablaze" is "thrown into the sea."

3. "A great star, blazing like a torch" falls from the sky, and "a third of the waters" turn bitter. "The name of the star is Wormwood."

4. A third of the light from the sun, moon, and stars turns dark. (Trumpets 5–7 now are described by a flying angel as "woes" about to befall the inhabitants of Earth.)

5. A "star" falls from heaven and is given "the key to the shaft of the Abyss." When he (it is usually assumed the "star" is a fallen angel)

opens the Abyss, smoke pours out, and an army looking like "locusts" comes forth. They have "hair like women's hair," "teeth like lion's teeth," and "breastplates of iron." The sound of their wings is "like the thundering of many horses." They have "tails and stings like scorpions," and they torment people "for five months. "They are led by a king "whose name in Hebrew is Abaddon, and in Greek, Apollyon."

6. Four angels are released who have been "bound at the great river Euphrates" and "kept ready for this very hour and day and month and year to kill a third of mankind." An army of 200 million "mounted troops" materializes to help carry out this task. These troops are riding on horses whose heads "resembled the heads of lions, and out of their mouths came fire, smoke and sulfur." Although a "third of mankind" is killed, the survivors still do not "repent of their murders, their magic arts, their sexual immorality or their thefts." (An angel comes down from heaven, places one foot on the sea and the other on the land, and shouts with the sound of "seven thunders." The content of his message is "sealed up." John is told "not to write it down." Instead, he is to "eat" a scroll the angel holds in his hand. It tastes "as sweet as honey" but turns his stomach sour. Two "witnesses" then appear on earth who "have power to shut up the sky so that it will not rain during the time they are prophesying; and they have power to turn the waters into blood and to strike the earth with every kind of plague as often as they want." "If anyone tries to harm them, fire comes from their mouths and devours their enemies." They prophesy for "1,260 days, clothed in sackcloth" to the "Gentiles," who "trample on the holy city for 42 months." The witnesses are finally killed and lie in the streets for "three and a half days" but then come to life and are transported to heaven.)

7. The seventh trumpet sounds, and the angelic choir breaks forth into the song immortalized by George Frideric Handel in the "Hallelujah!" chorus from his oratorio *Messiah*: "The kingdom of the world is become the kingdom of our Lord and of his Christ, and he will reign forever and ever."

Before the final set of seven "bowl judgments," a pageant takes place in heaven. Chapters 12 through 14 tell the story of a woman who appears "clothed with the sun and with the moon" and is about to give birth. A "red dragon with seven heads and ten horns" stands in front of her waiting to devour her child. A son is born to her but is "snatched up to God and to his throne" before the dragon can pounce. The woman then "flees to the desert to a place prepared for her by God, where she might be taken care of for 1,260 days."

War then breaks out in heaven. The archangel "Michael and his angels" fight "the dragon and his angels." The dragon, "that ancient serpent called

William Blake's 1805 artwork depicting the dragon and woman from chapters 12 through 14 of Revelation.

the devil, or Satan, who leads the whole world astray," is "hurled down."

Then, in chapter 13, John sees "a beast coming out of the sea" with "ten horns and seven heads, with ten crowns on his horns." The dragon gives this beast "his power and his throne and a great authority." "Men worshiped the dragon because he had given authority to the beast, and they also worshiped the beast." This beast is given "authority for forty-two months."

Finally, in the pageant, John sees another beast who has "two horns like a lamb" but speaks "like a dragon." He performs miracles, "causing fire to come down from heaven." He sets up an image of the first beast and orders humanity to worship it. He also forces "everyone, small and great, rich and poor, free and slave, to receive a mark on his right hand or on his forehead," and no one can "buy or sell" unless he has this mark, "which is the number of his name. This calls for wisdom. If anyone has insight, let him calculate the number of the beast, for it is a man's number. His number is 666."

John again sees the 144,000 Jews from chapter 7, but this time they are in heaven. They are described as "those who did not defile themselves with women, for they kept themselves pure" and as having been "purchased from among men and offered as first fruits to God and the Lamb."

Three angels then fly through the heavens warning humankind not to worship the beast or receive his mark. One "like a son of man" appears in the heavens, carrying a "sharp sickle." He is told to gather in his harvest, for "the time to reap is come ... the harvest of the earth is ripe." There follows the image that inspired the well-known words "he is trampling out the vintage where the grapes of wrath are stored" from the "Battle Hymn of the Republic": "The angel swung his sickle on the earth, gathered its grapes and threw them into the winepress of God's wrath. They were trampled in the winepress outside the city."

The stage is now set for the last seven plagues.

## The Seven Bowls of God's Wrath (Chapter 16)

1. Those who had received the mark of the beast are inflicted with "painful sores."

2. The sea turns to blood.

3. Fresh water turns to blood.

4. The sun scorches the earth with "intense heat."

5. Darkness covers the earth, and the sick fester in agony.

6. The Euphrates River dries up, preparing the way for "the kings from the East"; the armies of the earth gather for battle in a place that "in Hebrew is called Armageddon."

7. Tumultuous earthquakes, fires, explosions, and floods break out on the earth.

In Revelation 17, John is shown a woman "sitting on a scarlet beast" that has "seven heads and ten horns."

## The Final Battle (Chapters 17–20)

In chapter 17, John is shown the "punishment of the great prostitute, who sits on many waters." The woman is "sitting on a scarlet beast" that has "seven heads and ten horns." A title written on her forehead reads, in capital letters: "MYSTERY, BABYLON THE GREAT, THE MOTHER OF PROS- TITUTES AND OF THE ABOMINATIONS OF THE EARTH." When John wonders about all this, the angel "explains" things in a way that has only introduced more mystery over the past 2,000 years.

First, "the beast," according to the angelic interpreter, "once was, now is not, and will come up out of the Abyss and go to his destruction."

Second, as for the "seven heads and ten horns," the angel says:

> This calls for a mind with wisdom. The seven heads are seven hills on which the woman sits. They are also seven kings. Five have fallen, one is, the other has not yet come; but when he does come, he must remain for a little while. The beast who once was, and now is, is an eighth king. He belongs to the seven and is going to his destruction. The ten horns you saw are ten kings who have not yet received a kingdom, but who for one hour will receive authority as kings along with the

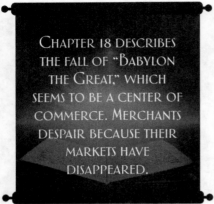

CHAPTER 18 DESCRIBES
THE FALL OF "BABYLON
THE GREAT," WHICH
SEEMS TO BE A CENTER OF
COMMERCE. MERCHANTS
DESPAIR BECAUSE THEIR
MARKETS HAVE
DISAPPEARED.

beast. They have one purpose and will give their power and authority to the beast. They will make war against the Lamb, but the Lamb will overcome them because he is Lord of lords and King of kings.

Having cleared up that mystery, the angel goes on to tackle the third part of the vision.

The prostitute is sitting "on many waters." According to the angel, "The waters you saw, where the prostitute sits, are peoples, multitudes, nations and languages."

To sum up the whole vision, the angel recaps:

> The beast and the ten horns you saw will hate the prostitute. They will bring her to ruin and leave her naked; they will eat her flesh and burn her with fire.... The woman you saw is the great city that rules over the kings of the earth.

Chapter 18 describes the fall of "Babylon the Great," which seems to be a center of commerce. Merchants despair because their markets have disappeared. Ships stay at sea, afraid to enter ports. Music is silenced in the streets, and workmen and tradesmen are no more. There is no light to be found in the city, and "the voice of the bridegroom and bride will never be heard in you again." By the "magic spell" of this great center of commerce and trade, "all the nations were led astray."

In chapter 19 the rider on a white horse comes to earth. "With justice he judges and makes war." This rider is called "faithful and true" but also "has a name written on him that no one but he himself knows," besides which "on his robe and on his thigh he has this name written," again in capital letters: "KING OF KINGS AND LORD OF LORDS."

The beast and the false prophet are captured and thrown alive "into the fiery lake of burning sulfur."

Chapter 20 sees the imprisonment of Satan "for a thousand years." This is the age called the Millennium. He is thrown into "the Abyss." Christ reigns on earth during this time, but at the end of the thousand years, Satan is released, gathers up an army, and is quickly defeated. He is, at last, "thrown into the lake of burning sulfur, where the beast and false prophet had been thrown. They will be tormented day and night forever and ever."

Then comes the final judgment from the "great white throne," when the "book of life" is opened and:

The dead were judged according to what they had done as recorded in the books. The sea gave up the dead that were in it, and death and Hades gave up the dead that were in them, and each person was judged according to what he had done.... If anyone's name was not found written in the book of life, he was thrown into the lake of fire.

Revelation ends with a message of hope as Jerusalem is restored along with the Tree of Life that heals all nations.

## The End (Chapters 21 and 22)

The final chapters paint a picture of life on a recycled earth. There is "a new heaven and a new earth ... and there was no longer any sea." The "New Jerusalem" comes down from heaven "prepared as a bride beautifully dressed for her husband." Here, "God himself" will live with men: "They will be his people, and God himself will be with them and be their God. He will wipe every tear from their eyes. There will be no more death or mourning or crying or pain, for the old order of things has passed away." He who calls himself the "Alpha and Omega," the "Beginning and the End," declares, "It is done."

The "tree of life," denied to Adam and Eve in the book of Genesis, now stands in the center of a restored Jerusalem. The "river of the water of life" brings it sustenance, and "the leaves of the tree are for the healing of the nations. No longer will there be any curse."

## Blessing and Warning

Revelation ends with both a blessing and a warning.

*Blessing*: "Blessed is he who keeps the words of the prophecy of this book.... Blessed are those who wash their robes, that they may have the right to the tree of life and may go through the gates into the city."

*Warning*: "Do not seal up the words of the prophecy of this book because the time is near.... I warn everyone who hears the words of the prophecy of this book: If anyone adds anything to them, God will add to him the plagues

A majority of Americans believe that Jesus is returning to earth, and he will be doing so in the near future.

described in this book. And if anyone takes words away from this book of prophecy, God will take away from him his share in the tree of life and in the holy city, which are described in this book."

The final words seek to offer hope to all who read the book, whatever their interpretive scheme:

He who testifies to these things says, "Yes, I am coming soon."

Amen. Come Lord Jesus. The grace of the Lord Jesus Christ be with God's people. Amen.

Largely based on a futurist reading of this final book of the Bible, there is a widespread feeling in Western cultures, especially the United States, that Jesus is coming soon. Gallup polls dating back to 1980 indicate that 62 percent of Americans (that is, all Americans, not just those identified as Christians) have "no doubts" that Jesus will someday return. During the weeks preceding Easter, it has become the custom for many news magazines to run articles citing polls indicating many people believe the return will be sooner rather than later. Obviously, Revelation has influenced many people, whether or not they have actually read the book and despite the fact that the message it conveys is debatable.

Still, in the words of Marcus Borg, "It is difficult to imagine a more powerful ending to the Bible."

That being said, there is no indication that a significant number of people, let alone political leaders, have changed their behavior for the better during these times. Wars and rumors of wars still fill the headlines. Pandemics and plagues scourge the earth. Pollution still runs amok. Religious writing, it seems, is much respected but almost totally ignored.

It's a form of censorship that is most insidious. To quote the immortal words of Walt Kelly's comic-strip character Pogo, it seems as though "we have met the enemy, and he is us."

# CONCLUSIONS

In Part III we have looked at four texts, all of which are well known to those who are versed in their context, although the *Corpus Hermeticum—The Lament of Hermes the Egyptian* is probably not as familiar as Daniel, 2 Timothy, and Revelation. They have been in plain sight for a long time. Why, then, do we need to consider them in a book about censorship when they have not, at least in an overt way, been censored?

To understand that, we need to define our concept of divine inspiration. Recall what was stated in the preface of this book:

> As we progress, we might come to remember the song that sings to our inner hearts and souls. That's where we'll hear it best. For even amid the clash and clamor of a noisy world, the music continues. It's not too late. We can still learn that beneath the song of Life, and even the song of Meaning, another song sings its eternal melody. It's a song called Purpose, and it must be sung by each one of us, individually.
>
> To hear the song of Purpose might be our ultimate existential goal. It underlies everything we are and do, and its music forms the soundtrack of our life on earth.

Language is tricky. When we say the words "divine inspiration," they mean vastly different things to different people.

- Some will picture Michelangelo's portrayal of the divine in the Sistine Chapel. They will visualize a god in the heavens, dictating words of wisdom to a few men who were chosen—whether for their purity or for some other reason—to receive them and write them down.

- Some will imagine a soft whisper that speaks to the inner heart and soul of one who is tuned to the music of the spheres.

- Others will think in terms of inspiration available to all who quiet their minds enough to hear mystical words from a Consciousness beyond human understanding.

- Still others will understand divine inspiration as that existential "Aha!" moment when something new breaks through to our understanding. Perhaps it will come through poetry or music. We won't be able to explain it in stodgy prose, but we will "get it" just the same.

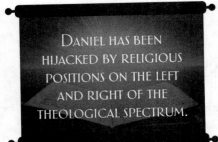

All these are viable options, and they are probably all correct in one way or another. What that means is that there are various levels of censorship when those avenues of inspiration are in any way muddled by gatekeepers who stand between the listener and the Source.

In the case of the four texts we have just considered, it is often the actions of those who believe in them the most that cloud their meaning to others, hindering their free imagination and preventing them from seeing through to their core meaning.

Take *The Lament of Hermes the Egyptian*, for instance. It is easy to see why any modern Egyptian wouldn't want to think the text was at all prophetic. It is a stinging rebuke to the current culture of a once proud nation, secure in its heritage as a manifestation of the gods on earth.

Daniel has been hijacked by religious positions on the left and right of the theological spectrum. Conservative Christian congregations have probably never heard a liberal interpretation of the book. And most liberal congregations tend to view conservative interpretations as contrived and almost laughable. Meanwhile, both groups probably never think to ask their Jewish friends about how the book is understood in their synagogue, even though it is a Hebrew text.

2 Timothy is the sneakiest of all when it comes to censorship. The whole book is a filtered rendition of early theology that represents a form of Christianity that brutally repressed other competing expressions, which might have been a lot closer to the ideas of Jesus but were buried by the triumphant Roman Church of the fourth century.

Revelation is only one of many examples of apocalyptic literature, selected for unknown reasons and interpreted in vastly different ways down through the last two millennia.

In other words, even books of the Bible that have received the official stamp of approval by the established Church often do more to block divine inspiration than advance it. Whenever a particular point of view or theological system is stamped on a biblical text, staking out a position of authority, it can be labeled censorship in the sense that it then attempts to crush any other, perhaps conflicting, view.

As an example of how this can be immensely important and of practical significance, imagine two Christian pastors preaching their sermons on the Sunday before the U.S. Civil War breaks out. Tensions are running high, and the issue of human enslavement is on everyone's mind. Both pastors, one from the North and the other from the South, decide to preach from the letters of Paul the Apostle on this particular Sunday.

The southern preacher chooses to read Ephesians 6:5, written by Paul:

> Slaves, obey your earthly masters with respect and fear, and with sincerity of heart, just as you would obey Christ.

The northern preacher chooses to preach from Galatians 3:28, also written by Paul:

> There is neither slave nor free, for you are all one in Christ Jesus.

Same author. Same Bible. Drastically different messages. Do you see the problem? The mere fact of choosing one and leaving out the other is, in effect, censorship.

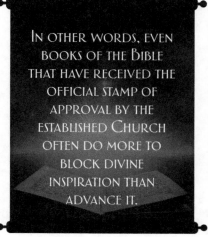

IN OTHER WORDS, EVEN BOOKS OF THE BIBLE THAT HAVE RECEIVED THE OFFICIAL STAMP OF APPROVAL BY THE ESTABLISHED CHURCH OFTEN DO MORE TO BLOCK DIVINE INSPIRATION THAN ADVANCE IT.

"But we don't want to confuse our congregations," argue the two preachers. "To read conflicting opinions from the same author will only raise questions that the people in the pew will not know how to handle."

So, the gatekeepers read the text they agree with and hope that if they preach loudly enough and with sufficient authority, "God's will" will be seen in clarity and precision.

If you don't think this is important, remember that war did break out, and, eventually, more than 600,000 people were killed. Some 360,000 died believing in Galatians 3:28. More than 258,000 died believing in Ephesians 6:5.

Divine censorship, no matter how it is defined, can result in drastic earthly consequences. It is better by far to allow the song of distant voices to ring forth in clarity than to stifle the melody, no matter what motives are held forth to justify the act. Who knows which songs come from the mind of God, however God is defined or understood?

# OF GATEKEEPERS AND CENSORSHIP:
## FINAL THOUGHTS

I shall be telling this with a sigh
Somewhere ages and ages hence:
Two roads diverged in a wood, and I—
I took the one less traveled by,
And that has made all the difference.

—Robert Frost, "The Road Not Taken"

Human beings stand on the shores of a great island of knowledge, surrounded by a vast sea of mystery.

Some of them face inward, toward the land, and think that what they see is all there is. Others face outward, toward the sea, and wonder what lies over the horizon. Does it go on forever? Will we ever travel there?

From time to time, throughout history, there have been a gifted few who have brought us tantalizing hints of the unknown that exists out there in the depths beyond the breakers.

Ancient shamans painted their visions on the walls of caves.

Musicians captured, in a few brief snatches of rhythm, melody, and harmony, the music of the spheres.

Poets found a fortunate turn of phrase and gave voice to that which is beyond language.

Mystics brought heaven down to earth to share a brief caress.

Artists conveyed, with a few splashes of color, something beyond our ability to explain.

Spiritual adepts showed us a glimpse of eternity.

And then their work was too often commandeered by gatekeepers who sought to systematize it all and preserve only their own interpretation of the miracle those unknown founders wrought.

Who is to say which written wisdom is divinely inspired and which isn't? The tragedy of censorship is not that it makes decisions based on a limited experiential framework that takes place within a specific cultural time and place. That is to be expected. The redactors and various committees who decided what sacred texts would be contained in holy writ couldn't possibly

IT DOESN'T TAKE MUCH
FOR GREAT INSIGHT TO
DIE IN THE DARK
WITHOUT EVER SEEING
THE LIGHT OF DAY.

have included everything. As we read in John 21:25, "If every one of them were written down, I suppose that even the whole world would not have room for the books that would be written."

No, the problem was not just in their selection. It was that, in many cases, the gatekeepers in charge of the selection process tried so desperately to destroy their rejects. It was as if they were afraid someone would look over their shoulders or in their wastebaskets and disagree with their decisions. That is the height of insecurity. It is also the height of hypocrisy. But that is what happened over and over again as history unfolded.

From the caves of Qumran to the deserts of Nag Hammadi, from the book burning of the Inquisition to the fires of the conquistadores, fear and hypocrisy were usually found in tandem. The suppression continues to this day. Even as I write these words, Buddhist shrines are being destroyed in Afghanistan and ancient Christian places of worship flooded in Turkey.

All of this is censorship—censorship of uniquely perceived, divine insights that were captured by ancient, vibrant, and spiritually alive people. We don't have to agree with their insights. They might not speak to our time and place. But to destroy them in the name of our particular brand of religious tradition is blasphemy.

Where would we be if a committee of gatekeepers decided we shouldn't like Mozart? Remember, as we said at the beginning of this book, Mozart died thinking he was a failure, as did Dutch artist Vincent van Gogh, American physicist Hugh Everett, German geophysicist Alfred Wegener, and many more artists and brilliant thinkers—all because their work was censored by people who had a different point of view or, even worse, a personal ax to grind.

It doesn't take much for great insight to die in the dark without ever seeing the light of day. Eckhart Tolle, the well-known author of *A New Earth* and *The Power of Now*, brought what some consider to be divinely inspired insight to millions of people. But he probably would not have achieved the success he did if Oprah Winfrey, the extremely popular talk-show host, had not brought his work to the attention of the public.

This is an example of how a gatekeeper with clout can use her position for the benefit of all. But how many actors with the same talent as Meryl Streep or Tom Hanks are still waiting on tables because they never got their big opportunity? How many musicians never achieved great popularity because they didn't connect with the public through that one big breakthrough of a hit song?

We cannot guarantee that true talent will inevitably rise to the top. Sometimes it doesn't. That's the way the world works. A lot of bad movies make a lot of money while artistic ones never get produced. Sometimes it happens because the actors and directors of those artistic movies failed to appeal to the fancy, and, as we have recently learned, sexual appetites of those who controlled the process.

Many great books will never be read because people just don't hear about them. That is a fact of life. But to deliberately destroy what might be the voice of divine inspiration because it utters words of wisdom someone rejected because it didn't fit within their spiritual or religious framework is blasphemy. Employing a rather broad phrase of metaphorical expression, I have called it "censoring God." That, and that alone, is the kind of suppression I have condemned in this book.

Read your Bible. Read your Quran. Read your Bhagavad Gita and Upanishads. Read your Popol Vuh. But know as you do so that what you hold in your hand might not be the complete spiritual expression of a Consciousness that is far greater than the sum of all its parts. For every text you digest, there are a hundred that never saw the light of day. Who knows what wisdom has been lost but is waiting to be rediscovered?

We have not reached the end of divine inspiration. Indeed, we might be only at the beginning.

# FURTHER READING

Ashton, John, and Tom Whyte. *The Quest for Paradise: Visions of Heaven and Eternity in the World's Myths and Religions*. New York: Harper Collins, 2001.

Borg, Marcus. *Meeting Jesus Again for the First Time: The Historical Jesus and the Heart of Contemporary Faith*. New York: Harper Collins, 1994.

———. *Reading the Bible Again for the First Time: Taking the Bible Seriously but Not Literally.* New York: Harper Collins, 1994.

Campbell, Joseph, with Bill Moyers. *The Power of Myth*. New York: Bantam, Doubleday Dell Publishing Group, 1988.

Drosnin, Michael. *The Bible Code*. New York: Simon & Schuster, 1997.

———. *Bible Code II: The Countdown*. New York: Viking Penguin, 2002.

Fell, Barry. *Saga America*. New York. NY: Times Books, 1980.

Felser, Joseph M. *The Way Back to Paradise: Restoring the Balance between Magic and Reason*. Charlottesville, VA: Hampton Roads Publishing, 2005.

Hancock, Graham. *The Sign and the Seal*. New York: Crown Publishers, 1992.

James, Simon. *The World of the Celts*. London, England: Thames & Hudson, 1993.

Johnson, Robert Bowie, Jr. *Genesis Characters and Events in Ancient Greek Art*. Annapolis, MD: Solving Light Books, 2004.

Jones, Prudence, and Nigel Pennick. *A History of Pagan Europe*. New York: Routledge, 1995.

Kauffman, Stuart A. *Reinventing the Sacred: A New View of Science, Reason, and Religion*. Philadelphia: Basic Books, 2008.

Lindsey, Hal. *The Late Great Planet Earth*. Grand Rapids, MI: Zondervan, 1970.

———. *There's a New World Coming*. Grand Rapids, MI: Zondervan, 1984.

*The Lost Books of the Bible and The Forgotten Books of Eden*. New York: The World Syndicate Publishing Co., 1926.

Minkoff, Harvey. *The Missing Books of the Bible*, Vols. 1–2. Reprint. Halo Press/Ottenheimer Publishers, 1996.

Osborne, Robert. *Civilization: A New History of the Western World*. New York: Pegasus Books, 2006.

Prabhupada, A. C. Bhaktivedanta. *Bhagavad-Gita As It Is*. Los Angeles, CA: International Society for Krishna Consciousness, 1984.

Sitchin, Janet. *The Anunnaki Chronicles: A Zecharia Sitchin Reader*. Rochester, VT: Bear & Co., 2015.

Sitchin, Zecharia. *Genesis Revisited*. New York: Avon Books. 1990.

Ulansey, David. *The Origins of the Mithraic Mysteries: Cosmology Salvation in the Ancient World*. New York: Oxford University Press, 1989.

Urquhart, David. *The Lebanon (Mount Souria): A History and a Diary*. BiblioBazaar, 2015.

Von Däniken, Eric. *Chariots of the Gods?* New York: Penguin Group, 1968.

Waters, Frank. *Book of the Hopi*. New York: Penguin Books, 1977.

Waziyatawin. *What Does Justice Look Like? The Struggle for Liberation in Dakota Homeland*. St. Paul, MN: Living Justice Press, 2008.

Willis, Jim. *Ancient Gods: Lost Histories, Hidden Truths and the Conspiracy of Silence*. Detroit: Visible Ink Press, 2016.

————. *Hidden Histories: Ancient Aliens, Conspiracies of Silence and the Secret Origins of Civilization*. Detroit: Visible Ink Press, 2020.

————. *Lost Civilizations: The Secret Histories and Suppressed Technologies of the Ancient*. Detroit: Visible Ink Press, 2019.

————. *The Religion Book: Places, Prophets, Saints and Seers*. Detroit: Visible Ink Press, 2004.

————. *Supernatural Gods: Spiritual Mysteries, Psychic Experiences and Scientific Truths*. Detroit: Visible Ink Press, 2017.

Willis, Jim, and Barbara Willis. *Armageddon Now: The End of the World, A–Z*. Detroit: Visible Ink Press, 2006.

Witzel, E. J. Michael. *The Origin of the World's Mythologies*. New York: Oxford University Press, 2012.

# INDEX

Note: (ill.) indicates photos and illustrations